Presented to:

By:

Date:

Occasion:

PRAYERS
that avail much®

Harrison House
Shippensburg, PA

PRAYERS that avail much®

Scriptural Prayers
— for your —
Daily Breakthrough

Germaine Copeland

Prayers and affirmations are paraphrased from the above-listed Bible versions unless otherwise stated or identified.

Previously published as *Prayers That Avail Much® Volumes 1, 2, and 3* and *Prayers That Avail Much ® 25th Anniversary Commemorative Edition, Prayers That Avail Much 40th Anniversary Commemorative Edition.* Previous ISBNs: *Prayers That Avail Much, Vol. 1-* 9781577945963. *Prayers That Avail Much, Vol.2-* 9781577946014. *Prayers That Avail Much, Vol. 3-* 9781577946021. *Prayers That Avail Much 25th Anniversary Commemorative Gift Edition* - Hardback- 9781577947523. *Prayers That Avail Much 40th Anniversary Commemorative Edition* - Hardback- 9781680314144

ISBN 13: 978-1-68031-824-1

Word Ministries, Inc.

P.O. Box 289

Good Hope, GA, 30641

Published by Harrison House

Shippensburg, PA 17257

For Worldwide Distribution, Printed in the U.S.A.

1 2 3 4 5 6 7 8 / 26 25 24 23 22

What Others Are Saying About

PRAYERS THAT AVAIL MUCH®
COMMEMORATIVE EDITION

Germaine Copeland's thoughtful, tried, and true collection of prayers, provides practical and scriptural insights that can equip believers to grow in prayer and to enjoy a vibrant connection with Jesus and His Word.

—Mike Bickle
International House of Prayer, Kansas City, MO

Around 30 years ago, I was introduced to the *Prayers That Avail Much* prayer book and to the ministry of Germaine Copeland. We were in the process of beginning our ministry, and the prayers in that book were an instrumental part of our intercession and prayers.

I remember during that time that I was trying to pray effectively for the president, and I felt inadequate to do so. The scope of the president's job was much greater than what I was able to pray! But once I found the prayer in *Prayers That Avail Much for the American Government,* I had found my answer; I pray that prayer for our president to this day! I thank God for Mrs. Copeland and for her ministry of *Prayers That Avail Much.* She and the book have been a great blessing and benefit to me and our ministry.

—E. Dwayne Brewington, Pastor
Victory Christian Church International
Gaithersburg, MD

I met Germaine Copeland almost 40 years ago and became acquainted with her powerful gift of praying the Word as we were "coincidentally" booked to speak at the same conventions in numerous places in the United States. It was a true joy to hear her minister and teach enthusiastic students how to pray and get results! I hear over and over the phrase, "the effectual fervent prayer," and I am sure others do too as they practice what they have learned through her teaching and her books.

We became friends and have shared many victories and prayed over many challenges over the years. I count her as a dear friend, a woman of strong faith and sensitivity to the Holy Spirit. For these many reasons, I highly endorse this book. Praying God's Word never goes out of style, and for this 40th Anniversary Edition, I prophesy success! His Word will not return void but will accomplish what it is sent to do. This Word is sent to you: Act on what you learn in these pages, and you will see great and mighty things in your life.

—Annette Capps, President
Capps Ministries, Tulsa, OK

There are very few books which I have read over and over. In fact, this is the only book I have read—more correctly prayed—repeatedly. I have worn the cover off several copies. I regard *Prayers That Avail Much* as the single most helpful resource I have ever used. I recommend it to everyone. You will not regret praying your way through this book.

—Dr. Jim Garlow, CEO
Well Versed, Inc., La Mesa, CA

James 5:16 states, "The effectual fervent prayer of a righteous man avails much." What a beautiful scriptural promise from the Lord to each of us as believers and pray-ers. Our heavenly Father is always faithful and through His Word He provides the promises and keys of how to be fervent and effectual prayer warriors in and for His kingdom plans and purposes. I am so honored to be able to endorse this classic book on intercession by Germaine Copeland.

It is a glory-anointed compilation of supernatural revelation and prayer birthed in the womb of intercession through His word, presence, and glory. Within the pages of this book are the revelation and prayer promises needed for breakthrough and victory. Thank you, Germaine, for providing this vital tool to the Body of Christ. It has impacted and changed my life as I have referred to it many times over the years.

To each reader of this book, I want to encourage you to be intentional in your prayers and intercession. Pray the prayers so beautifully scribed in this book, believe the Lord, and stand on His Word and promise. You will be ignited to be a fervent prayer warrior who has been captured by the heart of our Father to see tremendous power released through passionate, anointed, heartfelt intercession.

—Rebecca Greenwood
Christian Harvest International and
Strategic Prayer Apostolic Network, Falcon, CO
Author of *Authority to Tread, Let Our Children Go, Defeating Strongholds of the Mind,* and *Glory Warfare*

Germaine is a personal friend, and I am thrilled to endorse the 40th anniversary edition of her classic book, *Prayers That Avail Much.* Germaine's insights on the power of prayer will change your life! You will be blessed by reading her works.

—Barbie Cooper
Inspire Women's Ministry, Atlanta, GA

When I was first learning to pray 40 years ago, heaven used Germaine Copeland as such a spearhead for me. She has a gift to wrap words around the heart of God for specific situations. As you read this book, you will find yourself praying words that will ultimately translate the promises of God into life around you. If you lack words or utterance in prayer, this book will be such a blessing to you. You will find your heart inspired by her creative ability to empower everyday believers.

—Lynne Hammond
Living Word Christian Center, Brooklyn Park, MN

It was 40 years ago that I, still in my teens and newly filled with the Holy Spirit, obtained my first copy of *Prayers That Avail Much*. From that book, I learned to pray the Scriptures, which changed my life and set the foundation for my life and ministry. In every crisis I have faced, praying these prayers connected me to the Lord and His redeeming, delivering power in a very real way.

I want to recommend the 40th Anniversary Edition of *Prayers That Avail Much* to a new generation of believers who will take the Word of God, led by the Holy Spirit, and pray out the good plans of God for their lives, their families, their nation, and a world that desperately needs Jesus.

Oh, one more thing! Don't just skip to the prayers, but BE SURE to read the sections called "Effectual Prayer" and "How to Pray Prayers That Avail Much." The instruction contained there is vitally important!

—David Harris, Pastor
City on a Hill Church, Cumming, GA

What an honor to be asked to endorse this classic book that has so affected the Body of Christ with an empowerment to pray. It's amazing that it has been 40 years since the first release of this groundbreaking yet methodical call to pray that's seen breakthrough in countless of lives. My expectation is that just as with the original release this edition will stir a passion to cry out to God and see answers from heaven manifest. What a privilege we have been granted to stand before our God as Father and request His benevolent mercies in and over our lives. He is faithful and will answer the genuine cries of His people before His Throne.

—Robert Henderson
Waco, TX
Bestselling Author of *The Court of Heaven* Series

Prayers That Avail Much was my textbook on praying the Word. I first read this book in the '80s, and it gave me the foundation that I needed to become an effective intercessor. This is a much-needed read for every believer who wants to learn to pray effectually.

—Dr. Cindy Jacobs
Generals International
Ovilla, TX

Prayers That Avail Much comes directly from Germaine Copeland's own prayer history. This book emerged from a mother's heart for her son. In it, she shares a wonderful revelation: effective prayer always comes from adoration. Prayer begins with the awe of God. This book is a gift to those who desire to receive tools for their prayer life. It is rooted deeply in the Word, as Germaine shares the promises of God through scripture so we can see clearly how to pray.

—Beni Johnson
Bethel Church, Redding, CA
Author of *The Happy Intercessor* and *The Power of Communion*

Germaine Copeland did not intend to begin a ministry writing books on prayer, but the Body of Christ is greatly enriched because she yielded to the leadership of God's Spirit to write that first book. Over the last forty years, Germaine has continued to follow the Spirit's leading writing to encourage the people of God to come before the throne of God to pray the Word of God back to Him.

—Dr. Jimmy A. Long, Senior Pastor
Grace Fellowship of Greensboro, GA

Prayer and the Word of God are essential to having a personal relationship with God and to experiencing His supernatural power in and through our lives. When the Word of God is the substance of our prayers, and we are in right standing with Him through Jesus Christ, we can be certain that God will both hear and answer our prayers. It is only when we pray according to the Word, that we are truly praying the will of God. As we continue to consistently accumulate prayers before the presence of God, we can be sure that we will see His faithfulness, love, wisdom, and power through breakthroughs and answered prayers. It is for these reasons that I highly recommend Germaine Copeland's book, *Prayers That Avail Much.* It is a wonderful tool to help both leaders and believers develop and deepen a meaningful, powerful prayer life that will produce much fruit in every area of their lives.

—Guillermo Maldonado, Senior Apostle and Pastor
King Jesus International Ministry
Miami, FL

I was introduced to the first addition of *Prayers That Avail Much* written by Germaine Copeland as a first-year student at RHEMA Bible College. It was offered as one of the many books that we were required to read. Even being a minister, I had no idea that there were so many kinds of prayer. That first little book changed my life forever!

Now Germaine has once again invaded the realm of the spirit to bring to us a revised and improved edition to her first three volumes of *Prayers*

That Avail Much. As for me, no one on this planet has such insight to the wonderful privilege to pray prayers that bring heaven to earth. May you read this book and be blessed as much as it has blessed me.

—Dr. Mike Merritt
Little River, SC

Prayer is the most intimate time we can spend with God. As we communicate our gratitude, hopes, and concerns to Him, we form a direct connection that allows Him to transform our lives and circumstances. *Prayers That Avail Much* is filled with powerful prayers that will not only help you develop and strengthen your prayer life, but also will allow God to bless you in ways you never thought possible.

—Victoria Osteen, Co-Pastor
Lakewood Church, Houston, TX
New York Times bestselling author

Lord, teach me to pray! I was young in the Lord and new to the Word of God with an insatiable desire to connect the two through prayer. I needed mentoring, teaching, and disciplining! God answered my prayers when He directed me to Germaine's book, *Prayers That Avail Much*. The result of learning to pray scripture-based prayers accomplished two things. First, it was foundational to my relationship with the Father, Jesus, and the Holy Spirit and gave me language to begin God-conversations (prayers). Secondly, the book provided a foundation to praying God's will through His Word empowered by the Spirit. Trinity Praying.

This 40th anniversary edition of *Prayers That Avail Much* is priceless. Germaine has revisited this valuable prayer and intercession resource with enriched insight, focuses, and scriptures. This book will become a journal as you scribe your prayers on the pages and write God's promises next to the scriptures. Watching God answer prayers and realizing your prayers partnered with Him is priceless.

—Mary Jo Pierce, Pastor of Prayer and Intercession
Gateway Church, Southlake, TX
Author of *Adventures in Prayer* and *Follow Me: An Unending Conversation with Jesus*

In Ephesians 6:18, the apostle Paul said, "Praying always with all prayer and supplication...." The Greek actually means, "Pray anytime there's an opportunity—no matter where you are or what you're doing. Use every occasion, every season, every possible moment to pray. And when you do it, use every type of prayer that is at your disposal."

This verse explains why I love Germaine Copeland's powerful book Prayers That Avail Much. This 40th Commemorative Anniversary Edition will empower any believer with every available type of prayer to use on every occasion! This book will be a mighty tool in the hands of any praying saint!

—Rick Renner
Author, Teacher, Pastor, Broadcaster
Rick Renner Ministries and Moscow Good News Church
Tulsa, Oklahoma, and Moscow, Russia

God hears us when we pray according to His will (1 Jn 5:14). He will never set aside His purposes to answer our prayers. His purposes are the "gold" we mine from His promises. The Bible, His Word, is our spiritual treasure map! My friend, Germaine Copeland, understood this years ago when she began writing her remarkable books to equip us to pray scripture-focused prayers. Her masterful compilation is a powerful arsenal that will help us pray more effectively. She knows how to direct us...because she is a mighty time-tested prayer warrior. Each prayer can be a "launch pad" to activate our communication with the heavenly Father to pray according to His purposes. I encourage you to get your copy today!

—Alice Smith
U.S. Prayer Center
Houston, TX
Bestselling author of *Beyond the Veil, Entering into Intimacy with God through Prayer*

In 1974, I was a newly born-again teenager, hungry to learn about prayer and the Word of God. One day I came across a slim yellow copy of *Prayers That Avail Much* by Germaine Copeland. When I opened that book, a new door opened to me with an invitation to enter a lifelong adventure of communing with God through His Word in prayer.

The title suggested that prayer wasn't a hit-or-miss exercise but could actually be *effective*. I bought the book and read it aloud from cover to cover the same day! I quickly found that prayer in the Word was vibrant and alive. I was transfixed by how the author strung together scriptures like pearls, crafting profound appeals and declarations into prayers about matters I didn't even know the Bible addressed! Daily I knelt and prayed through the book, discovering that the voice of the Holy Spirit was becoming clearer and more recognizable to me as I prayed the Word. I often paused as He illuminated my heart with revelation and insight about the scriptures I had just prayed. I was awakening to the reality of the One Jesus said was sent to lead and guide me into truth and show me things to come.

The more I prayed the Scriptures, the more they prayed *me* — releasing God's presence and divine direction into my life, producing answers that were once elusive, and creating the confident assurance forged only by knowing God's Word *is* His will. *Prayers That Avail Much* laid in me a foundation and a framework for the Holy Spirit to build and breathe upon as He instilled within me an expectation that will not be cut off.

Above all, *Prayers That Avail Much* cultivated in me an understanding of what it means to know and walk with God by His Spirit through His Word in prayer. And this is available to anyone who will work by the Spirit with *Prayers That Avail Much.*

—Andrell Corbin Stevens
Tulsa, OK

Praise God for Word Ministries and *Prayers That Avail Much!*

Years ago, my wife, Trisha, and I were exposed to the prayer book that our friend in our church gave us. I would walk the aisle of our church and the altar area praying the prayers in first person. It was amazing to see a book of prayers that was actually praying the Word of God for different subject matters.

Trisha and I over the years have written names on the pages of different prayers Germaine has published in her prayer books. I can honestly say I have prayed those prays in all types of circumstances and situations throughout my ministry life.

When I was employed for the State of Michigan Department of Human Services, I had the *Prayers That Avail Much for Leaders* on my desk and prayed for my employees, staff, and other state leaders almost every day.

My go-to prayer is praying the names of God. It evokes the presence of God into any circumstance. When Trisha would pray this prayer to open a service, or when I would pray the prayer at a special meeting, the presence of God would fill the room.

Our devotion to these Word-based prayers has continued from volume to volume. We now use the 25th commemorative edition, which we give to all the couples we counsel before marriage, to families in crisis, and to graduates.

Germaine, thank you for obeying the Lord! Thank you for sharing your heart and teaching a generation how to pray effectively. And thank you for sharing with Trisha and me how to pray all manner of prayers. We love you and call you blessed in Jesus' name.

—James Tippin, MSW BA, Religious Ed.
Word Ministries, Inc. Board Member
Phoenix, AZ

Twenty-three years ago, this 44-year-old Jewish man accepted Yeshua (Jesus) as his Messiah. In the traditional synagogue, we were never asked to pray for someone, but in the Messianic Synagogue and churches I spoke in, I was asked to pray for people. I felt incredibly ill equipped for such an important assignment. I began to search for books on prayer and found great resources that explained what prayer was, but none taught me how to pray. As God would have it, just four blocks from where I lived and where I worshipped was a woman who had devoted her life to equipping the world in how to pray God's Word. Germaine Copeland sat down with me in Roswell, Georgia, and handed me the most profound book in my possession next to the Bible itself. Over the years, I added each volume as it was released until I was able to obtain the combined 25th Anniversary Edition. I have given out thousands of copies and consider it to be "Every Believers Guide to Praying the Scriptures" in almost every situation. It is my blessing to honor the gift of this mighty prayer warrior who equipped me to become the believer, minister, author, evangelist, teacher, and international talk show host that I have become using her gift of prayer and *Prayers That Avail Much* to change the lives of countless souls around the world. *Prayers That Avail Much* will forever be one of the most powerful tools in my arsenal and has stood the test of time as a classic.

—Rev./Rabbi Eric E. Walker,
Igniting a Nation Broadcasting Network, Executive Director and On-Air Host of *Revealing the Truth, Revealing the Bible, and Revealing Prophecy,* Birmingham, AL

Germaine Copeland has done it again! I remember purchasing Germaine's little yellow book so many years ago. The book changed my life! Today, her book, *Prayers That Avail Much 40th Anniversary Commemorative Edition,* is another book that will change the lives of all who read it. Germaine's scripture prayers are applicable for those longing for a closer relationship with the Lord. She continues through the book with prayers for numerous life situations including inmates and the parents of inmates. Whatever the life situation a person finds himself or herself in, this book will provide heartfelt prayers that are sure to reach the heart of God. I highly recommend this book for anyone desiring to shift their prayer life to a new level!

—Barbara Wentroble

President of International Breakthrough Ministries and Breakthrough Business Leaders, Argyle, TX

Author of *Prophetic Intercession; Praying with Authority, Fighting for Your Prophetic Promises,* and *The Council Room of the Lord* (series)

Often, I endorse books that I personally have not been impacted by. However, I happened to be in Atlanta in the '80s and a friend took me to one of Germaine's early prayer meetings. I neither knew her or what she was imparting concerning prayer, but one prayer meeting changed my prayer life. That Sunday night I quickly grasped the concept of praying the Word which is praying God's will. I am forever grateful to Germaine for imparting what she learned and then committing her knowledge of effective praying into a book, then several books. I will be first in line to buy this commemorative edition! I am forever grateful for Germaine Copeland because of her impact on my prayer life.

—Barbara Yoder

Ann Arbor, MI

I dedicate this book to my first prayer partner, Mrs. Doris Beasley, who shared my desire to know how to pray effectively.

Those years we prayed together became the foundation of *Prayers That Avail Much*®.

Together, we established Word Ministries, Inc., and Doris served as our first business manager.

Acknowledgments

THANK you to all the members of my first prayer group. This group assisted me in searching the Bible for answers to the prayer requests that began pouring in. I especially want to thank Carolyn East, who worked diligently to keep our records and mimeographed those first prayers for distribution. The written prayers were available to all who came from across the city of Atlanta, Georgia. I honor those who have transitioned from earth to heaven.

A special thank you to Jan Duncan, who walked around the dining room table observing all those written prayers and envisioned a book of prayers. That was the beginning of the book series known as *Prayers That Avail Much*®. Jan became the business manager for Word Ministries, and she and her husband, Earle, served as board members.

Another thank you goes to Linda Whitaker, who served Word Ministries as secretary. Gently, she taught me much more than she can ever imagine. Thank you for encouraging me and teaching me how to be a leader.

I owe Donna Walker a debt of gratitude. She was the editor who read those first handwritten yellow pages, marked them up in red and persuaded me that I could be a prolific writer.

There are a host of others I could name who served as personal assistants, travel companions, prayer leaders, office personnel, conference organizers, etc. etc. etc. Each one contributed to the success of the *Prayers That Avail Much*® book series.

Thank you, David Copeland, Vice-President of *Prayers That Avail Much*®, for praying for me and talking me through those stress-filled days when nothing seems to be working. Also, I can't say thank you enough for taking care of the business of the ministry with the help of our board members, Andy and Gail Lee, James and Trisha Tippin, Lynn Copeland Sutton, and last but certainly not least, my husband, Everette Copeland.

This revised and improved edition of the first three volumes of *Prayers That Avail Much*® involved many others. I especially want to thank Brad Herman, publisher of Harrison House; Kaye Mountz, editor; and the entire team for your guidance and support.

This is the confidence we have before him: If we ask anything according to his will, he hears us. And if we know that he hears whatever we ask, we know that we have what we have asked of him.

—1 John 5:14-15, CSB

Contents

Part II: Group Prayers

A Letter from Germaine

Dear Friend,

It was 1980 when Harrison House first published *Prayers That Avail Much*®. The original book was a collection of prayers the Holy Spirit orchestrated from the depths of my heart and the pages of God's Word as my husband, Everette, and I faced great adversity fighting for the life of our son who had become addicted to drugs and alcohol.

Those many years ago, we recognized that the personality of our intelligent, charismatic son was changing, and we had begun a search for help. We had heard about a hospital that was a rehabilitation center for those wanting to recover from their addictions. Today, I realize the psychiatrist we consulted knew that we were parents seeking help for our son who was not seeking help.

The cost of the required six-month stay was astronomical, but we were willing to mortgage our home and whatever else it might take to rescue our son. As we drove home, the last words spoken to us by the psychiatrist hung there in space: "I cannot guarantee you anything. After six months in rehab, your son may walk out drug-free or just the same."

Silence carried me as we climbed in the car and drove toward home. Finally, I said, "I know Someone who offers a guarantee, and I suggest we believe God's Word and trust Him for David's deliverance." I knew that my pragmatic husband would consider all sides of the issue before speaking. The next day we decided against rehab and affirmed our faith in God, who knew the kinds of prayer that would be required before David would be ready to choose between life and death.

Only three years before, I had an experience with God that had drastically changed my life. I knew full well that Jesus was not a myth. He was real and to know Him is to know God. God talked to me through the pages of the Bible, and I talked to Him. I was just "hanging out with God." God loved me, and I loved Him. Life was exciting as I learned more of God and His Word. And when trouble knocked at our door, I knew the One who had the answers.

My Holy Ghost bubble was shattered when the drug epidemic of the 1970s invaded our home, and I turned to God for answers. The day came when I made the decision to trust God and count it all joy! It was not easy, but my son's life was threatened by the thief who comes to steal, kill, and destroy. By this time in my life, I knew that I knew that God hears and answers prayers according to His will. Though I knew nothing about spiritual warfare or the prayer of intercession, I embarked on another level of Bible study and practiced prayer.

Even though no one else seemed to notice, I questioned our son's strange behavior and cried out, "Lord, teach me to pray!" This was the beginning of my education and training in the art of intercessory prayer. It was all trial and error. I made mistakes, and those mistakes were stepping stones to exciting prayer revelations. I lived in the pages of the Bible, and my mind was expanded to understand the dividing of soul and spirit so I could cooperate with my Divine Teacher who knows the mind of the Father (see Rom. 8:26-28 NLT).

During chaos, I had peace and joy. Then one day, after another session with the school counselor about David, I drove home and made my way to the bedroom where I dissolved into a pool of tears completely broken. The Voice which I had learned to recognize responded to my anguish, "You are broken, but not crushed. I will put you back together." Later, while reading the Bible, I learned that my outpouring of emotions was made up of tears from a mother's broken heart plus tears from a spirit of travail. Hannah, a woman who lived long before me, had also been broken-hearted, and God answered her prayer (see 1 Sam. 1).

There is power in agreement, and my constant prayerful study revealed *two* divine intercessors who were praying. My focus changed from "deliverance from drugs" to David's divine destiny and his eternal salvation. Jesus was praying for David. Satan had come to sift him like wheat, but Jesus pleaded in prayer for him that David's faith should not fail, and when he had come through he would strengthen others (see Luke 22:31-33 NLT).

Intercessor in Training

Little did I understand the depth of all that was happening with me. I became addicted to reading my Bible, seeking the face of my Father that I might know Him. And I prayed. Having prayed ineffectual prayers in the past, I searched for effectual prayers. I searched for answers from my Father who loved David and me. I learned to recognize the voice of God, and my life motto took on more meaning: *To be ever learning, ever growing, and ever achieving to the glory of the Father.*

Born in 1934, I can now look back over my life and connect the dots—the events that have led me to where I am today. Sometimes David and I talk about the millions who are experiencing emotional and physical healing and transformation as they pray scriptural prayers written from the heart of a mother who searched out God's answers to life's challenges.

A fellow believer who was the local director of the Atlanta chapter of a national Christian organization asked me to teach one of their home Bible studies. Ladies came to study the Bible with me and soon the very first prayer group was formed. We were surprised when people from far and near sent in prayer requests. Together we searched the Scriptures for answers. Volume I of *Prayers That Avail Much* was penned by members of that first prayer group and me.

The first "little yellow book" with its mission to equip pray-ers circulated far and wide and turned up in unusual places. Since then, in response to personal requests for additional written prayers, the Lord has orchestrated many more books of scriptural prayers and now millions are learning to stand and pray with confidence and boldness. They are offering their petitions to the Father with thanksgiving, and the testimonies we receive continue to come in.

This classic collection of three prayer volumes is designed to enhance your ability to pray effectively for specific needs and prepare you to go out into the marketplace as a living witness empowered by the Holy Spirit. Whether you are a seasoned pray-er or a novice, never forget the power of prayer. It is the very foundation that enables you to go from faith to faith and glory to glory. My dear pray-er, you are a world-changer—strong in the Lord and the power of His might!

> *Proclaim his majesty, all you mighty champions, you sons of Almighty God, giving all the glory and strength back to him! Be in awe before his majesty. Be in awe before such power and might! Come worship wonderful Yahweh, arrayed in all his splendor, bowing in worship as he appears in the beauty of holiness. Give him the honor due his name. Worship him wearing the glory-garments of your holy, priestly calling!* (Psalm 29:1-2 TPT)

Always remember, you have a friend praying for you!

Sincerely in His Love,
Germaine Copeland
President of Word Ministries, Inc.
The home of *Prayers That Avail Much*® Family Books

Effectual Prayer

The effective, fervent prayer of a righteous man avails much.
—James 5:16 NKJV

WITHOUT a doubt, there are effective prayers and ineffective prayers. James, the half-brother of Jesus, writes to the churches and includes instructions on prayer. He tells us in James 5:16 that it is the effective, fervent prayer of a righteous person that avails much.

Thank God that I grew up in a home where prayer was something we did as a family every morning and every night. Kneeling, my siblings and I knew to remain quiet as our dad or mother prayed. Then, at the end of their prayers, we recited the Lord's Prayer together. I knew God heard the prayers of my parents and my grandparents, but I was not convinced He would hear mine, much less answer. Never would I have dreamed that I was righteous or that I could ever pray an effective, fervent prayer. In fact, believe me when I tell you that I have prayed many ineffective prayers. Yet, when we desire truth, God will meet us where we are and show us His salvation.

The Beginning of Effective, Fervent Prayer

Effectual prayer begins with a personal relationship with God, and fellowship with God is fellowship with His Word. I wanted to know

Him and understand who He is, and therefore, I had to realize that "the Word was with God, and the Word was God" (John 1:1 NLT). He talks to you through the pages of the Bible, and prayer is talking to Him. This is sweet communication—your vital, personal contact with God, who is more than enough. Effectual prayer is uttered in words, and your words have the power of life or death—positive or negative. You have His Word that God hears the prayers you pray according to His will. But keep in mind that negative prayers also have the power to set circumstances into motion. That is not to scare you but to inspire you to learn to pray effectual prayers to the glory of the Father.

> *If you want to enjoy life and see many happy days, keep your tongue from speaking evil and your lips from telling lies. Turn away from evil and do good. Search for peace, and work to maintain it. The eyes of the Lord watch over those who do right, and his ears are open to their prayers. But the Lord turns his face against those who do evil* (1 Peter 3:10-12 NLT).

Prayer is not a religious obligation without power. Personal prayer time is that special time when you can talk with the Father one on one. You come just as you are without pretense. You come because He is your Father and you are His child. To know Jesus is to know the Father, and He instructs us to go directly to the Father and ask Him for anything.

> *For here is eternal truth: When that time comes you won't need to ask me for anything, but instead you will go directly to the Father and ask him for anything you desire and he will give it to you, because of your relationship with me. Until now you've not been bold enough to ask the Father for a single thing in my name, but now you can ask, and keep on asking him! And you can be sure that you'll receive what you ask for, and your joy will have no limits!* (John 16:23-24 TPT)

Effectual prayer changes you, and prayer becomes a way of life. Your prayers become more accurate as you learn God's will and His ways as revealed in His Word. God is the Word, and He watches over His Word to perform it (see Jer. 1:12). The effectual prayer is the prayer that God answers. You can be confident that He hears every request you pray according to His will. And if you know that He hears you in whatever you ask, you also know that you have obtained the requests you ask of Him (see John 5:14-15).

Effectual prayer is the "living" Word in your mouth. When you pray scriptural prayers, you are releasing your faith in His mighty power to answer your requests.

> *For we have the living Word of God, which is full of energy* [all effective], *and it pierces more sharply than a two-edged sword. It will even penetrate to the very core of our being where soul and spirit, bone and marrow meet! It interprets and reveals the true thoughts and secret motives of our hearts* (Hebrews 4:12 TPT).

When prayers are not effectual, ask the Holy Spirit to help you to know how to pray. Be ready for God's "living" Word to reveal if you are in conflict and fighting to have your own way and fulfill your own desires. When you do not receive what you ask for, go back to the Scriptures. God is faithful, and He desires to answer the prayers of His children.

A Study on Answered Prayer

> *What is the cause of your conflicts and quarrels with each other? Doesn't the battle begin inside of you as you fight to have your own way and fulfill your own desires? You jealously want what others have so you begin to see yourself as better than others. You scheme with envy and harm others to selfishly obtain what you crave—that's why you quarrel and fight.*

> *And all the time you don't obtain what you want because you won't ask God for it! And if you ask, you won't receive it for you're asking with corrupt motives, seeking only to fulfill your own selfish desires* (James 4:1-3 TPT).

Effectual prayer changes you. As your mind is renewed to God's Word, your motives and desires are transformed. God's Word is our contact with Him. Your perceptions of God change, and you make Him the utmost delight and pleasure of your life, and He will provide for you what you *desire* the most (see Ps. 37:4 TPT).

We put Him in remembrance of His Word (see Isa. 43:26), asking Him for what we need in the name of Jesus, who is the Word. The woman in Mark 5:25-34 placed a demand on the Word of God (Jesus) when she touched the hem of His garment. We do not know how long this woman had been waiting to see Jesus. She had obviously heard about His power to heal and to perform miracles—about blind eyes opened and the lame walking. And she believed. She defied tradition and ventured out not only to see Him but to touch Him! When she saw Jesus, she released her faith in this prayer. "If I can but touch the hem of His garment, I will be healed." She acted on her faith with her words and her actions. She placed a demand on His power to heal.

Effectual prayer brings prodigals home. Faith comes by hearing and hearing by the Word. The book you are reading today began the day I chose to believe God that our prodigal son would come home. I had read Jesus' story of the prodigal son; I heard testimonies of prodigals. By faith I began to place a demand on the power of God to deliver our prodigal out of the strange land of addictions and bring him home. Again, we learn from the book of James to fix our minds on God's Word and become single-minded. Our faith will remain strong while surrounded by circumstances that contradict our prayer, and we "will continue to experience the untold blessings of God!" (James 1:12 TPT).

The prayers in this book are composed of God's Word that does not return to Him void—without producing any effect, useless—but it shall accomplish that which He pleases and purposes, and it shall prosper in the thing for which He sent it (see Isa. 55:11). He did not leave us without His thoughts and His ways, for we have His Word—His bond. God tells us, "Call to me and I will answer you, and will tell you great and hidden things that you have not known" (Jer. 33:3 ESV). Prayer is an exciting adventure—not drudgery.

God is looking for an intercessor in each generation—someone who will come before Him and pray! God's power is released from heaven when the believer prays in faith—believing! The eyes of the Lord search the whole earth in order to strengthen those whose hearts are fully committed to him (see 2 Chron. 16:9 NLT). So, let us come boldly to the throne of our gracious God. There we will receive His mercy, and we will find grace to help us when we need it most (see Heb. 4:16 NLT).

Effectual prayer is developed when you become a doer of the Word. Practice, practice, practice praying the Word that the Father may be glorified.

> *Jesus said, "This is how you should pray: 'Father, may your name be kept holy. May your Kingdom come soon. Give us each day the food we need, and forgive us our sins, as we forgive those who sin against us. And don't let us yield to temptation'"* (Luke 11:2-4 NLT).

Prayer is an exciting journey with the great Three-in-One. Prayer is not a boring task you hope will win you brownie points with God. Prayer is a meeting with God who has raised you from the dead along with Christ and seated you with Him in the heavenly realms because you are united with Christ Jesus! (See Eph. 2:6 NLT.) Here is where you learn the strategies of prayer, the different forms of prayer, with the help of the Holy Spirit. The more you pray, the more you will desire to pray because you have His divine help.

There are different types of prayer and all are effective when uttered from the believer's heart of hope, faith, and love. The greatest of these is love.

Effectual prayer begins with adoration from a believing heart in awe of the majesty of God. Prayer does not cause faith to work, but faith causes prayer to work. Always remember, faith works by love—and therefore, prayers must be prayed from a place of love.

Your Prayers Will Avail Much

You have been made the righteousness of God in Christ Jesus, and you have the mind of Christ. Your prayers will bring salvation to the sinner, deliverance to the oppressed, healing to the sick, and hope to the poor. God desires that all may be healed and prosper even as their souls prosper.

United in prayer, we will usher in the next move of God on planet Earth! It is harvest time! In the process of praying, our lives will be changed as we move from faith to faith and from glory to glory.

> *God, glorify your name! Yes, your name alone be glorified, not ours. For you are the one who loves us passionately, and you are faithful and true* (Psalm 115:1 TPT).

How to Pray Prayers That Avail Much

THIS is not a book of formulas, but a book of living prayers that will impart wisdom and spiritual understanding to you. Do not hurry through but take time to read and meditate on the scriptures included with each prayer. The Holy Spirit will unlock the treasures of true knowledge and empower you to reign in life. Your commitment to pray scriptural prayers will be the beginning of a glorious experience. Be intentional about prayer! You will become spiritually strong, and the Father will be glorified.

If you are just embarking on your personal journey of prayer, the A.C.T.S. method is an effective tool. You do not have to achieve every step every time. Your prayers will expand as you continue to practice the prayer of Adoration, Confession, Thanksgiving, and Supplication. The Holy Spirit is your divine Helper, and He will be your guide. Confession is a time for you to examine yourself (see 1 Cor. 13:5 NLT).

A question I'm often asked about prayer is this: "How long do I pray these beautiful prayers?" The answer is simple. Pray a prayer until the words become written on the tablets of your heart and your mind. You will discover that your doubts and fears dissolve as your faith in God's Word increases. Effectual prayer is a prayer based on the will of the Father. Your mind will be renewed if you choose to exchange wrong, misguided thought patterns for God's Word. Faith comes by hearing and hearing by the Word of God (see Rom. 10:17).

God is patient and kind even when we have the audacity to tell Him exactly how He should answer our prayers. God's Word is for correction and discipline! (See 2 Tim. 3:16-17 AMPC.) Praying the Scriptures changed my false perceptions about who God is. As you pray the Word, you will come to know the Scriptures in a meaningful way, and you will experience transformation in your every-day-going-to-work life. You will become strong in the Lord and in His mighty power.

When you pray, be sure to take your time and pause for reflection. If you have not already done so, be sure you do not allow your cell phones and other devices to rob you of your listening time. Use this time to develop your spiritual imagination. See your Father inviting you into His Throne Room (see Heb. 4:16). He wants to hear your voice, and He is ready and willing to extend mercy and grace just when you need it. Ask the Holy Spirit to make the Word a reality in your heart and mind. One believer who had been diagnosed with terminal cancer began praying the written prayers page by page. She received a miracle; God's Word healed her. Another believer prayed each prayer every day, sometimes several times each day. At the end of seven days, he was delivered from depression. Prayer is not magic! God is not withholding any good thing from His children. Effectual prayer is deep calling to deep—a loving Father answering the prayers of His children.

These prayers will help you ask and keep on asking, seek and keep on seeking, knock and keep on knocking until the door is opened! (See Matt. 7.) The King of glory will come in!

Take the time to research and contemplate the spiritual significance of each verse listed at the end of the prayers. Praying in the name of Jesus is the prayer Jesus would offer in your situation. Tacking "in the name of Jesus" at the end of your prayers is not just a token saying. It's the authority to pray the prayer, knowing that Jesus releases the power to back it up.

These prayers are a guide for you to get to know your heavenly Father intimately. How do you become acquainted with anyone? By spending time with that individual. Never run from God even when you've sinned; instead, run to Him. If you confess your sins, He is faithful to forgive you and cleanse you from all unrighteousness (see 1 John 1:9). Remember, the Father will never leave you or forsake you. He will never leave you without support (see Heb. 13:5 AMPC).

Practical Steps to a Vibrant Prayer Life

- Have an appointed time to pray deliberately. I have found if I do not keep my early morning time with God, the day gets away. "Each morning you listen to my prayer, as I bring my requests to you and wait for your reply" (Ps. 5:3 CEV). "Every *morning* I will move my soul toward him. Every waking hour I will worship only him, and he will hear and respond to my cry" (Ps. 55:17 TPT).

- Read your Bible. If you do not like to read or have time to read, listen to an audio reading of the Scriptures. The Bible is food to your spirit being. Feed your heart and mind on the Word of God.

- Enter your prayer time with praise and thanksgiving. "Proclaim his majesty, all you mighty champions, you sons of Almighty God, giving all the glory and strength back to him! Be in awe before his majesty. Be in awe before such power and might!" (Ps. 29:1-2 TPT).

- Meditate on God's Word. Choose a verse of scripture for your meditation. Be patient with yourself; you have the power of choice and can learn to capture your thoughts and focus on the Word. Learning to meditate was not easy for me; my mind was never still. Instrumental music helped me get my mind focused. (I recommend music albums by Nick Syrett and Maurice Sklar.) "I long for more revelation of your truth, for I love the light of your Word as I *meditate* on your decrees" (Ps. 119:48 TPT).

Keep on Keeping On

Be prepared! Prayer is not an invitation to tiptoe through the tulips. Scriptural prayers pierce the darkness, and Satan will apply pressure and tempt you just as he did Jesus in Matthew 4. Do what Jesus did. Answer every lie with Scripture and have the prayer available to reinforce your faith. Satan's only weapon is deception. The enemy has been stripped of power, and you alone can draw the "line in the sand." Do not let go! Remember, you are strong, not in human strength, but "strong in the Lord, and in the power of His might" (Eph. 6:10).

God will give you even more strength to stand against all such evil longings. "As the Scripture says, God gives strength to the humble but sets himself against the proud and haughty. So give yourselves humbly to God. Resist the devil and he will flee from you" (James 4:6-7 TLB).

You are salt and you are light! You are the Body of Christ! Put on your prayer armor! (See Eph. 6:12-18.)

As you pray the prayers that follow, you will be reinforcing your prayer armor, which we have been instructed to put on in Ephesians 6:11. The fabric from which the armor is made is the Word of God. We are to live by every word that proceeds from the mouth of God. We desire the whole counsel of God because we know it changes us. By receiving that counsel, you will be "transformed (changed) by the [entire] renewal of your mind [by its new ideals and its new attitude], so that you may prove [for yourselves] what is the good and acceptable and perfect will of God, even the thing which is good and acceptable and perfect [in His sight for you]" (Rom. 12:2 AMPC).

If Satan brazenly attempted to stop Jesus from doing the Father's will, he will not hesitate to attack those who dare to believe the Word of God! Thoughts come out of nowhere to undermine your confidence, and you may even question your salvation. The accuser is no respecter of persons. Satan's tactics change from attempting to stop you from accepting Jesus to attempting to deceive you. One night, as I was preparing to leave for a speaking engagement, a sneering thought came from nowhere: *Who do you think you are?* Immediately, I declared, "I am a daughter of the Most High God! That's who I am!"

Turn to the next page and speak aloud the personal affirmations to reinforce who you are. Write the affirmations on index cards and post them around your house. Keep God's Word before your eyes, and remember, you are created in the image of God. You are intelligent and of great valor.

And keep on keeping on. Never give up, never give in, and never draw back. When you are victorious, God is glorified.

Your prayers will avail much!

They will bring salvation to the sinner, deliverance to the oppressed, healing to the sick, and prosperity to the poor. They will usher in the next move of God on the earth. In addition to affecting outward circumstances and other people, your prayers will also affect you. In the very process of praying, your life will be changed as you go from faith to faith and from glory to glory in Him—the One who called you to pray.

Personal Affirmations

- I have a spirit of power, love, and self-discipline (2 Tim. 1:7 NLT).
- I choose life that I and my offspring may live (Deut. 30:19 ESV).
- I am the righteousness of God in Christ Jesus (2 Cor. 5:21).
- My prayers avail much! (James 5:16b).
- I can do all things through Christ who strengthens me (Phil. 4:13).
- The Lord is my shepherd; I shall not want (Ps. 23:1 ESV).
- My God supplies all my need according to His riches in glory in Christ Jesus (Phil. 4:19).
- In everything by prayer and supplication with thanksgiving, I choose to make my requests known to God (Phil. 4:6).
- I choose to honor God and bring glory to Him in my body (1 Cor. 6:20).
- I have the mind of Christ and hold the thoughts, feelings, and purposes of His heart (1 Cor. 2:16).

- I choose to walk in the Kingdom of light, in love, in the Word; and the wicked one touches me not (Rom. 5:5; 1 John 4:16; 1 John 5:18).
- I have the power to tread upon serpents and scorpions and over all the power of the enemy (Luke 10:19).
- I take my shield of faith and quench Satan's every fiery dart (Eph. 6:16).
- Greater is He that is in me than he that is in the world (1 John 4:4).
- I am seated with Christ in heavenly places (Eph. 2:6).
- The law of the Spirit of life in Christ Jesus has made me free from the law of sin and death (Rom. 8:2).
- If God be for me, who can be against me? (Rom. 8:31).
- I hear the voice of the Good Shepherd. I hear my Father's voice, and the voice of a stranger I will not follow (John 10:27).
- I roll my works upon the Lord. I commit and trust them wholly to Him. He will cause my thoughts to become agreeable to His will, and so shall my plans be established and succeed (Prov. 16:3).
- I am God's masterpiece (Eph. 2:10).
- I will fulfill the destiny God has given me for I am joined to Jesus (Eph. 2:10).

PART I

Personal Prayers

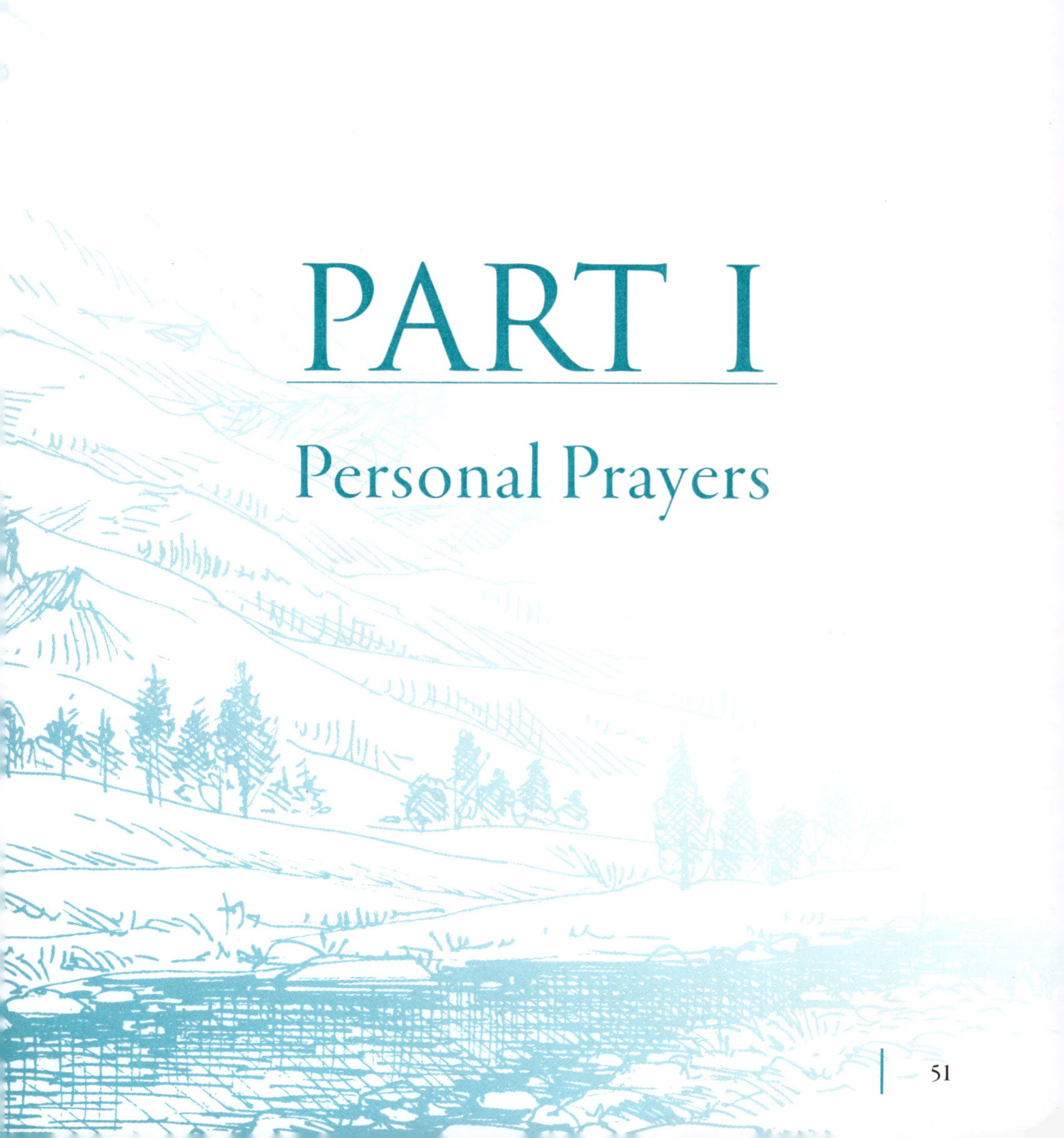

PRAYERS
of Commitment

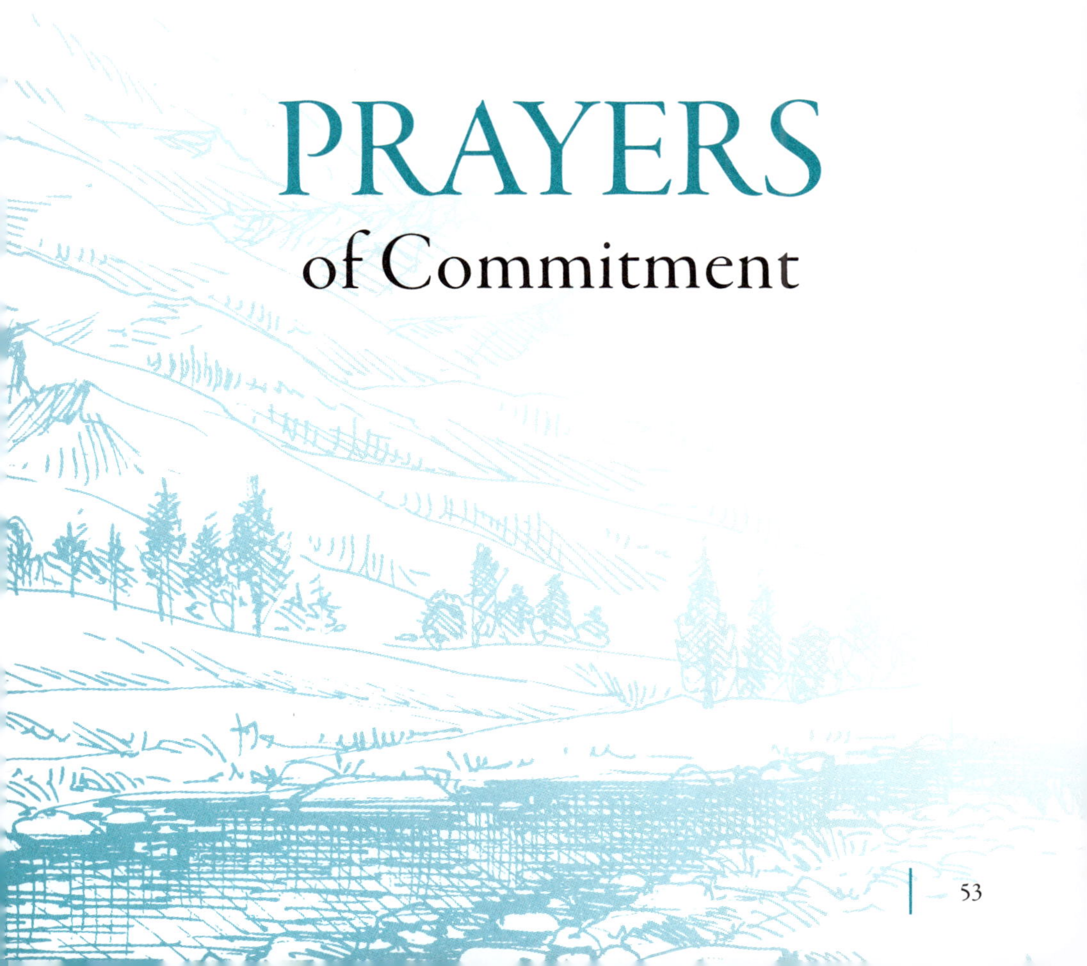

1

To Receive Jesus as Savior and Lord

FATHER, it is written in Your Word that if I confess with my mouth that Jesus is Lord and believe in my heart that You have raised Him from the dead, I will be saved.

Therefore, Father, I confess that Jesus is my Lord. I make Him Lord of my life right now. I believe in my heart that You raised Jesus from the dead. I renounce my past life with Satan and close the door to any of his devices.

Thank You, Father, for forgiving me of all my sin. Jesus, You are my Lord! I am a new creation. The past is finished and gone, everything has become fresh and new. The old life is gone; a new life has begun in Jesus' name, amen.

SCRIPTURE REFERENCES

John 3:16 • John 14:6 • John 6:37 • Romans 10:9-10 • John 10:10
Romans 10:13 • Romans 3:23 • Ephesians 2:1-10 • 2 Corinthians 5:19
2 Corinthians 5:17 TPT, PHI, NLT • John 16:8-9 • John 1:12
Romans 5:8 • 1 Corinthians 5:21

— 2 —

To Commit to Pray

FATHER, in the name of Jesus, I thank You for calling me to be a fellow workman—a joint promoter and a laborer together—with You. I commit to pray and to not give up.

Jesus, You are the Son of God, and I will never stop trusting You. You are my High Priest, and You understand my weaknesses. So I come boldly to Your throne, my gracious Father. There I receive Your mercy and find grace to help me when I need it most.

There are times I do not know what I ought to pray for. Holy Spirit, I submit to Your leadership and thank You for interceding for us with groans that words cannot express. You search hearts and know the mind of the Spirit, because You intercede for the saints in accordance with God's will.

Therefore, I am assured and know that with God being a partner in my labor all things work together and are fitting into a plan for my good, because I love God and am called according to His design and purpose.

Lord, teach me to pray that I might be a house of prayer for all the nations. I commit to pray without ceasing as the Holy Spirit helps me. The Lord is at hand; I choose not to be anxious about anything, but in everything by prayer and supplication with thanksgiving let my requests be made known to God. Whatever I ask for in prayer, I believe that it is granted to me, and I will receive it.

I choose to watch and pray that I may not enter into temptation. Even though the flesh is weak, I am strong in the Lord and the power of His might. Father, I bow my head, and with thanksgiving I am here to thank You for placing me in right standing with You. I am the righteousness of God because of Your great mercy. Now my earnest, heartfelt, and continued) prayer makes tremendous power available—dynamic in its working. Father, I live in You—abide vitally united to You—and Your words remain in me and continue to live in my heart. Therefore, I ask whatever I will, and it shall be done for me. When I produce much fruit, it brings great glory to You—the Father of my Lord Jesus Christ. Amen.

SCRIPTURE REFERENCES

1 Corinthians 3:9 NIV • Hebrews 4:16 NLT • Mark 11:17
Mark 11:24 AMP • Luke 18:1 NIV • 2 Corinthians 5:21 NLT
Romans 8:26-27 NIV • James 5:16 AMPC • Romans 8:28 AMPC
Philippians 4:6 ESV • John 15:7-8 AMPC

— 3 —

To Align My Thoughts with God's Word

FATHER, I am a spirit being learning to live in a polarized world of light and darkness. I have a soul (mind, will, and emotions), and I live in a physical body. I have the mind of Christ. I am in the world, but I am not of the world. God of peace, I ask You to sanctify me in every way, and may my whole spirit and soul and body be kept blameless until that day when Jesus comes again.

Father, You called me, and You are completely dependable. You said it, and You will do it. Thank You for the Spirit who guides me into all truth as I am being transformed by the renewal of my mind, bringing every thought into proper alignment with the Word of God.

I am a child of God, born of the Spirit of God, filled with the Spirit of God, and led by the Spirit of God. I choose to listen to the voice of the Good Shepherd.

Thank You, Holy Spirit, for directing me and illuminating my mind. You lead me in the way I should go. Thank You for leading me by an inward witness. The eyes of my understanding are being enlightened. Wisdom is in my inward parts. God's love is perfected in me. I have an unction from the Holy One.

Father, by grace I am becoming alert to my thoughts, attitudes, and feelings. I demolish every deceptive fantasy that opposes God and break through every arrogant attitude raised up in defiance of the true knowledge of God. I capture, like a prisoner of war, every thought and insist that it bow in obedience to the Anointed One.

I trust in You, Lord, with all of my heart and lean not to my own understanding. In all of my ways, I acknowledge You, and You direct my paths. I walk in the light of the Word. Holy Spirit, You are my Counselor, teaching me to educate, train, and bring my thoughts into alignment with the mind of Christ. The Word of God shall not depart out of my mouth. I meditate therein day and night. Therefore, I shall make my way prosperous, and I will have good success in life. I am a doer of the Word and put Your Word first.

SCRIPTURE REFERENCES

1 Thessalonians 5:23-24 • 1 John 4:12 • John 16:13 • Romans 12:1-2
1 John 2:20 • Proverbs 20:27 NLT • Romans 8:1 • 1 Corinthians 2:12 NLT
John 10:4 • Proverbs 3:5-6 • Romans 8:14,16 • Psalm 119:105
John 3:6-7 • John 14:26 • Ephesians 5:18 • Joshua 1:8 • Isaiah 48:17
James 1:22 • Ephesians 1:18 • 2 Corinthians 10:5 TPT

— 4 —

To Put on the Armor of God

FATHER, I put on the whole armor that You have given me that I may be able to stand against the wiles of the devil; for I wrestle not against flesh and blood, but against principalities, powers, the rulers of the darkness of this world, and spiritual wickedness in high places.

Therefore, I take unto myself the whole armor of God, that I may be able to withstand in the evil day, and having done all, to stand. I stand victorious with the force of Your explosive power flowing in and through me. My waist is girded with truth. Your Word, Lord, which is truth, contains all the weapons of my warfare, which are not carnal, but mighty through God to the pulling down of strongholds.

I have on the breastplate of righteousness, which is faith and love. My feet are shod with the preparation of the Gospel of peace. In Christ Jesus I have peace and pursue peace with all men. I am a minister of reconciliation, proclaiming the good news of the Gospel.

I take the shield of faith, wherewith I am able to quench all the fiery darts of the wicked; the helmet of salvation holding the thoughts, feelings, and purpose of God's heart; and the Sword of the Spirit, which is the Word of God. In the face of all trials, tests, temptations, and tribulation, I cut to pieces the snare of the enemy by speaking the Word of God. Greater is He that is in me than he that is in the world.

Thank You, Father, for the armor. I will pray at all times—on every occasion, in every season—in the Spirit, with all manner of prayer. To that end, I will keep alert and watch with strong purpose and perseverance, interceding in behalf of all the saints. My power and ability and sufficiency are from God who has qualified me as a minister and a dispenser of a new covenant of salvation through Christ. Amen.

SCRIPTURE REFERENCES

Ephesians 6:11-18 NKJV, TPT • Psalm 34:14 • John 17:17 • 2 Corinthians 5:18
2 Corinthians 10:4 • Ephesians 6:16-17 AMPC • Ephesians 6:14-15 AMPC
1 John 4:4 • Ephesians 2:14

— 5 —

To Rejoice in the Lord

FATHER, this is the day the You have made. I rejoice and I am glad in it! I rejoice in You always. And, again, I say rejoice. I delight myself in You, Lord. Happy am I because You are my Lord!

Father, thank You for loving me and rejoicing over me with joy. Hallelujah! I am redeemed. I come with singing, and everlasting joy is upon my head. I obtain joy and gladness—sorrow and sighing flee away. The spirit of rejoicing, joy, and laughter is my heritage. Where the Spirit of the Lord is, there is liberty—freedom and emancipation from bondage. I walk in that liberty.

Father, I praise You with joyful lips. I am ever filled and stimulated with the Holy Spirit. I speak out in psalms and hymns and make melody with all my heart to You, Lord. My happy heart is a good medicine and my cheerful mind works healing. The light in my eyes rejoices the hearts of others. I have a good report. My countenance radiates the joy of the Lord.

Father, I thank You that I bear much prayer fruit. I ask in Jesus' name, and I will receive, so that my joy, gladness, and delight may be full, complete, and overflowing. The joy of the Lord is my *strength*. Therefore, I count it all joy, all strength, when I encounter tests or trials of any sort because I am strong in You, Father.

I have the *victory* in the name of Jesus. Satan is under my feet. I am not moved by adverse circumstances. I have been made the righteousness of

God in Christ Jesus. I dwell in the Kingdom of God and have peace and joy in the Holy Spirit! Praise the Lord! In Jesus' name I pray, amen.

SCRIPTURE REFERENCES

Psalm 118:24 • Philippians 4:8 • Philippians 4:4 • Proverbs 15:13
Philippians 3:1 • John 15:7-8 • Psalm 144:15 • John 16:23
Zephaniah 3:17 • Nehemiah 8:10 • Isaiah 51:11 • James 1:2
2 Corinthians 3:17 • Ephesians 6:10 • James 1:25 • 1 John 5:4
Psalm 63:5 • Ephesians 1:22 • Ephesians 5:18-19
2 Corinthians 5:7 • Proverbs 17:22 • 2 Corinthians 5:21
Proverbs 15:30 • Romans 14:17

6

To Glorify God

FATHER, I offer my body as a living sacrifice, holy and pleasing to God—this is my spiritual act of worship. It is not in my own strength. For it is You, Lord, who are all the while effectually at work in me—energizing and creating in me the power and desire—both to will and work for Your good pleasure and satisfaction and delight.

Father, I will not draw back or shrink in fear, for then Your soul would have no delight or pleasure in me. I was bought for a price—purchased with a preciousness and paid for, made Your very own. So, I honor You, Lord, and bring glory to You in my body.

I called on You in the day of trouble, and You delivered me. I will honor and glorify You. I rejoice because You delivered me and drew me to Yourself out of the control and dominion of darkness and transferred me into the Kingdom of the Son of Your love. I will confess and praise You, Father, with my whole united heart, and I will glorify Your name forevermore.

As a bond servant of Jesus Christ, I receive and develop the talents that have been given me, for I would have You say of me, "Well done, you honorable, admirable, and faithful servant!" I make use of the gifts, talents, and qualities according to the grace given me. I let my light so shine before men that they may see my moral excellence and my praiseworthy, noble, and good deeds and recognize and honor and praise and glorify my Father who is in heaven.

In the name of Jesus, I allow my life to lovingly express truth in all things—speaking truly, dealing truly, living truly. Whatever I do—no matter what it is—in word or deed, I do everything in the name of the Lord Jesus. I depend on Him, giving praise to God the Father through Him. Whatever may be my task, I work at it heartily as something done for the Lord and not for men. To God the Father be all glory and honor and praise. Amen.

SCRIPTURE REFERENCES (AMPC)

Romans 12:1 • Matthew 25:21 • Philippians 2:13 • Romans 12:6
Hebrews 10:38 • Matthew 5:16 • 1 Corinthians 6:20 • Ephesians 4:15
Psalm 50:15 • Colossians 3:17 • Colossians 1:13 • Colossians 3:23
Psalm 86:12

7

To Walk in God's Wisdom and His Perfect Will

LORD and God, You are worthy to receive glory and honor and power, for You created all things. You created me and adopted me as Your child through Jesus Christ, in accordance with Your pleasure and will. I pray that I may be active in sharing my faith, so I will have a full understanding of every good thing I have in Christ.

Father, I ask You to give me a complete understanding of what You want to do in my life, and I ask You to make me wise with spiritual wisdom. Then the way I live will always honor and please You, and I will continually do good, kind things for others. All the while, I will learn to know You better and better.

I roll my works upon You, Lord, and You make my thoughts agreeable to Your will, so my plans are established and succeed. You direct my steps and make them sure. I understand and firmly grasp what the will of the Lord is for I am not vague, thoughtless, or foolish. I stand firm and mature in spiritual growth, convinced and fully assured in everything You will.

Father, You have destined and appointed me to come progressively to know Your will—that is to perceive, to recognize more strongly and clearly, and to become better and more intimately acquainted with Your will. Thank You, Father, for the Holy Spirit who abides permanently in me and who guides me into all the truth—the whole, full truth—and speaks whatever He hears from the Father and announces and declares to me the things that are to come. I have the mind of Christ and hold the thoughts, feelings, and purposes of His heart.

So, Father, I have entered into that blessed rest by adhering to, trusting in, and relying on You, in the name of Jesus. Hallelujah! Amen.

SCRIPTURE REFERENCES

Revelation 4:11 NIV • Colossians 4:12 AMPC • Ephesians 1:5 NIV
Acts 22:14 • Colossians 1:9-10 NLT • 1 Corinthians 2:16 AMPC
Proverbs 16:3,9 AMPC • Hebrews 4:10 • Ephesians 5:16 AMPC

8

To Walk in the Word

FATHER, in the name of Jesus, I commit myself to walk in the Word. Your Word living in me produces Your life in this world. I recognize that Your Word is integrity itself—steadfast, sure, eternal—and I trust my life to its provisions.

You have sent Your Word forth into my heart. I let it dwell in me richly in all wisdom. I meditate in it day and night so that I may diligently act on it. The Incorruptible Seed, the Living Word, the Word of Truth is abiding in my spirit. That Seed is growing mightily in me now, producing Your nature, Your life. It is my counsel, my shield, my buckler, my powerful weapon in battle. The Word is a lamp to my feet and a light to my path. It makes my way plain before me. I do not stumble, for my steps are ordered in the Word.

The Holy Spirit leads and guides me into all the truth. He gives me understanding, discernment, and comprehension so that I am preserved from the snares of the evil one.

I delight myself in You and Your Word. Because of that, You put Your desires within my heart. I commit my way unto You, and You bring it to pass. I am confident that You are at work in me now both to will and to do all Your good pleasure.

I exalt Your Word, hold it in high esteem, and give it first place. I make my schedule around Your Word. I make the Word the final authority to settle all questions that confront me. I choose to agree with the Word of God, and I choose to disagree with any thoughts, conditions, or circumstances contrary to Your Word. I boldly and confidently say that my heart is fixed and established on the solid foundation—the living Word of God! Amen.

SCRIPTURE REFERENCES

Hebrews 4:12 • 1 Peter 3:12 • Colossians 3:16 • Colossians 4:2
Joshua 1:8 • Ephesians 6:10 • 1 Peter 1:23 • Luke 18:1 • Psalm 91:4
James 5:16 • Psalm 119:105 • Psalm 37:4-5 • Psalm 37:23 • Philippians 2:13

— 9 —

To Walk in Love

FATHER, in Jesus' name, I thank You that the love of God has been poured forth into my heart by the Holy Spirit who has been given to me. I keep and treasure Your Word. The love of and for You, Father, has been perfected and completed in me, and perfect love casts out all fear.

Father, I am Your child, born of love. Your love that is poured out in my heart is *large* and incredibly patient. Holy Spirit, remind me to be gentle and consistently kind to all. Father, I submit to Your love that refuses to be jealous when blessing comes to someone else. I choose not to brag about my achievements nor inflate my own importance. Thank You, for love does not traffic in shame and disrespect nor selfishly seek its own honor. I choose to walk in the love of God that is not easily irritated or quick to take offense. I joyfully celebrate honesty and find no delight in what is wrong. Love is a safe place of shelter, and I will never stop believing the best for others even when I'm tempted. Love never takes failure as defeat, for it never gives up.

Father, I have no control over persecution from those who dislike me or what they say about me, but I can choose my reaction. I choose to let go of hurt and disappointment, and I purpose to *bless* and *pray* for those who are cruel in their attitude toward me. I bless them and do not curse them. Therefore, my love abounds yet more and more in knowledge and in all judgment. I approve things that are excellent. I am sincere and without offense till the day of Christ. I am filled with the fruits of righteousness.

Everywhere I go I commit to plant seeds of love. Thank You, Father, for preparing hearts ahead of time to receive this love. I know that these seeds will produce Your love in the hearts where they are sown.

Father, thank You that as I flow in Your love and wisdom, people are being blessed by my life and ministry. You make me to find favor, compassion, and loving-kindness with others (name them).

I am rooted deep in love and founded securely on love, knowing that You are on my side and nothing is able to separate me from Your love, Father, which is in Christ Jesus my Lord. Thank You, Father, in Jesus' precious name. Amen.

SCRIPTURE REFERENCES

Romans 5:5 • Philippians 1:9-11 • 1 John 2:5 • John 13:34 • 1 John 4:18
1 Corinthians 3:6 • 1 Corinthians 13:4-8 TPT • Daniel 1:9 AMPC
Romans 12:14 AMPC • Ephesians 3:17 AMPC • Matthew 5:44
Romans 8:31,39

10

To Walk in Forgiveness

FATHER, in the name of Jesus, I make a fresh commitment to You to live in peace and harmony, not only with the other brothers and sisters of the Body of Christ, but also with my friends, associates, neighbors, and family.

Father, I repent of holding on to bad feelings toward others. I bind myself to godly repentance and loose myself from bitterness, resentment, envying, strife, and unkindness in any form. Father, I ask Your forgiveness for the sin of ______________. By faith, I receive it, having assurance that I am cleansed from all unrighteousness through Jesus Christ. I ask You to forgive and release all who have wronged and hurt me. I forgive and release them. Deal with them in Your mercy and loving-kindness.

From this moment on, I purpose to walk in love, to seek peace, to live in agreement, and to conduct myself toward others in a manner that is pleasing to You. I know that I have right standing with you, and Your ears are attentive to my prayers.

I choose to forgive so I will not be exploited by the adversary, Satan, for I know his clever schemes.

It is written in Your Word that the love of God has been poured forth into my heart by the Holy Ghost who is given to me. I believe that love flows forth into the lives of everyone I know, that we may be filled with and abound in the fruits of righteousness, which bring glory and honor unto You, Lord, in Jesus' name. So be it! Amen.

SCRIPTURE REFERENCES

Romans 12:16-18 • Mark 11:25 • Romans 12:10
Ephesians 4:32 • Philippians 2:2 • 1 Peter 3:8,11-12
Ephesians 4:31 • Colossians 1:10 • Ephesians 4:27 • Romans 5:5
John 1:9 • Philippians 1:9,11 • 2 Corinthians 2:10-12 TPT

11

To Receive the Infilling of the Holy Spirit

My heavenly Father, I am Your child, for I believe in my heart that Jesus has been raised from the dead, and I confess Him as my Lord.

Jesus, the love I have for You empowers me to obey Your commands. Thank You for sending the Holy Spirit of Truth, who will be in me and never leave me.

Heavenly Father, I ask You for the Holy Spirit's fullness. If imperfect parents know how to lovingly take care of their children and give them what they need, how much more will You give me the Holy Spirit's fullness.

I receive the promise of the Holy Spirit, and I will be filled with power. I desire to be Your messenger to my city and nation—even to the remotest places on earth!

I thank You for filling me with the Holy Spirit and giving me the ability to speak in other tongues as the Holy Spirit gives me utterance.

Here in Your presence is fullness of joy and at Your right hand are pleasures forevermore. It's all in the name of Jesus! Praise the Lord and Amen!

SCRIPTURE REFERENCES

Romans 10:9-10 • John 14:15 TPT • Luke 11:12-14 TPT • Acts 1:8
Acts 2:4 NASB

— 12 —

To Walk in Sanctification

FATHER, thank You for sanctifying me by the truth; Your Word is truth. Jesus, You consecrated Yourself for my sake, so I will be truth-consecrated in my mission. In the name of Jesus, I repent and turn from my wicked ways. I wash myself, make myself clean. I cease to do evil, and I am learning to do right.

Father, You dwell in me and walk with me. So I leave the corruption and compromise; I leave it for good. You are my Father, and I will not link up with those who would pollute me, because You want me all for Yourself. I purify myself from everything that contaminates body and spirit, perfecting holiness out of reverence for God.

Father, I confess my sins. You are faithful and just to forgive me my sins and to cleanse me from all unrighteousness. Jesus has been made unto me wisdom, righteousness, sanctification, and redemption.

I submit myself to You, Lord—spirit, soul, and body. I strip myself of my old, unrenewed self and put on the new nature, changing whatever needs to be changed in my life. The desire of my heart is to be a vessel unto honor, sanctified, fitting for Your use, and prepared for every good work.

Thank You, Lord, that I eat the good of the land, because You have given me a willing and obedient heart. Amen.

SCRIPTURE REFERENCES

John 17:17,19 • Isaiah 1:16-17 • 2 Corinthians 6:17 MSG
2 Corinthians 7:1 NIV • 1 John 1:9 NKJV • 1 Corinthians 1:30
Ephesians 4:22-24 • 2 Timothy 2:21 • Isaiah 1:19

13

To Bear Fruit

Lord Jesus, You chose me and appointed me to go and bear fruit—fruit that will last. Then the Father will give me whatever I ask in Your name. Father, You are the Gardener. You prune every branch that bears fruit, so it will be even more fruitful.

The apostle Paul said to be filled with the fruit of righteousness and that he desired that fruit might abound to our account. Therefore, I commit myself to bring forth the fruit of the Spirit: love, joy, peace, longsuffering, gentleness, goodness, faith, meekness, and temperance. I renounce and turn from the fruit of the flesh, because I belong to Jesus Christ and have crucified the flesh with its affections and lusts.

A seed cannot bear fruit unless it first falls into the ground and dies. I confess that I am crucified with Christ. Nevertheless I live; yet not I, but Christ lives in me. And the life that I now live in the flesh I live by the faith of the Son of God, who loved me and gave Himself for me.

Father, thank You that I am good ground, that I hear Your Word and understand it, and that the Word bears fruit in my life—sometimes a hundredfold, sometimes sixty, sometimes thirty. I am like a tree planted by the rivers of water that brings forth fruit in its season. My leaf shall not wither, and whatever I do shall prosper.

Father, in Jesus' name, thank You for filling me with the knowledge of Your will in all wisdom and spiritual understanding that I may walk worthy of You, Lord, being fruitful in every good work and increasing in the knowledge of You. Amen.

SCRIPTURE REFERENCES

John 15:16 • Galatians 2:20 • Philippians 1:11 • Matthew 13:23
Philippians 4:17 • Psalm 1:3 • Galatians 5:22-24 • Colossians 1:9-10
John 12:24

14

To Help Others

FATHER, I will treat others the way I want to be treated. I will go after a life of love as if my life depended on it—because it does. I purpose to make loving and helping others my aim, my great quest in life.

In the name of Jesus, I will look not only to my own interests, but also to the interests of others. I will forget myself and lend a helping hand. I am strong in the Lord and in the power of His might. I will make it a practice to please (make happy) my neighbors, (bosses, co-workers, teachers, parents, children, brothers and sisters, etc.) for their good and for their true welfare, to edify them—that is, to strengthen and build them up in all ways—spiritually, socially, and materially.

I desire to imitate my heavenly Father, and as a child of light I will walk in love and wisdom. Help me to encourage, admonish, and exhort others and edify them.

Father, in the name of Jesus, I love my enemies (as well as my business associates, fellow church members, neighbors, those in authority over me) and am kind and do good—doing favors so that someone derives benefit from them. I lend expecting and hoping for nothing in return but considering nothing as lost and despairing of no one.

Thank You, Father, for imprinting Your laws upon my heart and inscribing them on my mind—on my inmost thoughts and understanding. According to Your Word, as I would like and desire that men would do to me, I do exactly so to them, in the name of Jesus. Amen.

SCRIPTURE REFERENCES

Luke 6:31 TPT • 1 Thessalonians 5:11 AMPC
1 Corinthians 14:1 MSG, AMPC • Luke 6:35-36 AMPC
Philippians 2:4 NLT, MSG • Ephesians 5:1-2 AMPC
Ephesians 6:10 • Hebrews 10:16 AMPC • Romans 15:2 AMPC
Luke 6:31 AMPC

15

To Watch What You Say

FATHER, today I make a commitment to You in the name of Jesus. I will guard my speech and watch the way I talk. I will forsake obscenities, worthless insults, and nonsensical words that bring disgrace and are unnecessary. I will lay aside ugly, hateful, and bitter words. Instead I will let my words become beautiful gifts that encourage others by speaking words of grace to help them. I will let worship fill my heart and spill out in my words.

In the name of Jesus, I submit to godly wisdom that I might learn to control my tongue. I am determined that hell will not set my tongue on fire. I dedicate my mouth to speak excellent and right things. My mouth shall utter truth. I purpose to guard my mouth and my tongue that I might keep myself from calamity for the tongue has the power of life and death.

Father, Your Words are top priority to me. They are spirit and life. I let the Word dwell in me richly in all wisdom. The ability of God is released within me by the words of my mouth and by the Word of God. I speak Your Words out of my mouth. They are alive in me. You are alive and working in me. So, I can boldly say that my words are words of faith, words of power, words of love, and words of life. They produce good things in my life and in the lives of others because I choose Your Words for my lips, and Your will for my life, in Jesus' name. Amen.

SCRIPTURE REFERENCES

Ephesians 5:4 MSG, TPT • Ephesians 4:27-32 MSG, TPT • Proverbs 21:23
2 Timothy 2:16 • Proverbs 18:21 • Ephesians 4:27 • James 3:6
James 1:6 • Proverbs 8:6-7 • John 6:63 • 2 Corinthians 5:21
Colossians 3:16 • Proverbs 4:23 • Philemon 6

— 16 —

To Live Free from Worry

FATHER, I thank You that I have been delivered from the power of darkness and translated into the Kingdom of Your dear Son. I choose to live free from worry in the name of Jesus, for the law of the Spirit of life in Christ Jesus has made me *free* from the law of sin and death.

I humble myself under Your mighty hand that in due time You may exalt me. I cast the whole of my cares—all my anxieties, all my worries, all my concerns (name them)—once and for all on You. You care for me affectionately and care about me watchfully. You sustain me. You will never allow the consistently righteous to be moved—made to slip, fall, or fail!

Father, I delight myself in You, and You perfect that which concerns me.

I cast down imaginations, reasonings, and every high thing that exalts itself against the knowledge of You, and I bring into captivity every thought to the obedience of Christ. I strip off every weight that slows me down, especially the sin that so easily trips me up. And I run with endurance the race God has set before me. I do this by keeping my eyes on Jesus, the Champion, who initiates and perfects my faith.

I thank You, Father, that You are able to keep that which I have committed unto You. I fix my mind on those things that are true, honest, just, pure, lovely, of good report, virtuous, and deserving of praise. I will not let my heart be troubled. I abide in Your Word, and Your Word abides in me. Therefore, Father, I do *not* forget what manner of person I am. I look into the perfect law of liberty and continue therein, being *not* a forgetful hearer, but a *doer of the Word* and, thus, blessed in my doing!

Thank You, Father. *I am carefree.* I walk in that peace that passes all understanding, in Jesus' name! Amen.

SCRIPTURE REFERENCES

Colossians 1:13 • Hebrews 12:1-2 NLT • Romans 8:2 • 2 Timothy 1:12
1 Peter 5:6-7 AMPC • Philippians 4:8 • Psalm 55:22 • John 14:1
Psalm 138:8 • James 1:22-25 • 2 Corinthians 10:5 • Philippians 4:6

PRAYERS to the Father

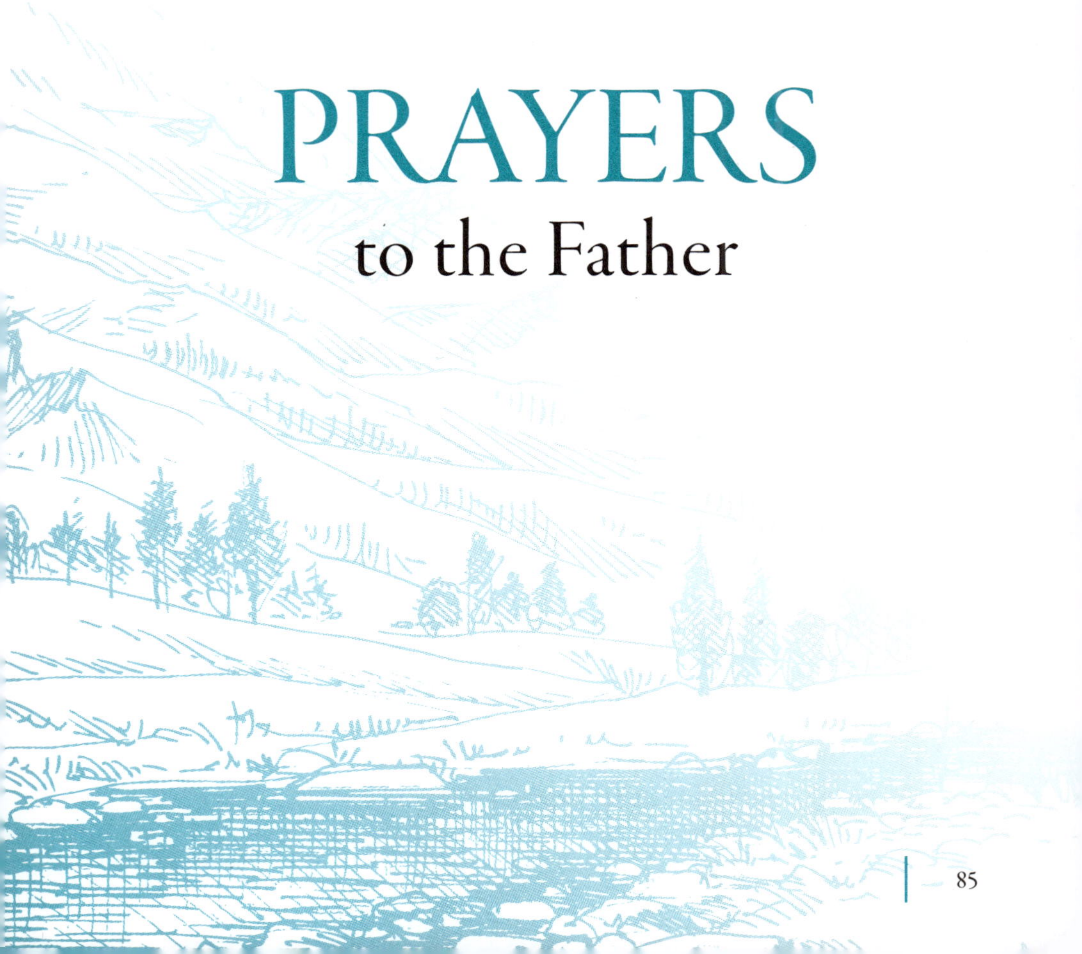

17

Adoration: "Hallowed Be Your Name"

OUR Father, dwelling in the heavenly realms, may the glory of Your name be the center on which our lives turn. Manifest Your kingdom realm and cause Your every purpose to be fulfilled on earth, just as it is fulfilled in heaven. Hallowed be Your name!

Bless the Lord, O my soul, and all that is within me bless Your holy name. I adore You and make known to You my adoration and love this day.

I bless Your name, *Elohim,* the Creator of heaven and earth, who was in the beginning. It is You who made me, and You have crowned me with glory and honor. You are the God of might and strength. Hallowed be Your name!

I bless Your name, *El-Shaddai,* the God Almighty of blessings. You are the Breasty One who nourishes and supplies. You are all-bountiful and all-sufficient. You are God of the Mountain and God the Destroyer of Enemies. You are God Almighty! Hallowed be Your name!

I bless Your name, *Adonai,* my Lord and my Master. You are Jehovah—the Completely Self-Existing One, always present, revealed in Jesus, who is the same yesterday, today, and forever. Hallowed be Your name!

I bless Your name, *Jehovah-Jireh,* the One who sees my needs and provides for them. Hallowed be Your name!

I bless Your name, *Jehovah-Rapha,* my Healer and the One who makes bitter experiences sweet. You sent Your Word and healed me. You forgave all my iniquities, and You healed all my diseases. Hallowed be Your name!

I bless Your name, *Jehovah-M'Kaddesh,* the Lord my Sanctifier. You have set me apart for Yourself. Hallowed be Your name!

Jehovah-Nissi, You are my Victory, my Banner, and my Standard. Your banner over me is love. When the enemy comes in like a flood, You lift up a standard against him. Hallowed be Your name!

Jehovah-Shalom, I bless Your name. You are my Peace—the peace that transcends all understanding, which garrisons and mounts guard over my heart and mind in Christ Jesus. Hallowed be Your name!

I bless You, I bless You, *Jehovah-Tsidkenu,* my Righteousness. Thank You for becoming sin for me that I might become the righteousness of God in Christ Jesus. Hallowed be Your name!

Jehovah-Rohi, You are my Shepherd, and I shall not want for any good or beneficial thing. Hallowed be Your name!

Hallelujah to *Jehovah-Shammah,* the One who will never leave or forsake me. You are always there. I take comfort and am encouraged and confidently and boldly say the Lord is my Helper; I will not be seized with alarm—I will not fear or dread or be terrified. What can man do to me? Hallowed be Your name!

I worship and adore You, *El-Elyon,* the Most High God. You are the First Cause of everything, the Possessor of the heavens and earth. You are the everlasting God, the great God, the living God, the merciful God, the faithful God, the mighty God. You are Truth, Justice, Righteousness, and Perfection. You are *El-Elyon*—the Highest Sovereign of the heavens and the earth. Hallowed be Your name!

Father, You have exalted above all else Your name and Your Word, and You have magnified Your Word above all Your name. The Word was made flesh and dwelt among us, and His name is Jesus. Hallowed be Your name!

In Jesus' name I worship and adore You, my Father, Son and Holy Spirit—the great three in One!

SCRIPTURE REFERENCES

Matthew 6:9 TPT • Song of Solomon 2:4 • Psalm 103:1
Isaiah 59:19 • Genesis 1:1-2 • Judges 6:24 • Psalm 8:5
Philippians 4:7 AMPC • Genesis 49:24-25 • Jeremiah 23:5-6
Genesis 15:1-2,8 • 2 Corinthians 5:21 • Hebrews 13:8 • Psalm 23:1
Genesis 22:14 • Psalm 34:10 • Psalm 147:3 AMPC • Hebrews 13:5
Exodus 15:23-26 AMPC • Hebrews 13:6 AMPC • Psalm 107:20
Genesis 14:19,22 • Psalm 103:3 • Psalm 91:1 • Leviticus 20:7-8
Psalm 138:2 AMPC • Exodus 17:15 • John 1:14

18

Divine Intervention: "Your Kingdom Come"

FATHER, in Jesus' name, I pray according to Matthew 6:10: "Your Kingdom come." Thank You for rescuing me completely from the tyrannical rule of darkness and translating me into the kingdom of Your beloved Son. In Jesus all my sins are cancelled, and I have the release of redemption through His very blood.

Your kingdom is not coming with signs and wonders. It is already here. Your kingdom is within us, and we are seated together with Jesus Christ in heavenly places in Him.

Dear Father, dwelling in the heavenly realms, may the glory of Your name be the center on which our lives turn. Manifest Your kingdom realm and cause Your every purpose to be fulfilled on earth, just as it is fulfilled in heaven.

Father, we are looking forward to the day when Jesus who ascended into heaven will come back in the same way.

This is exactly who I am—a child of God. And that's only the beginning. Who knows how I will end up! What I know is that when Christ is openly revealed, I will see Him—and in seeing Him, become like Him. I look forward to His coming and stay ready, with the glistening purity of Jesus' life as a model for my own.

God's marvelous grace has manifested in person, bringing salvation for everyone. This same grace teaches me how to live each day as I turn my back on ungodliness and indulgent lifestyles, and it equips me to live a self-controlled, upright, godly life in this present age. For I continue to look forward to the joyful fulfillment of our hope in the dawning splendor of the glory of my great God and Savior, Jesus, the Anointed One.

For the Lord Himself shall descend from heaven with a shout, with the voice of the archangel, and with the trump of God, and the dead in Christ shall rise first. Then we who are alive and remain shall be caught up together with them in the clouds to meet the Lord in the air, and so shall we ever be with the Lord.

Thank You, Father, that the Lord shall come to earth and all the saints and angels with Him; and the Lord shall be King over all the earth; in that Day He shall be one Lord, and His name one. The government shall be upon His shoulder.

Father, thank You that we shall join the great voices in heaven saying, "The kingdoms of this world are become the kingdoms of our Lord, and of His Christ; and He shall reign for ever and ever."

Yours, O Lord, is the greatness and power and the glory and the victory and the majesty; for all that is in the heavens and the earth is Yours; Yours is the Kingdom, O Lord; and Yours it is to be exalted as Head over all. Your Kingdom come. Hallelujah! Amen.

SCRIPTURE REFERENCES

Colossians 1:13-14 TPT • Luke 17:21 • Matthew 6:10-11 TPT • Acts 1:11
1 John 3:2-3 MSG • Isaiah 9:6 AMPC • Titus 2:11-13 TPT
Revelation 11:15 • 1 Thessalonians 4:16-17 • 1 Chronicles 29:11 AMPC
Zechariah 14:5,9 AMPC

19

Submission: "Your Will Be Done"

Father, in the name of Jesus, I pray that the will of God be done in my life as it is in heaven. I am Your masterpiece, created anew in Christ Jesus, so I can do the good things You planned for me long ago.

Teach me to do Your will, for You are my God. Let Your good Spirit lead me into a plain country and into the land of uprightness. Jesus, You gave Yourself up to atone for my sins and to save and sanctify me, in order to rescue and deliver me from this present, wicked world order, in accordance with the will and purpose and plan of our God and Father.

In the name of Jesus, I am not conformed to this world, but I am transformed by the renewing of my mind, that I may prove what is that good and acceptable and perfect will of God. Holy Spirit, thank You for teaching me to appreciate and give dignity to my body, not abusing it.

Father, thank You that You chose me—actually picked me out for Yourself as Your own—in Christ before the foundation of the world; that I should be holy (consecrated and set apart for You) and blameless in Your sight, even above reproach before You in love, having predestinated me unto the adoption of a child by Jesus Christ to Yourself, according to the good pleasure of Your will.

Your will be done on earth in my life as it is in heaven. Amen and so be it!

SCRIPTURE REFERENCES

Matthew 6:9-10 • Romans 12:2 • Ephesians 2:10 NLT
1 Thessalonians 4:4-5 MSG • Psalm 143:10 AMPC • Ephesians 1:4 AMPC
Galatians 1:4 AMPC • Ephesians 1:5

— 20 —

Provision:
"Give Us This Day Our Daily Bread"

In the name of Jesus, I confess with the psalmist David that I have not seen the righteous forsaken, nor Your seed begging bread.

Father, thank You for food, clothing, and shelter. In the name of Jesus, I am learning to stop being perpetually uneasy (anxious and worried) about my life, what I shall eat and what I shall drink, or about my body, what I shall put on. My life is greater in quality than food, and my body is far above and more excellent than clothing.

I will not eat the bread of idleness (gossip, discontent, and self-pity). It is You, Father, who will liberally supply—fill to the full—my every need according to Your riches in glory in Christ Jesus.

In the name of Jesus, I shall not live by bread alone, but by every word that proceeds from the mouth of God. Your words were found, and I did eat them, and Your Word was to me a joy and the rejoicing of my heart.

And the Word became human and made His home among us. Jesus, You are the Bread of Life that gives me life, the Living Bread.

Thank You, Father, in the name of Jesus, for spiritual bread—manna from heaven. Amen.

SCRIPTURE REFERENCES

Matthew 6:9-11 • Matthew 4:4 • Psalm 37:25 • Jeremiah 15:16 AMPC
Matthew 6:25 AMPC • John 1:14 NLT • Proverbs 31:27 AMPC
John 6:48-51 AMPC • Philippians 4:19 AMPC

21

Forgiveness: "Forgive Us Our Debts"

FATHER, forgive us the wrongs we have done as we ourselves release forgiveness to those who have wronged us. You have graciously forgiven me, and because of Your love and forgiveness, I choose to graciously forgive others in the depths of Christ's love.

Because of Your great love, I'm asking You for the grace to walk out the decision to forgive. Father, I choose to forgive the betrayal of even my intimate friends—those with whom I once worshiped in unity as one.

As a follower of Jesus, I choose to love my enemy and bless the one who curses me. Holy Spirit, show me something wonderful that I can do for the one who hates me. Rather than reacting, I choose to respond to the very ones who persecute me by praying for them.

Father, not only will I pray for ____________, but I set myself to treat him/her well (do good and act nobly toward him/her). I will be merciful, sympathetic, tender, responsive, and compassionate toward ________, even as You are, Father.

My desire is to be an imitator of You, and I can do all things through Christ Jesus who strengthens me.

Father, thank You that I have great peace in this situation, for I love Your law and refuse to take offense toward __________.

Jesus, I am blessed—happy [with life—joy and satisfaction in God's favor and salvation apart from outward conditions] and to be envied—

because I take no offense in You and refuse to be hurt or resentful or annoyed or repelled or made to stumble, whatever may occur.

And now, Father, I roll this work upon You—commit and trust it wholly to You; and I believe that You will cause my thoughts to become in agreement to Your will, and so my plans shall be established and succeed. In Jesus' name, amen.

SCRIPTURE REFERENCES

Matthew 6:12 TPT • Ephesians 4:32 TPT • Ephesians 5:1 AMPC
Psalm 55:20-23 • Matthew 5:44 TPT • Matthew 6:14-15
Philippians 4:13 AMPC • Psalm 119:165 AMPC • Luke 6:27 AMPC
Luke 7:23 AMPC • Matthew 5:44 AMPC • Proverbs 16:3 AMPC
Luke 6:28 AMPC

22

Guidance and Deliverance: "Do Not Lead Us into Temptation"

FATHER, there has no temptation taken me but such as is common to man. Thank You for Your faithfulness. I am confident that You will not suffer me to be tempted above that which I am able but will with the temptation also make a way to escape, that I may be able to bear it.

You have not given me a spirit of fear but a spirit of love, power, and a sound mind. I choose to gaze upon You, join my life with Yours, and joy will come. When I cry out to You, my Lord, You hear me and bring Your miracle-deliverance when I need it most.

I choose to count it all joy when I fall into various temptations, knowing this—that the trying of my faith works patience.

I will not say when I am tempted, "I am tempted from God," for God is incapable of being tempted by what is evil, and He Himself tempts no one.

Thank You, Jesus, for giving Yourself for my sins, that You might deliver me from this present evil world, according to the will of God and our Father—to whom be glory for ever and ever.

Father, in the name of Jesus, and according to the power that is at work in me, I will keep awake, give strict attention, be cautious, and watch and pray that I may not come into temptation. In Jesus' name, amen.

SCRIPTURE REFERENCES

1 Corinthians 10:13 • Psalm 34:5-6 TPT • 2 Timothy 1:7
Galatians 1:4-5 • James 1:2-3 • Ephesians 3:20 • James 1:13 AMPC
Matthew 26:41 AMPC

23

Praise: "For Yours Is the Kingdom, and the Power, and the Glory"

COME, let us tell of the Lord's greatness; let us exalt His name together.

Father God, Your way is perfect! The Word of the Lord is tested and tried, and You are a shield to all those who take refuge and put their trust in You.

I pray my spoken words and unspoken thoughts be pleasing to You, Lord, my Rock and my Redeemer.

Your Word has revived me and given me life.

Forever, O Lord, Your Word is settled in heaven.

Your Word is a lamp to my feet and a light to my path.

The sum of Your Word is truth, and every one of Your righteous decrees endures forever.

Father, I will praise Your name for Your loving-kindness and for Your truth and faithfulness. You have exalted above all else Your name and Your Word, and You have magnified Your Word above all Your name!

Father, let my prayer be as the evening sacrifice that burns like fragrant incense, rising as my offering to you as I lift up my hands in surrendered worship. Father, give me grace to guard my lips from speaking what is wrong.

I bring an offering of praise and thanksgiving to honor and glorify You, for Your Word says that true praise is a worthy sacrifice that really honors You. I'm overflowing with Your praise for all You've done, and Your splendor thrills me all day long.

Your tender mercies mean more to me than life itself. How I love and praise You, my Father. Daily I will worship You passionately and with all my heart. My arms will wave to You like banners of praise.

Your commandments are my counselors; Your Word is my light and delight. In Jesus' name, I pray, amen.

SCRIPTURE REFERENCES

Psalm 34:3 NLT • Psalm 138:2 • Psalm 18:30 • Psalm 141:2-3
Psalm 19:14 TLB • Psalm 50:23 TLB • Psalm 119:50
Psalm 71:8 TPT • Psalm 119:89 • Psalm 63:3-4 TPT • Psalm 119:105
Psalm 119:24 TPT • Psalm 119:160

PRAYERS
for the Needs and Concerns of the Individual

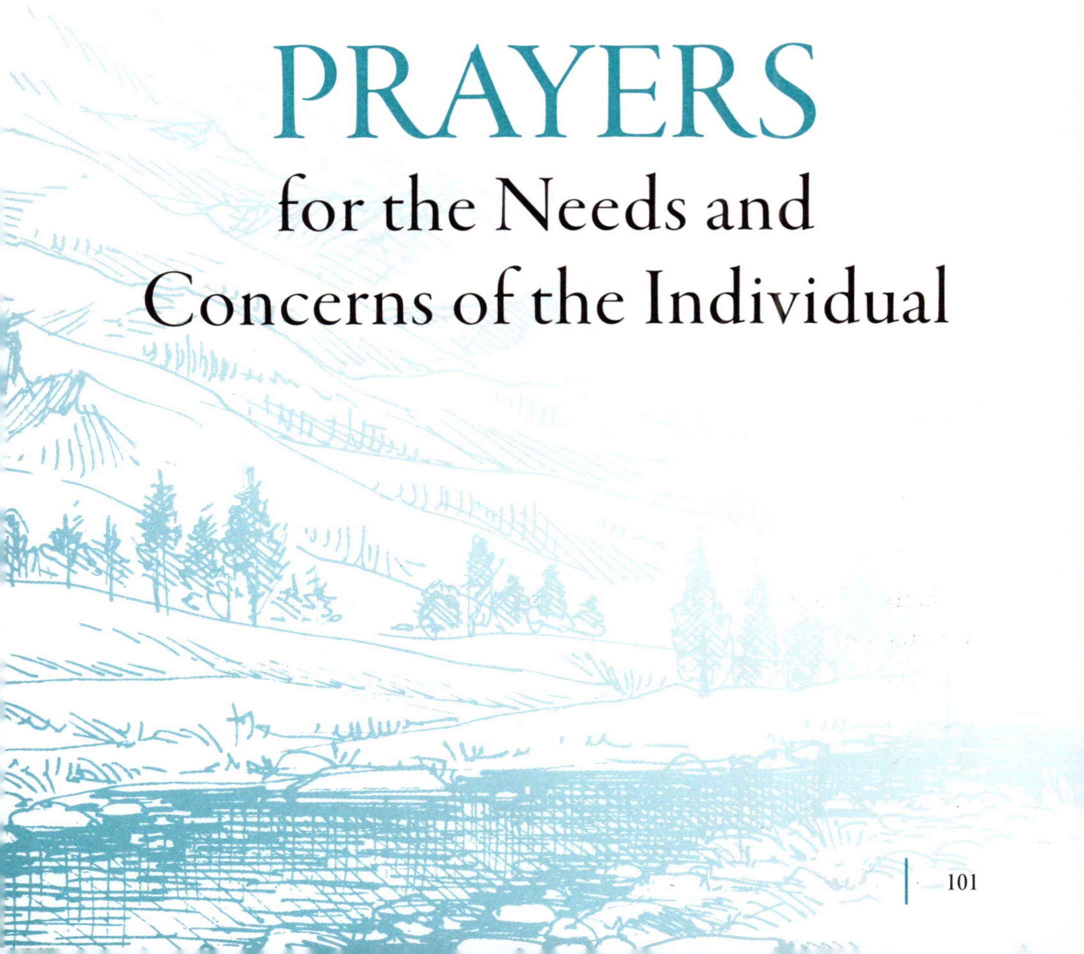

24

Submitting All to God

FATHER, I acknowledge You are the Supreme Authority—a God of order. You have instituted other authority structures that will support healthy relationships and maintain harmony. I surrender my will to You, that I might find protection and dwell in Your secret place, Most High.

Father, thank You for pastors and leaders of the church—those who are submitted to You and are examples to the congregation. I submit to the church elders (the ministers and spiritual guides of the church), giving them due respect and yielding to their counsel.

Lord, You know just how rebellious I have been. I ask Your forgiveness for manipulating circumstances and people—for trying to manipulate You to get my own way. May Your will be done in my life, even as it is in heaven.

Father, when I feel that my life is spiraling out of control, I bind my mind to the mind of Christ and my emotions to the control of the Holy Spirit. I loose my mind from obsessive thought patterns that try to confuse me.

Father, I understand that obedience is far better than sacrifice. You are much more interested in my listening to You than in my offerings of material things to You. Father, once I was blind but now I can see that my rebellion was as bad as the sin of witchcraft, and stubbornness was as bad as worshiping idols. I repent of these sins and ask You to cleanse me of all unrighteousness.

Father, You deserve honesty from the heart—yes, utter sincerity and truthfulness. Thank You for this wisdom. Sprinkle me with the cleansing blood, and I shall be clean again. Wash me, and I shall be whiter than snow. You have rescued me from the dominion of darkness and brought me into the Kingdom of the Son You love, in whom I have redemption, the forgiveness of sins.

Lord, I want to follow You. I am putting aside my own desires and conveniences. I yield my desires that are not in Your plan for me. Even in the midst of my fear, I surrender and entrust my future to You. I choose to take up my cross and follow You [cleave steadfastly to You, conforming wholly to Your example in living and, if need be, in dying also]. I desire to lose my lower life on Your account that I might find the higher life.

Father, You gave Jesus to be my Example. He has returned to You, Father, and has sent the Holy Spirit to be my Helper and Guide. In this world there are temptations, trials, and tribulations. But Jesus has overcome the world, and I am of good cheer—confident and undaunted!

Jesus is my Lord. I choose to become His servant, but He calls me His friend and brother.

Lord, help me to walk through the process of surrendering my all to You. I exchange rebellion and stubbornness for a willing and obedient heart. When I refuse to listen, anoint my ears to hear; when I am blinded by my own desires, open my eyes to see.

I belong to Jesus Christ, the Anointed One, who breaks down and destroys every yoke of bondage. In His name and in obedience to Your will, Father, I submit to the control and direction of the Holy Spirit whom You have sent to live in me. I am Your child. All to You I surrender. I am an overcomer by the blood of the Lamb and by the word of my testimony! In Jesus' name I pray, amen.

SCRIPTURE REFERENCES

1 Corinthians 14:33 • Psalm 51:6-7 TLB • 1 Timothy 2:2
Colossians 1:13-14 NIV • Psalm 91:1 • Matthew 10:38-39 AMPC
1 Peter 5:5 AMPC • John 16:33 AMPC • Matthew 6:10 • John 15:15
James 4:7 • Revelation 12:11 • 1 Samuel 15:22-23 TLB

25

Receiving Forgiveness

FATHER, Your Word promises that if I ask for forgiveness, You are faithful to forgive me and cleanse me from all unrighteousness. In Jesus' name, I choose to also forgive myself. I confess Jesus as my Lord and believe in my heart that You raised Him from the dead, and I am saved.

Father, I count myself blessed, how happy I am—I get a fresh start, my slate's wiped clean. I count myself happy, fortunate, to be envied. You, Father, are holding nothing against me, and You're not holding anything back from me.

Father, before I confessed my sins, I kept it all inside; my dishonesty devastated my inner life, causing my life to be filled with frustration, irrepressible anguish, and misery. I don't depend on my own strength to accomplish this; however, I do have one compelling focus—I forget all of the past as I fasten my heart to the future instead. I've got my eye on the goal, where God is beckoning us onward—to Jesus. I'm off and running, and I'm not turning back.

In the face of this feeling of guilt and unworthiness, I receive my forgiveness, and the pressure is gone—my guilt dissolved, my sin disappeared. I am blessed, for You have forgiven my transgressions—You have covered my sins. I am blessed, for You will never count my sins against me.

Thank You, Father, for choosing me to be Your very own, for joining me to Jesus Christ even before You laid the foundation of the universe!

Because of Your great love, You ordained me so that I would be seen as holy in Your eyes with an unstained innocence.

Lord, I have received Your Son, Jesus; I believe in His name, and He has given me the right to become Your child. I acknowledge You, Lord, as my Father. Thank You for forgiving me and absolving me of all guilt. I am an overcomer by the blood of the Lamb and by the word of my testimony. In the name of Jesus, amen.

SCRIPTURE REFERENCES

1 John 1:9 • Psalm 32:1-6 TPT • Romans 10:9-10 • Romans 4:7-8 NIV
Philippians 3:13 TPT • Philippians 3:14 MSG • Mark 11:23
Ephesians 1:4 TPT • Matthew 21:22 AMPC • John 1:12 NIV
Mark 9:24 • Revelation 12:11 • Psalm 32:1 AMPC

26

Walking in Humility

FATHER, I wrap around myself the apron of a humble servant, for You resist the proud but multiply grace and favor to the humble. I renounce pride and arrogance, and I choose to humble myself under Your mighty hand, that in due time You may exalt me.

In the name of Jesus, I cast the whole of my care (all my anxieties, all my worries, all my concerns for my future, once and for all) on You, for You care for me affectionately and care about me watchfully. I expect a life of victory and awesome deeds because my actions are done on behalf of a spirit humbly submitted to Your truth and righteousness.

Father, in the name of Jesus, I refuse to be wise in my own eyes, but I choose to fear You and shun evil. This will bring health to my body and nourishment to my bones.

Father, I humble myself and submit to Your Word that speaks (exposes, sifts, analyzes, and judges) the very thoughts and purposes of my heart. I test my own actions so that I might have appropriate self-esteem, without comparing myself to anyone else. The security of Your guidance will allow me to carry my own load with energy and confidence.

I listen carefully and hear what is being said to me. I incline my ear to wisdom and apply my heart to understanding and insight. Humility and fear of You bring wealth and honor and life.

Father, I hide Your Word in my heart that I might not sin against You. As one of Your chosen people, holy and dearly loved, I clothe myself with compassion, kindness, humility, gentleness, and patience. I bear with others and forgive whatever grievances I may have against anyone. I forgive as You forgave me. And over all these virtues I put on love, which binds them all together in perfect unity. I let the peace of Christ rule in my heart, and I am thankful for Your grace and the power of the Holy Spirit.

Father, may Your will be done on earth in my life as it is in heaven. In Jesus' name, amen.

SCRIPTURE REFERENCES

1 Peter 5:5-7 TPT, AMPC • Proverbs 22:4 NIV • Proverbs 3:7-8 NIV
Psalm 119:11 • Hebrews 4:12 AMPC • Colossians 3:12-15 NIV
Galatians 6:4-5 NIV • Matthew 6:10 NIV • Proverbs 2:2 NIV

27

Giving Thanks to God

God saw you when you were in your mother's womb (see Ps. 139:13-16). He knew your mother and father and the circumstances of the home where you were to grow up. He knew the schools you would attend and the neighborhood in which you would live.

God gave you the ability to survive and walked with you through good times and bad. He gave you survival techniques and guardian angels to keep and protect you (see Ps. 91:11). He chose you before the foundation of the world to be holy and without blame before Him in love (see Eph. 1:4).

He cried with you when you cried. He laughed with you when you laughed. He was grieved when you were misunderstood and treated unfairly. He watched and waited, looking forward to the day when you would receive Jesus as your Savior. To as many as received Him gave He the power, the right, and the authority to become the sons of God (see John 1:12 AMPC). He longs for your fellowship, desiring for you to know Him more and more intimately.

Your survival techniques were probably different than mine. Whatever they were, and whatever your life may have been like up to this point, the peace of God can change the regrets and the wounds of the past into thanksgiving and praise. You can experience wholeness by earnestly and sincerely praying this prayer.

I. Daily Prayer of Thanksgiving

Father, I come to You in the name of Jesus. With the help of the Holy Spirit and by Your grace, I join with the heavenly host making a joyful noise to You and serving You with gladness! I come before Your presence with singing!

Lord, I know (perceive, recognize, and understand with approval) that You are God! It is You who made us, not we ourselves, and we are Yours! We are Your people and the sheep of Your pasture.

Father, I enter into Your gates with thanksgiving and present an offering of thanks. I enter into Your courts with praise! I am thankful and delight to say so. I bless and affectionately praise Your name! For You are good, and Your mercy and loving-kindness are everlasting. Your faithfulness and truth endure to all generations. It is a good and delightful thing to give thanks to You, Most High.

Lord, by Your Holy Spirit, perfect the fruit of my lips. Help me draw thanksgiving forth from my innermost resources; reach down into the most secret places of my heart that I may offer significant thanksgiving to You, Father.

Thank You for my parents who gave me life. I am grateful for the victories and achievements I have experienced in spite of my hurts—the bruises and the abuses that boxed me in when I was a small child. You used them for good even though Satan intended them for my destruction. Father, I refuse to be a critic full of bias toward my parents, former teachers, and counselors. Forgive me for blaming them for my mistakes and failures. Judging them has not served me well. Today, I choose to overturn my table of judgment and let go of my grievances toward others. I choose to surrender to love that holds no record of wrong.

Thank You for Your grace, which is teaching me to trust myself and others. Thank You for life—life in all its abundance. It was You who gave me a desire to pray, and I am grateful for the prayer closet where we meet.

Thank You for Your Word. Life is exciting, and I am grateful that I am alive for such a time as this.

Thank You for past and present relationships. I learn from both those who oppose me and those who are for me. You taught me to recognize and understand my strengths and weaknesses. You gave me discernment and spiritual understanding. I enter Your gates with thanksgiving in my heart. You are my Father, and I am Your child, loved by You unconditionally. I rejoice in You, Lord, and give thanks to You every time I reflect on Your holiness. I am an overcomer by the blood of the Lamb and by the word of my testimony. In the name of Jesus, amen.

SCRIPTURE REFERENCES

Psalm 100:1-5 AMP • Matthew 7:1-5 TPT • Philippians 2:13
Psalm 92:1 AMP • Esther 4:14 • Psalm 138:8 • Psalm 100:4
Hebrews 13:15 • Philippians 3:1 • Genesis 50:20 NIV
Psalm 30:4 TPT • John 10:10 • Revelation 12:11

II. Prayer of Thanksgiving for Food Eaten While Traveling

Father, I ask for the wisdom to order that which is healthy and nourishing to my body.

In the name of Jesus, I resist the lust of the flesh and the lust of the eye as I scan the menu. When I am in doubt about what I am to order, I will pause and ask for wisdom, which You will give generously without finding fault with me.

Should I unknowingly eat or drink any deadly thing, it will not harm me, for the Spirit of life makes me free from the law of sin and death.

Father, everything You have created is good. We should not reject any of it but receive it with thanks. It is made acceptable by the Word of God and prayer.

I receive this food with thanksgiving and will eat the amount that is sufficient for me. In the name of Jesus, amen.

SCRIPTURE REFERENCES

James 1:5 • Romans 8:2 • 1 John 2:16 • 1 Timothy 4:4-5 NLT
Mark 16:18 • Psalm 136:1,25

28

Committing to a Fast

I. Beginning a Fast

Introduction

There are different kinds of fasts: a total fast from food and liquid for a short interval; a liquid fast, allowing only water; a juice fast, allowing water and given amounts of juices at mealtimes; and a fast from meats, allowing only fruits and vegetables.

It is important to understand the effects of fasting on the spirit, soul, and body. Before committing to a fast, I encourage you to study the Word of God and read books that provide important nutritional and other health information. Understanding will help to avoid harm and injury—both physically and spiritually.

Do not flaunt your fast, but do talk with your family and close associates, if necessary, to let them know what you are doing.

(Personal note: During times of fasting, I continue to prepare meals at home for my family.)

Prayer

Father, I consecrate this fast to You and purpose in my heart and my mind to gain understanding in these matters for which I am concerned.

(Write your concerns out and keep them before your eyes. Do not lose sight of the reason for your fast.)

I humble myself before You, Most High God. In accordance with Daniel 10:1-3, I will eat no __________ for the period of __________.

I obey the words of Jesus so that when I fast it is not obvious. Instead, I wash my face and groom myself and realize that my Father in the secret place is the One who is watching me.

I look to You for my reward, Father. I am assured that You hear me when I pray according to Your will, and I know that I will have the petitions that I desire of You. I delight myself in You, and You cause my desires to be agreeable to Your will.

Father, I submit to the fast You have chosen—to loose the chains of injustice and untie the cords of the yoke, to set the oppressed free and break every yoke. I share my food with the hungry and provide the poor wanderer with shelter. When I see the naked, I will clothe him, and I will not turn away from my own flesh and blood. Then my light will break forth like the dawn, and my healing will quickly appear; then my righteousness will go before me, and Your glory, Lord, will be my rear guard.

Father, thank You for cleansing me—spirit, soul, and body. All my ways seem innocent to me, but my motives are weighed by You, my Lord and my Master. I commit this fast to You, and my plans will succeed. Thank You, Father, that even though I make plans, it is ultimately You who directs my steps.

Forever, O Lord, Your Word stands firm in heaven. Your faithfulness extends to every generation, like the earth You created; it endures by Your decree, for everything serves Your plans. In Jesus' name, amen.

SCRIPTURE REFERENCES

Matthew 6:17-18 TPT • 1 Thessalonians 5:23 • 1 John 5:14-15
Proverbs 16:2-3 NIV • Psalm 37:4 • Proverbs 16:1 TPT
Proverbs 16:3 AMPC • Isaiah 58:6-8 TLB • Psalm 119:89-91 TLB

II. Ending a Fast

Introduction

It is best to break a fast by eating fruit, broth, or a light salad, gradually adding other foods day by day depending upon the length of the fast.

Prayer

Father, in the name of Jesus, You are my Light and my Salvation; whom shall I fear? You are the Strength of my life; of whom shall I be afraid?

Father, You have given me the desires of my heart. You have heard and answered my prayers. To You be the glory! Great things You have done!

I rest in You, awaiting the manifestation of all that I required and inquired of You.

Thank You for giving me Your strength to face each day full of spiritual vitality. Today, I break this fast as You have directed. I thank You for this food because it is consecrated by Your Word and prayer. In Jesus' name, amen.

SCRIPTURE REFERENCES

Psalm 27:1 • Psalm 92:14 TLB • Psalm 37:4
1 Timothy 4:4-5 AMPC • Psalm 34:4 AMPC

29

Pleading the Blood of Jesus

I. Morning Prayer[1]

FATHER, I come in the name of Jesus to plead the blood of Jesus on my life, on all property that belongs to me, and on all over which You have made me a steward.

I plead the blood of Jesus on the portals of my mind, my body (the temple of the Holy Spirit), my emotions, and my will. I believe that I am protected by the blood of the Lamb, which gives me access to the Holy of Holies.

I plead the blood on my children, on my grandchildren and their children, and on all those whom You have given me in this life.

Lord, You have said that the life of the flesh is in the blood. Thank You for this blood that has cleansed me from sin and sealed the New Covenant of which I am a partaker. In Jesus' name, amen.

Scripture References

Exodus 12:7,13 • Leviticus 17:11 • 1 Corinthians 6:19 • 1 John 1:7
Hebrews 9:6-14 • Hebrews 13:20 AMPC

1 Based on a prayer written by Joyce Meyer in *The Word, the Name and the Blood* (Tulsa: Harrison House, 1995).

II. Evening Prayer[2]

Father, as I lie down to sleep, I plead the blood of Jesus upon my life—within me, around me, and between me and all evil and the author of evil. In Jesus' name, amen.

2 Based on a prayer written by Mrs. C. Nuzum as recorded by Billye Brim in *The Blood and the Glory* (Tulsa: Harrison House, 1995).

— 30 —

Handling the Day of Trouble or Calamity

Introduction

During a time of trouble or calamity, it is sometimes difficult to remember the promises of God. The pressures of the moment may seem overwhelming. At such times, it is often helpful to read, meditate on, and pray the entire chapter of Psalm 91.

It may be that during a stressful time you will find this entire prayer too long. If so, draw from the scriptures included in the following prayer. You may find yourself praying one paragraph or reading it aloud to yourself or to your family and friends.

I also encourage you to meditate on this prayer during good times. At all times, remember that faith comes by hearing, and hearing by the Word of God (see Rom. 10:17).

Sometimes, others create the problems you are facing. If so, remember that you are not responsible for what they did; you are only responsible for your reactions. God has given you a spirit of power, love, and a sound mind (see 2 Tim. 1:7). You have the power to choose to forgive and bring your thoughts into alignment with God's forgiveness.

> *Beloved, don't be obsessed with taking revenge, but leave that to God's righteous justice. For the Scriptures say: "If you don't*

take justice in your own hands, I will release justice for you," says the Lord (Romans 12:19 TPT).

Prayer

Father, I come to You in the name of Jesus, acknowledging You as my Refuge and High Tower. You are a refuge and a stronghold in these times of trouble, high cost, destitution, and desperation.

In the day of trouble, You will hide me in Your shelter; in the secret place of Your tent will You hide me; You will set me high upon a rock. And now shall my head be lifted up above my enemies round about me; in Your tent I will offer sacrifices and shouting of joy; I will sing, yes, I will sing praises to You, O Lord. Hear, O Lord, when I cry aloud; have mercy and be gracious to me and answer me!

On the authority of Your Word, I declare that I have been made the righteousness of God in Christ Jesus. When I cry for help, You, Lord, hear me and deliver me out of all my distress and troubles. You are close to me, for I am of a broken heart, and You save such who are crushed with sorrow for sin and are humbly and thoroughly penitent. Lord, many are the evils that confront me, but You deliver me out of them all.

Thank You for being merciful and gracious to me, O God, for my soul takes refuge and finds shelter and confidence in You; yes, in the shadow of Your wings I take refuge and am confident until calamities and destructive storms are past. You perform on my behalf and reward me. You bring to pass Your purposes for me, and surely You complete them!

God, you're such a safe and powerful place to find refuge! You're a proven help in time of trouble—*more than enough* and always available whenever I need You. So I will never fear even if every structure of support were to crumble away. I will not fear even when the earth quakes and shakes, moving mountains and casting them into the sea. For the raging roar of stormy winds and crashing waves cannot erode our faith in you.

Lord, like Paul I pleaded with You to relive me of this trouble. I choose to believe Your grace is always more than enough for me and Your power finds its full expression through my weakness. So I celebrate my weaknesses, for when I'm weak I sense more deeply the mighty power of Christ living me in. So I'm not defeated by my weakness, but delighted! For when I feel my weakness and endure mistreatment—when I'm surrounded with troubles on every side and face persecution because of my love for Christ—I am made yet stronger. For my weakness becomes a portal to God's power.

Lord, You have given me Your peace. By Your grace, I will not let my heart be troubled, neither will I let it be afraid. With the help of the Holy Spirit, I will stop allowing myself to be agitated and disturbed. I refuse to permit myself to be fearful, intimidated, cowardly, and unsettled.

By faith, I respond to these troubles and calamities: I am full of joy now! I exult and triumph in my troubles and rejoice in my sufferings, knowing that pressure and affliction and hardship produce patient and unswerving endurance. And endurance (fortitude) develops maturity of character (approved faith and tried integrity). And character of this sort produces the habit of joyful and confident hope of eternal salvation. Such hope never disappoints or deludes or shames me, for Your love has been poured out in my heart through the Holy Spirit who has been given to me. In Jesus' name, amen.

SCRIPTURE REFERENCES

Psalm 9:9 AMPC • Psalm 57:1-2 AMPC • Psalm 27:5-7 AMPC
Psalm 46:1 TPT • 2 Corinthians 5:21 • 2 Corinthians 12:8-10 TPT
John 14:27 AMPC • Psalm 34:17-20 AMPC • Romans 5:3-5 AMPC

— 31 —

Breaking the Curse of Abuse

Introduction

> *Christ redeemed us from the curse of the law by becoming a curse for us, for it is written: "Cursed is everyone who is hung on a tree"* (Galatians 3:13 NIV).

On a Sunday morning after I had taught a lesson titled "Healing for the Emotionally Wounded," a young man wanted to speak with me. I listened intently as he told me that he had just been released from jail and was now on probation for physically abusing his family. His wife had filed for divorce, and he was living alone. It was not easy for him to confess his sin to me, and I was impressed by his humble attitude.

He said, "I am glad that this message is being given in the church and the abused can receive ministry. Is there anywhere that the abuser can go to receive spiritual help?"

He shared with me that he was attending a support group for abusers. He desired to commit to a church where he could receive forgiveness and acceptance. He knew that any lasting change would have to be from the inside out by the Spirit. I prayed with him, but it was sometime later before I could write a prayer for the abuser.

As I read, studied, and sought the Lord, I discovered that the abuser is usually a person who has been abused. Often the problem is a generational curse that has been in the family of the abuser for as far back as anyone can remember. Many times, the abuser declares that he will never treat his wife and children as he has been treated, but in spite of his resolve he finds himself reacting in the same violent manner.

Unfortunately, when we focus on the "never" we draw that to ourselves. I know an adult man who vowed when he was very young that no matter what his alcoholic dad had done, he would do the opposite, and he did. His dad had been outgoing, but he was always guarded and kept his walls up even with his wife and children. The power of forgiveness cannot be overstated. In this case, the abuser frees himself. His blind eyes are opened, and he walks into the light of wholeness. He is free to choose to let go of judgment and walk in the fullness of life. The generational curse is reversed!

If you are an abuser, I encourage you to pray this prayer for yourself until it becomes a reality in your life.

If you know someone who is an abuser, pray this as a prayer of intercession in the third person.

Prayer

I receive and confess that Jesus is my Lord, and I ask that Your will be done in my life.

Father, You have rescued me from the dominion of darkness and have brought me into the Kingdom of the Son of Your love. Once I was darkness, but now I am light in You; I walk as a child of light. The abuse is exposed and reproved by the light—it is made visible and clear, and where everything is visible and clear there is light.

Help me to grow in grace (undeserved favor, spiritual strength) and recognition and knowledge and understanding of my Lord and Savior, Jesus Christ, so that I may experience Your love and trust You to be a Father to me.

The history of my earthly family is filled with abusive behavior, much hatred, strife, and rage. The painful memory of past abuse (verbal, emotional, physical, and/or sexual) has caused me to be hostile and abusive to others.

I desire to be a doer of the Word and not a hearer only. No matter which way I turn, I can't make myself do right. I want to, but I can't. When I want to do good, I don't; and when I try not to do wrong, I do it anyway. It seems that sin still has me in its evil grasp. This pain has caused me to hurt myself and others. In my mind I want to be Your willing servant, but instead I find myself still enslaved to sin.

I confess my sin of abuse, resentment, and hostility toward others, and I ask You to forgive me. You are faithful and just to forgive my sin and cleanse me from all unrighteousness. I am tired of reliving the past in my present life, perpetuating the generational curse of anger and abuse.

Jesus was made a curse for me; therefore, Lord, I put on Your whole armor that I may be able to successfully stand against all the strategies and the tricks of the devil. I thank You that the evil power of abuse is broken, overthrown, and cast down in my life. I submit myself to You and resist the devil. The need to hurt others no longer controls me or my family. In Jesus' name, amen.

SCRIPTURE REFERENCES

Romans 10:9 • Romans 7:18-25 TLB • Matthew 6:10
1 John 1:9 • Colossians 1:13 AMPC • Galatians 3:13 • Ephesians 5:8,13 AMPC
Ephesians 6:11-12 TLB • 2 Peter 3:18 AMPC • 2 Corinthians 10:5

32

Healing from Abuse

Introduction

This prayer can be applied to any form of abuse—physical, mental, emotional, or sexual. I wrote it after reading T.D. Jakes' book, *Woman, Thou Art Loosed.*[3] By praying it, I personally have experienced victory and freedom—I am no longer a victim but an overcomer.

Prayer

Lord, You are my High Priest, and I ask You to loose me from this "infirmity." The abuse I suffered pronounced me guilty and condemned. I was bound in an emotional prison, crippled, and could in no wise lift up myself. You have called me to Yourself, and I have come.

The anointing that is upon You is present to bind up and heal the brokenness and emotional wounds of the past. You are the Truth that makes me free.

Thank You, Lord, for guiding me through the steps to emotional wholeness. You have begun a good work in me, and You will perform it until the day of Christ Jesus.

Father, I desire to live according to the Spirit of life in Christ Jesus. This Spirit of life in Christ, like a strong wind, has magnificently cleared

3 (Shippensburg, PA: Destiny Image, 2006).

the air, freeing me from a fated lifetime of brutal tyranny at the hands of abuse.

Thank You for the living Word, which is all effective, full of energy. I am grateful that Your Word interprets and reveals the true interpretations and the revelations of my true thoughts and secret motives of my heart. With a sensitive spirit I absorb Your Word, which has been implanted within my nature, for the Word of Life has power to continually transform my soul (my mind, will, and emotions). Reveal all unacknowledged hurts and unresolved issues that have hindered my spiritual growth and emotional wholeness.

Father, thank You for exposing the painful experiences of my childhood when my eyes were blinded and I believed Satan's lies. You love me unconditionally and have opened my eyes. Those experiences do not identify me, and I am no longer a victim. When I was a child, I spoke about childish matters, for I saw things like a child and reasoned like a child. But the day came when I matured, and I set aside my childish ways.

My understanding is incomplete now, but one day I will understand everything, just as everything about me has been fully understood. Until then, there are three things that remain: faith, hope, and love—yet love surpasses them all.

Because I am now free, I forget all of the past as I fasten my heart to the future instead. I press on to reach the end of the race and receive the heavenly price for which God—through Christ Jesus—is calling us. I have my eye on the goal where God is beckoning us onward. I'm off and running, and I'm not turning back.

Praise You, Father! I am a new creature in Christ Jesus. Old things have passed away; and, behold, all things have become new. I declare and decree that henceforth I will walk in newness of life.

Forgive me, Father, for self-hatred and self-condemnation. I am Your child. You sent Jesus that I might have life and have it more abundantly. Thank You for the blood of Jesus that makes me whole.

It is my desire to throw all spoiled virtue and cancerous evil in the garbage. In simple humility, I let my Gardener, You Lord, landscape me with the Word, making a salvation-garden of my life.

Father, by Your grace, I forgive my abuser/abusers and ask You to bring him/her/them to repentance. In the name of Jesus, I pray. Amen.

SCRIPTURE REFERENCES

Luke 13:11-12 • Romans 6:4 • John 14:6 • 1 John 3:1-2 • John 8:32
John 10:10 • Philippians 1:6 • 1 John 1:7 • Romans 8:2 MSG
James 1:21 MSG • Philippians 3:13-14 TPT, MSG • Matthew 5:44
2 Corinthians 5:17 • 2 Peter 3:9

33

Letting Go of the Past

FATHER, I realize my helplessness in saving myself, and I glory in what Christ Jesus has done for me. I let go—put aside all past sources of my confidence—counting them worth less than nothing, in order that I may experience Jesus and become one with Him.

Lord, I have received Your Son, and He has given me the authority (power, privilege, and right) to become Your child.

I unfold my past and put into proper perspective those things that are behind. I have been crucified with Christ and no longer live, but Christ lives in me. The life I live in the body, I live by faith in the Son of God, who loved me and gave Himself for me. I trust in You, Lord, with all of my heart and lean not on my own understanding. In all of my ways I acknowledge You, and You will make my paths straight.

I want to know Christ and the power of His resurrection and the fellowship of sharing in His sufferings, becoming like Him in His death, and so, somehow, to attain to the resurrection from the dead. So, whatever it takes, I will be one who lives in the fresh newness of life of those who are alive from the dead.

Father, I am made in Your image. I haven't learned all I should, but inwardly I am being transformed by the Holy Spirit through a total reformation of how I think. This empowers me to discern God's will as I live a beautiful life, satisfying and perfect in Your eyes.

I'm leaving my old life behind, putting everything on the line. I am sprinting toward the only goal that counts—to cross the line, to win the prize, and to hear God's call to resurrection life found exclusively in Jesus. In His name I pray, amen.

SCRIPTURE REFERENCES

Philippians 3:7-9 TLB • Proverbs 3:5-6 NIV • John 1:12 AMPC
Philippians 3:10-11 NIV • Psalm 32:5 AMPC • Romans 6:4
Philippians 3:13 • Philippians 3:12-14 VOICE • Galatians 2:20 NIV
Romans 12:2 TPT

— 34 —

Strength to Overcome Cares and Burdens

WHY are you down in the dumps, dear soul? Why are you crying the blues? I will fix my eyes on God—soon I'll be praising again. You put a smile on my face. You are my God.

Father, You set Yourself against the proud and haughty, but You give grace continually unto the humble. I submit myself therefore to You, God. In the name of Jesus, I resist the devil, and he will flee from me. I resist the cares of the world, which try to pressure me daily. Except the Lord builds the house, they labor in vain who build it.

Jesus, I come to You for I am weary and carry a heavy burden, but You cause me to rest—You will ease and relieve and refresh my soul. You are my Oasis.

I take Your yoke upon me and learn of You; for You are gentle, humble, and easy to please. I find refreshment and rest in You. For Your burden is light and all that You require of me will be pleasant and easy to bear.

I cast my burden on You, Lord, releasing the weight of it. You will sustain me. Thank You that You will never allow me, the consistently righteous, to be moved—made to slip, fall, or fail.

In the name of Jesus, I withstand the devil. I am firm in my faith against his onset—rooted, established, strong, immovable, and determined. And now, dear Father, I enter into Your rest. I cease from my own works, trusting You, for Your Word says whoever enters Your rest will cease from his own works, as You did from Yours.

Father, I thank You that Your presence goes with me and that You give me rest. My heart is fixed on you—quiet and confident. You left me with a gift—peace of mind and heart. And the peace You give is a gift the world cannot give. So, I will not be troubled or afraid, discouraged or disturbed, for I know my God will break through for me. Then I'll have plenty of reasons to praise You all over again. Yes, living before Your face is my saving grace! In Jesus' name, amen.

SCRIPTURE REFERENCES

Psalm 42:11 MSG • Hebrews 4:10-11 TPT • James 4:6-7 AMPC
Exodus 33:14 MSG • Psalm 127:1 AMPC • Psalm 37:7 • Matthew 11:28-30 TPT
John 14:27 TPT • Psalm 55:22 AMPC • Psalm 42:11 TPT • 1 Peter 5:9 AMPC

35

Renewing the Mind

FATHER, in Jesus' name, I thank You that I shall prosper and be in health, even as my soul prospers. I have the mind of Christ, the Messiah, and do hold the thoughts, feelings, and purposes of His heart. I trust in You, Lord, with all of my heart; I lean not unto my own understanding, but in all of my ways I acknowledge You, and You shall direct my paths.

Today I submit myself to Your Word, which exposes and sifts and analyzes and judges the very thoughts and purposes of my heart. For the weapons of my warfare are not carnal, but mighty through You to the pulling down of strongholds—intimidation, fears, doubts, unbelief, and failure. I refute arguments and theories and reasonings and every proud and lofty thing that sets itself up against the true knowledge of God; and I lead every thought and purpose away captive into the obedience of Christ, the Messiah, the Anointed One.

Today I shall be transformed by the renewing of my mind, that I may prove what is that good and acceptable and perfect will of God. Your Word, Lord, shall not depart out of my mouth; but I shall meditate on it day and night, that I may observe to do according to all that is written therein—for then I shall make my way prosperous, then I shall have good success.

My thoughts are the thoughts of the diligent, which lead to abundance. Therefore, I am not anxious about anything, but in everything, by prayer and petition,[4] with thanksgiving, I present my requests to God. And the peace of God, which transcends all understanding, will guard my heart and my mind in Christ Jesus.

Today I fix my mind on whatever is *true,* whatever is *worthy of reverence* and is *honorable* and *seemly,* whatever is *just,* whatever is *pure,* whatever is *lovely* and *lovable,* whatever is *kind* and *winsome* and *gracious.* If there is any *virtue* and *excellence,* if there is anything *worthy of praise,* I will think on and weigh and take account of these things.

Today I roll my works upon You, Lord. I commit and trust them wholly to You. You will cause my thoughts to become agreeable to Your will, and so shall my plans be established and succeed. In Jesus' name I pray, amen.

SCRIPTURE REFERENCES

3 John 2 • Romans 12:2 • 1 Corinthians 2:16 AMPC • Joshua 1:8
Proverbs 3:5-6 • Proverbs 21:5 ESV • Hebrews 4:12 AMPC
Philippians 4:6-8 NIV • 2 Corinthians 10:4 • Proverbs 16:3 AMPC
2 Corinthians 10:5 AMPC

4 I encourage you to keep a prayer journal, writing down your petitions (definite requests) in prayer form.

36

Conquering the Thought Life

In the name of Jesus, I take authority over my thought life. Even though I walk (live) in the flesh, I am not carrying on my warfare according to the flesh and using mere human weapons. For the weapons of my warfare are not physical weapons of flesh and blood, but they are mighty before God for the overthrow and destruction of strongholds. I refute arguments and theories and reasonings and every proud and lofty thing that sets itself up against the true knowledge of God; and I lead every thought and purpose away captive into the obedience of Christ, the Messiah, the Anointed One.

With my soul I will bless the Lord with every thought and purpose in life. My mind will not wander out of the presence of God. My life shall glorify the Father—*spirit, soul, and body.* I take no account of the evil done to me—I pay no attention to a suffered wrong. It holds no place in my thought life. I am ever ready to believe the best of every person. I gird up the loins of my mind, and I set my mind and keep it set on what is above—the higher things—not on the things that are on the earth.

Whatever is true, whatever is worthy of reverence and is honorable and seemly, whatever is just, whatever is pure, whatever is lovely and lovable, whatever is kind and winsome and gracious, if there is any virtue and excellence, if there is anything worthy of praise, I will think on and weigh and take account of these things—I will fix my mind on them.

I have the mind of Christ, the Messiah, and do hold the thoughts, feelings, and purposes of His heart. In the name of Jesus, I will practice what I have learned and received and heard and seen in Christ and model my way of living on it, and the God of peace—of untroubled, undisturbed wellbeing—will be with me. In Jesus' name, amen.

SCRIPTURE REFERENCES (AMPC)

2 Corinthians 10:3-5 • Colossians 3:2 • Psalm 103:1 • Philippians 4:8
1 Corinthians 6:20 • 1 Corinthians 2:16 • 1 Corinthians 13:5,7
Philippians 4:9

37

Casting Down Imaginations

FATHER, though I live in the world, I do not wage war as the world does. The weapons I fight with are not the weapons of the world. On the contrary, they have divine power to demolish strongholds. I demolish arguments and every pretension that sets itself up against the knowledge of You, and I capture, like prisoners of war, every thought and insist that it bow in obedience to the Anointed One.

In the name of Jesus, I ask You, Father, to bless those who have despitefully used me. Whenever I feel afraid, I will trust in You. When I feel miserable, I will express thanksgiving; and when I feel that life is unfair, I will remember that You are more than enough.

When I feel ashamed, help me to remember that I no longer have to be afraid; I will not suffer shame. I am delivered from the fear of disgrace; I will not be humiliated. I relinquish the shame of my youth.

It is well with my soul, for You have redeemed me. You have called me by my name.

I am in Your will for my life at this time. I am being transformed through the renewing of my mind. I am able to test and approve for myself what Your will is—Your good and acceptable and perfect will.

You have good things reserved for my future. All my needs will be met according to Your riches in glory. I will replace worry for my family with asking You to protect and care for them.

You are love, and perfect love casts out fear. In Jesus' name, amen.

SCRIPTURE REFERENCES

2 Corinthians 10:3-5 TPT • Romans 12:2 AMPC • Luke 6:28
Jeremiah 29:11 AMPC • Isaiah 54:4 NIV • Philippians 4:19 • Isaiah 43:1
1 Peter 5:7 • Romans 12:2 • 1 John 4:8,18

38

Healing for Damaged Emotions

FATHER, in the name of Jesus, I come to You with a feeling of shame and emotional hurt. I confess my transgressions to You, continually unfolding the past till all is told. You are faithful and just to forgive me and cleanse me of all unrighteousness. You are my Hiding Place, and You, Lord, preserve me from trouble. You surround me with songs and shouts of deliverance. I have chosen life. According to Your Word, You saw me while I was being formed in my mother's womb; and on the authority of Your Word, I was wonderfully made.

Now I am Your handiwork, recreated in Christ Jesus.

Father, You have delivered me from the spirit of fear, and I shall not be ashamed. Neither shall I be confounded and depressed. You gave me beauty for ashes, the oil of joy for mourning, and the garment of praise for the spirit of heaviness that I might be a tree of righteousness, the planting of the Lord, that You might be glorified. I speak out in psalms, hymns, and spiritual songs, offering praise with my voice and making melody with all my heart to the Lord. Just as David did in 1 Samuel 30:6, I encourage myself in the Lord.

I believe in God who raised Jesus from the dead. Jesus was betrayed and put to death because of my misdeeds and was raised to secure my acquittal, absolving me from all guilt before God. Father, You anointed Jesus and sent Him to bind up and heal my broken heart and liberate me from the shame of my youth and the imperfections of my caretakers.

In the name of Jesus, I choose to forgive all those who have wronged me in any way. You will not leave me without support as I complete the forgiveness process. I take comfort and am encouraged and confidently say, "The Lord is my Helper; I will not be seized with alarm. What can man do to me?"

My spirit is the candle of the Lord searching all the innermost parts of my being, and the Holy Spirit leads me into all truth. When reality exposes shame and emotional pain, I remember that the sufferings of this present life are not worth being compared with the glory that is about to be revealed to me and in me and for me and conferred on me!

Jesus wore a crown of thorns for the chastisement of my peace. My wellbeing was upon Jesus, and with the stripes that wounded Him, I was healed and made whole. As Your child, Father, I have a joyful and confident hope of eternal salvation. This hope will never disappoint, delude, or shame me, for God's love has been poured out in my heart through the Holy Spirit who has been given to me. In His name I pray, amen.

SCRIPTURE REFERENCES

Psalm 32:5-7 AMPC • Romans 4:24-25 • 1 John 1:9
Isaiah 61:1 • Deuteronomy 30:19 • Mark 11:25 • Psalm 139
Hebrews 13:5-6 • Ephesians 2:10 • Proverbs 20:27 • 2 Timothy 1:7
John 16:13 • Isaiah 54:4 • Romans 8:18 • Isaiah 61:3
Isaiah 53:5 WEB, NASB • Ephesians 5:19 • Romans 5:3-5

39

Victory Over Depression

Father, You are my Refuge and my High Tower and my Stronghold in times of trouble. I lean on You and confidently put my trust in You, for You have not forsaken me. I know I can count on You for help no matter what. I put my hope in You. I praise You—my Savior and my God!

Lord, You lift up those who are bowed down. Therefore, I am strong and my heart takes courage. I establish myself on righteousness—right standing in conformity with Your will and order. I am far even from the thought of oppression or destruction, for I fear not. I am far from terror, for it shall not come near me.

Father, You have thoughts and plans for my welfare and peace. *My mind is stayed on You,* for I stop allowing myself to be agitated and disturbed and intimidated and cowardly and unsettled.

In the name of Jesus, I loose my mind from wrong thought patterns. I tear down strongholds that have protected bad perceptions about myself. I submit to You, Father, and resist fear, discouragement, self-pity, and depression. I will not give place to the devil by harboring resentment and holding on to anger. I surround myself with songs and shouts of deliverance from depression, and I will continue to be an overcomer by the word of my testimony and the blood of the Lamb.

Father, I thank You that I have been given a spirit of power and of love and of a calm and well-balanced mind. I have discipline and self-control. I have the mind of Christ and hold the thoughts, feelings, and purposes of His heart. I have a fresh mental and spiritual attitude, for I am constantly renewed in the spirit of my mind with Your Word, Father.

Therefore, I brace up and reinvigorate and cut through and make firm and straight paths for my feet—safe and upright and happy paths that go in the right direction. I arise from the depression and prostration in which circumstances have kept me. I rise to new life; I shine and am radiant with the glory of the Lord.

Thank You, Father, in Jesus' name, that I am set free from every evil work. I praise You that the joy of the Lord is my strength and stronghold! Hallelujah! Amen.

SCRIPTURE REFERENCES

Psalm 9:9-10 AMPC • Ephesians 4:27 • Psalm 42:5,11 • Luke 4:18-19
Psalm 146:8 • 2 Timothy 1:7 AMPC • Psalm 31:22-24 AMPC
1 Corinthians 2:16 AMPC • Isaiah 35:3-4 • Philippians 2:5 • Isaiah 54:14
Ephesians 4:23-24 AMPC • Isaiah 50:10 • Hebrews 12:12-13 AMPC
Jeremiah 29:11-13 AMPC • Isaiah 60:1 AMPC • Isaiah 26:3
Galatians 1:4 • John 14:27 AMPC • Nehemiah 8:10 AMPC • James 4:7

40

Victory Over Pride

FATHER, Your Word says that You hate a proud look, that You resist the proud but give grace to the humble. I submit myself, therefore, to You. In the name of Jesus, I resist the devil, and he will flee from me. I renounce every manifestation of pride in my life as sin; I repent and turn from it.

As an act of faith, I clothe myself with humility and receive Your grace. I humble myself under Your mighty hand, Lord, that You may exalt me in due time. I refuse to exalt myself. I do not think of myself more highly than I ought. I empty myself of self-promotion and do not create a false image of my importance. I honestly assess my worth by using Your faith as the standard of measurement, so I see my true value with an appropriate self-esteem.

Proverbs 11:2 says, "When pride cometh, then cometh shame: but with the lowly is wisdom." Father, I set myself to resist pride when it comes. My desire is to be counted among the lowly, so I take on the attitude of a servant.

Father, thank You that You dwell with one who is of a contrite and humble spirit. You revive the spirit of the humble and revive the heart of the contrite one. Thank You that the reward of humility and the reverent and worshipful fear of the Lord is riches and honor and life. In Jesus' name I pray, amen.

SCRIPTURE REFERENCES

Proverbs 6:16-17 • Proverbs 11:2 • James 4:6-7 • Matthew 23:11
Proverbs 21:4 • Isaiah 57:15 • 1 Peter 5:5-6 • Proverbs 22:4 AMPC
Romans 12:3 TPT

41

Victory in a Healthy Lifestyle

FATHER, I am Your child, and Jesus is Lord over my spirit, soul, and body. I praise you because I am fearfully and wonderfully made. Your works are wonderful; I know that full well.

Lord, thank You for declaring Your plans for me—plans to prosper me and not to harm me, plans to give me hope and a future. I choose to align my mind to Your plans for a healthy lifestyle. You have given me superabundant grace that is already powerfully working in me, releasing within me all forms of wisdom and practical understanding. Therefore, I give thought to my steps.

Teach me knowledge and good judgment. I choose to abandon every form of evil, deceit, hypocrisy, and feelings of jealousy and slander. I crave the pure spiritual milk of Your Word, for this "milk" will cause me to grow into maturity, fully nourished and strong for life—especially now that I have had a taste of Your goodness and have experienced Your kindness.

Your words are spirit and life. I listen carefully to everything that You teach me and pay attention to all that You have to say. Daily, I fill my thoughts with Your words until they penetrate deep into my spirit. Your words impart true life and radiant health into the very core of my being. I guard the affections of my heart for they affect all that I am. Holy Spirit, with Your help I will pay attention to the welfare of my innermost being for from there flows the wellspring of life.

My body is for the Lord. So here is what I want to do with Your help, Father God. I choose to take my every day, ordinary life—my sleeping, eating, going-to-work, and walking-around life—and place it before You as an offering. Embracing what You do for me is the best thing I can do for You.

Christ, the Messiah, will be magnified and receive glory and praise in this body of mine and will be boldly exalted in my person. Thank You, Father, in Jesus' name! Hallelujah! Amen.

SCRIPTURE REFERENCES

Psalm 139:14 • Ephesians 1:8 TPT • Psalm 119:66 • Jeremiah 29:11
Romans 12:1 MSG • Proverbs 14:15 • Philippians 1:20 AMPC
Proverbs 4:20-23 TPT • 1 Peter 2:1-3 TPT

42

Victory Over Fear

FATHER, when I am afraid, I will put my confidence in You. Yes, I will trust Your promises. And because I trust You, what can mere man do to me?

You have not given me a spirit of fear but of power and love and self-control. Therefore, I am not ashamed of the testimony of my Lord. I have not received a spirit of slavery leading to fear again, but I have received a spirit of adoption as a son or daughter, by which I cry out, "Abba! Father!"

Jesus, You delivered me, who, through fear of death, had been living all my life as a slave to constant dread. I receive the gift You left me—peace of mind and heart! And the peace You give isn't fragile like the peace the world gives. I cast away troubled thoughts, and I choose not to be afraid. I believe in You.

Lord, You are my Light and my Salvation; You protect me from danger—whom shall I fear? When evil men come to destroy me, they will stumble and fall! When besieged, I am calm as a baby. When all hell breaks loose, I'm collected and cool. My heart knows no fear because I'm confident in You!

Thank You, Holy Spirit, for bringing these things to my remembrance when I am tempted to be afraid. I will trust in my God. In the name of Jesus, I pray. Amen.

SCRIPTURE REFERENCES

Psalm 56:3-5 TLB • Hebrews 2:15 TLB • 2 Timothy 1:7-8 TPT
John 14:1,17 TLB • Romans 8:15 NASB • Psalm 27:1-3 TLB, MSG

43

Overcoming a Feeling of Abandonment

Introduction

Even if my father and mother abandon me, the Lord will and hold me close (Psalm 27:10 NLT).

This prayer was prompted by a letter I received from someone who is incarcerated. According to his letter, he grew up in a family of fighters and felt abandoned by his family and so-called friends. His pugnacious attitude controlled him, and eventually his aggressive temperament caused him to almost kill someone.

In prison he was ridiculed and harassed by inmates who encouraged him to fight. His wife divorced him, and again he was left alone. Thoughts that "no one likes me" continually tormented him, but he desired to know how to change his thinking.

A laborer of the harvest introduced him to Jesus and my book, *Prayers That Avail Much, Volume 1.* He still had trouble controlling his temper even with those who might have been his friends. His letter was filled with the pain of loneliness and abandonment. The following is a revised and expanded version of the original prayer I wrote, encouraging him to pray for himself.

Prayer

Father, I have confessed Jesus as my Lord and believe in my heart that You raised Him from the dead. I ask for the power of the Holy Spirit to overcome the resentment I feel toward those who abused and abandoned me.

Now I am Your child. When other people leave me and I feel unloved, I am thankful that You will never, ever leave me alone or reject me.

Jesus gave His life for me and called me His friend. He lives in my heart, and I am on my way to heaven. Those are plenty of reasons to be thankful. So when I am lonely or discouraged, I can think of things that are pure and holy and good, even when I am apart from everyone.

Heavenly Father, I ask You to strengthen me and help me while in the presence of the dangers surrounding me. You have assigned angels who will accompany, defend, and preserve me in all my ways of obedience and service. I am not alone. Your Word says that there is nothing that can separate me from the love of Christ—not pain nor stress nor persecution. I will come to the top of every circumstance or trial through Jesus' love.

You are concerned with the smallest detail that concerns me, and You are my Help. I ask You for friends who will admonish and encourage me. Teach me how to trust others and be a friend who sticks closer than a brother. Help me to walk in Your love and show myself friendly. In Jesus' name, amen.

Scripture References

Romans 10:9-10 NIV • Psalm 91:11 AMPC • Hebrews 13:5 NIV Romans 8:35,39 • John 15:13-15 NIV • Psalm 138:8 AMPC • 1 Thessalonians 5:18 TLB • Psalm 46:1 MSG • Philippians 4:8 TLB • Proverbs 18:24 Isaiah 41:10 TLB • Psalm 27:10 NLT, ESV

44

Overcoming Discouragement

Introduction

Moses returned to the Lord and said, "O Lord, why have you brought trouble upon this people? Is this why you sent me? Ever since I went to Pharaoh to speak in your name, he has brought trouble upon this people, and you have not rescued your people at all" (Exodus 5:22-23 NIV).

HERE in this passage, we find Moses discouraged and complaining to God. Most of us have done the same. It is important that we approach God with integrity and in an attitude of humility, but because we fear making a negative confession, we sometimes cross the line of honesty into the line of denial and delusion.

Let's be honest. God already knows what we are feeling. He can handle our anger, complaints, and disappointments. He understands us. He is aware of our human frailties (see Ps. 103:14) and can be touched with the feelings of our infirmities (see Heb. 4:15).

Whether your "trouble" is a business failure, abandonment, depression, a mental disorder, a chemical imbalance, oppression, a marriage problem, a child who is in a strange land of drugs and alcohol, financial disaster, or anything else, the following prayer is for you.

Sometimes when you are in the midst of discouragement, it is difficult to remember that you have ever known any Scripture. I admonish you to read this prayer aloud until you recognize the reality of God's Word in your spirit, soul, and body. Remember, God is watching over His Word to perform it (see Jer. 1:12 AMPC). He will perfect that which concerns you (see Ps. 138:8).

Prayer

Father, on my own, I am powerless to change my situation and circumstances, and I've exhausted all my possibilities. But I'm not on my own, for You have said, "Don't panic. I'm with you. There's no need to fear for I'm your God. I'll give you strength. I'll help you. I'll hold you steady, keep a firm grip on you" (Isa. 41:10 MSG). Thank You, dear Father, that with You all things are possible.

I have a great High Priest who has gone through the heavens: Jesus, Your Son. And I hold firmly to the faith I profess. My High Priest is able to sympathize with my weaknesses. He was tempted in every way, just as I am—yet was without sin. I approach Your throne of grace with confidence, so that I may receive mercy and find grace to help me in my time of need.

In the face of discouragement, disappointment, and anger, I choose to believe that Your word to Moses is Your word to me. You are mighty to deliver. Because of Your mighty hand, You will drive out the forces that have set themselves up against me. You are the Lord, Yahweh, the Promise-Keeper, the Almighty One. You appeared to Abraham, to Isaac, and to Jacob and established Your covenant with them.

Father, I believe that You have heard my groaning, my cries. I will live to see Your promises of deliverance fulfilled in my life. You have not forgotten one word of Your promise; You are a Covenant-Keeper.

It is You who will bring me out from under the yoke of bondage and free me from being a slave to ____________________. You have redeemed me with an outstretched arm and with mighty acts of judgment. You have taken me as Your own, and You are my God. You are a father to me. You have delivered me from the past that has held me in bondage and translated me into the Kingdom of love, peace, joy, and righteousness. I will no longer settle for the pain of the past. Where sin abounds, grace does much more abound.

Father, what You have promised, I will go and possess, in the name of Jesus. I am willing to take the chance, to take the risk, to get back into the good fight of faith. It is with patient endurance and steady and active persistence that I run the race, the appointed course set before me. I rebuke the spirit of fear, for I am established in righteousness. Oppression and destruction shall not come near me. Behold, they may gather together and stir up strife, but it is not from You, Father. I am more than a conqueror through You and Your love for me. In Jesus' name I pray, amen.

SCRIPTURE REFERENCES

This prayer is based on Exodus 5:22-6:11 and includes other verses where applicable.

Mark 9:24 NIV • Deuteronomy 26:8 • Luke 18:27 • Colossians 1:13
1 Peter 5:6 NIV • Romans 5:20 • Hebrews 4:14-16 NIV • 1 Timothy 6:12
Exodus 6:3-4 AMPC • Hebrews 12:1 AMPC • Genesis 49:22-26 AMPC
Isaiah 54:14-16 • 1 Kings 8:56 • Romans 8:37

45

Overcoming Intimidation

FATHER, I come to You in the name of Jesus, confessing that intimidation has caused me to stumble. I ask Your forgiveness for thinking of myself as inferior, for I am created in Your image, and I am Your workmanship. Jesus said that the Kingdom of God is in me. Therefore, the power that raised Jesus from the dead dwells in me and causes me to face life with hope and divine energy.

The Lord is my Light and my Salvation; whom shall I fear? The Lord is the Strength of my life; of whom shall I be afraid? Lord, You said that You would never leave me or forsake me. Therefore, I can say without any doubt or fear that You are my Helper, and I am not afraid of anything that mere man can do to me. Greater is He that is in me than he that is in the world. If God is for me, who can be against me? I am free from the fear of man and public opinion.

Father, You have not given me a spirit of timidity—of cowardice, of craven and cringing and fawning fear—but You have given me a spirit of power and of love and of a calm and well-balanced mind and discipline and self-control. I can do all things through Christ who gives me the strength. In Jesus' mighty name, amen.

SCRIPTURE REFERENCES

1 John 1:9 • Ephesians 2:10 • Luke 17:21 • Ephesians 1:19-20
Colossians 1:29 • Psalm 27:1 • Hebrews 13:5 • 1 John 4:4
Romans 3:31 • Proverbs 29:25 • Joshua 1:5 • Philippians 4:13 • 2 Timothy 1:7

46

Overcoming a Sense of Hopelessness

FATHER, as Your child I boldly come before Your throne of grace that I may receive mercy and find grace to help in this time of need.

Father, I know Your ears are open to my prayers, so hear my prayer and answer me. I am worn out by my worries and crushed by oppression. I am gripped by fear and trembling. Oh, that I had wings like a dove! I would fly away and be at rest. Yes, I would wander far away; I would lodge in the wilderness. I would hasten to escape and to find a shelter from the stormy wind and tempest.

I am calling upon You, my God, to rescue me. You redeem my life in peace from the battle of hopelessness that is against me. I cast my burden on You, Lord, releasing the weight of it. You sustain me. You will never allow the consistently righteous to be moved—made to slip, fall, or fail.

Hopelessness lies in wait for me to swallow me up or trample me all day long. Whenever I am afraid, I will have confidence in and put my trust and reliance in You. By Your help, God, I will praise Your Word; on You I lean, rely, and confidently put my trust; I will not fear.

You know my every sleepless night. Each tear and heartache is answered with Your promise. I am thanking You with all my heart. You pulled me from the brink of death, my feet from the cliff edge of doom. Now I stroll at leisure with You in the sunlit fields of life.

What, what would have become of me, Lord, had I not believed that I would see Your goodness in the land of the living! I wait and hope for and expect You; I am brave and of good courage, and I let my heart be stout and enduring. Yes, I wait for and hope for and expect You.

Father, I give You all my worries and cares, for You are always thinking about me and watching everything that concerns me. I am well-balanced and careful—vigilant, watching out for attacks from Satan, my great enemy. By Your grace I am standing firm, trusting You, and I remember that other Christians all around the world are going through these sufferings too. You, God, are full of kindness through Christ and will give me Your eternal glory.

In the name of Jesus, I am an overcomer by the blood of the Lamb and by the word of my testimony. Amen.

SCRIPTURE REFERENCES

Hebrews 4:16 • Psalm 56:5,8 MSG • Psalm 55:1-5 GNT • Psalm 56:13 MSG
Psalm 27:13-14 AMPC • Psalm 55:6-8 AMPC • 1 Peter 5:7-9 AMPC, TLB
Psalm 55:16,18,22 AMPC • Revelation 12:11 • Psalm 56:2-4 AMPC

47

Overcoming a Feeling of Rejection

Introduction

Rejection seems to create an identity crisis. Rejection by those in the Body of Christ is especially cruel. It happens more often than it should. When you are thrown into an identity crisis, you have the opportunity to erase old recordings that have played in your mind for a long time and replace those self-destructive thoughts with God-thoughts. One of your most powerful weapons is forgiving those who have hurt you. Forgiving others is a choice, not a feeling.

Your heavenly Father saw you and approved of you even while you were in your mother's womb (see Ps. 139:13-16). He gave you survival tools that would bring you to the place where you are today. He is a Father who has been waiting for you to come home to truth—the truth that will set you free (see John 8:32).

Do not allow a feeling to hinder your prayers. Whenever you stand praying, if you find that you are guarding this feeling and resenting anyone, choose to forgive and be set free (see Mark 11:25).

Future rejection may hurt, but it will be only for a season (see 1 Pet. 1:6). The Word of God is your shield against all the fiery darts of the devil (see Eph. 6:16-17).

For victory over your feeling of rejection, pray the following prayer in faith and joy.[5]

Prayer

Lord, Your Son, Jesus, is my High Priest. He understands and sympathizes with my weaknesses and this excruciating pain of rejection. In His name I approach Your throne of grace with confidence, so I may receive mercy and find grace to help me in my time of need. I ask You to forgive my sins, and I receive Your mercy. I expect Your healing grace to dispel the agony of rejection I have suffered because of the false accusations and demeaning actions of another.

Father, Jesus was despised and rejected—a Man of Sorrows, acquainted with bitterest grief. The grief of ____________ turning against me and treating me as an outcast has consumed me, just as my rejection consumed Your Son, who freely gave His life for me.

Forgive me for turning my back on Jesus and looking the other way—He was despised, and I didn't care. Yet it was my grief He bore, my sorrows that weighed Him down. He was wounded and bruised for my sins. He was beaten that I might have peace; He was lashed, and with His stripes I was healed.

In the face of rejection, I will declare, "The Lord is my Light and my Salvation—whom shall I fear or dread? The Lord is the Refuge and Stronghold of my life—of whom shall I be afraid?" (Ps. 27:1 AMPC).

I know right from wrong and cherish Your laws in my heart; I won't be afraid of people's scorn or their slanderous talk. Slanderous talk is temporal and fades away. Your Word will never pass away.

Father, I choose to look at the things that are eternal—Your justice and mercy shall last forever, and Your salvation from generation to generation.

---

5 For further support, I encourage you to read Psalm 27 and the book of Ephesians in their entirety.

Your eyes are upon me, for I have right standing with You, and Your ears are attentive to my prayer. You spoke to me and asked, "Now who is going to hurt you if you are a zealous follower of that which is good?"

In Jesus' name, I will refuse to give the opposition a second thought. Through thick and thin, I will keep my heart at attention, in adoration before Christ, my Master. I will be ready to speak up and tell anyone who asks why I'm living the way I am with the utmost courtesy. I will keep a clear conscience before God so that when people throw mud at me, none of it will stick. They will end up realizing that they are the ones who need a bath. For God has said, it's better to suffer for doing good than to be punished for doing bad. That's what Jesus did definitively (see 1 Pet. 3:15-18 MSG).

There is wonderful joy ahead, even though the going has been rough for a while down here. These trials are only to test my faith, to see whether it is strong and pure. It is being tested as fire tests gold and purifies it—and my faith is far more precious to You, Lord, than mere gold; so if my faith remains strong after being tried in the test tube of fiery trials, it will bring me much praise and glory and honor on the day of Jesus' return.

In spite of the rejection I have experienced, I declare that everything You say about me in Your Word is true:

I am blessed with all spiritual blessings in heavenly places in Christ (Eph. 1:3).

I am chosen by You, my Father (Eph. 1:4).

I am holy and without blame (Eph. 1:4).

I am Your child according to the good pleasure of Your will (Eph. 1:5).

I am accepted in the Beloved (Eph. 1:6).

I am redeemed through the blood of Jesus (Eph1:7).

I am a person of wisdom and prudence (Eph. 1:8).

I am an heir (Eph. 1:11).

I have a spirit of wisdom and revelation in the knowledge of Christ (Eph. 1:17).

I am saved by Your grace (Eph. 2:5).

I am seated in heavenly places in Christ Jesus (Eph. 2:6).

I am Your workmanship (Eph. 2:10).

I am near to You by the blood of Christ (Eph. 2:13).

I am a new creation (2 Cor. 5:17).

I am of Your household (Eph. 2:19).

I am a citizen of heaven (Eph. 2:19).

I am a partaker of Your promises in Christ (2 Pet. 1:4).

I am strengthened with might by Your Spirit (Eph. 3:16).

I allow Christ to dwell in my heart by faith (Eph. 3:17).

I am rooted and grounded in love (Eph. 3:17).

I speak the truth in love (Eph. 4:15).

I am renewed in the spirit of my mind (Eph. 4:23).

I am Your follower (Eph. 5:1).

I walk in love (Eph. 5:2).

I am light in You (Eph. 5:8).

I walk circumspectly (Eph. 5:15).

I am filled with the Spirit (Eph. 5:18).

I am more than a conqueror (Rom. 8:37).

I am an overcomer (Rev. 12:11).

I am the righteousness of God in Christ Jesus (1 Cor. 1:30).

I am healed (1 Pet. 2:24).

I am free (John 8:36).

I am salt (Matt. 5:13).

I am consecrated (1 Cor. 6:11 AMPC).

I am sanctified (1 Cor. 6:11).

I am victorious (1 John 5:4).

Everything You say about me is true, Lord. In Your name I pray, amen.

SCRIPTURE REFERENCES

Hebrews 4:14-16 NIV • Isaiah 51:7-8 TLB • Isaiah 53:3-5 TLB
1 Peter 3:12-18 MSG • 2 Corinthians 4:18 • 1 Peter 1:6-7 TLB

48

Overcoming Worry

FATHER, I depart from evil and do good. I seek, inquire for, and crave peace. I pursue and go after it! When my ways please You, Lord, You make even my enemies to be at peace with me.

Lord, You have given me Your peace. Your own peace You have bequeathed to me. It is not the peace that the world gives. I will not let my heart be troubled, neither will I let it be afraid. I refuse to be agitated and disturbed; and I will not permit myself to be fearful, intimidated, cowardly, and unsettled.

Instead of worrying, I will pray. I will let petitions and praises shape my worries into prayers, letting You, Father, know my concerns, not forgetting to thank You for the answers. Your peace will keep my thoughts and my heart quiet and at rest as I trust in Christ Jesus, my Lord. It is wonderful when Christ displaces worry at the center of my life.

Thank You for guarding me and keeping me in perfect and constant peace. You will keep in perfect peace all who trust in You, all whose thoughts are fixed on You! So, I commit myself to You, lean on You, and hope confidently in You.

I let the peace (soul harmony that comes) from Christ rule (act as umpire continually) in my heart deciding and settling with finality all questions that arise in my mind. I am thankful (appreciative), giving praise to You always. In Jesus' name, amen.

SCRIPTURE REFERENCES

Philippians 4:6-7 • Colossians 3:15 AMPC, MSG, TLB
Proverbs 16:7 AMPC • Psalm 34:14 AMPC • John 14:27 AMPC
Isaiah 26:3 NLT

49

Overcoming Hypersensitivity

Introduction

A new command I give you: Love one another. As I have loved you, so you must love one another. By this all men will know that you are my disciples, if you love one another (John 13:34-35 NIV).

THE royal law of love is the counteragent for hypersensitivity.

First Corinthians 13:5 AMPC reveals that love "is not conceited (arrogant and inflated with pride); it is not rude (unmannerly) and does not act unbecomingly. Love (God's love in us) does not insist on its own rights or its own way, for it is not self-seeking; it is not touchy or fretful or resentful; it takes no account of the evil done to it [it pays no attention to a suffered wrong]."

The hypersensitive person has usually experienced deep hurt from rejection and needs a lot of approval from others. This individual is excessively sensitive to remarks that may or may not be intended to be hurtful. Sometimes, he or she is offended simply by a facial expression. It is difficult for a person of this nature to trust others, to accept constructive criticism or advice; and this weakness hinders positive relationships.

When presentations or suggestions are rejected, that action is taken as a personal attack.

Hypersensitivity is an enemy that can be overcome through spiritual warfare. In waging the good warfare, we have God-given weapons to overthrow our adversary. These weapons include, among other things, the anointing that is upon Jesus to bind up and heal the brokenhearted (see Luke 4:18), the Sword of the Spirit, which is the Word of God (see Eph. 6:17), the shield of faith (see Eph. 6:16), and the help of the Holy Spirit (see John 14:16 AMPC), which may come through a Christian counselor, a minister, or a friend.

James instructed us, "Confess to one another therefore your faults (your slips, your false steps, your offenses, your sins) and pray [also] for one another, that you may be healed and restored [to a spiritual tone of mind and heart]. The earnest (heartfelt, continued) prayer of a righteous man makes tremendous power available [dynamic in its working]" (James 5:16 AMPC). We are overcomers by the blood of the Lamb and by the word of our testimony (see Rev. 12:11)!

Prayer

Father, forgive me for my attempts to hurt and dominate others. I realize that I have released my anger inappropriately. I confess this as sin and receive Your forgiveness, knowing that You are faithful and just to forgive my sin and cleanse me from all unrighteousness. I forgive those who have wronged me, and I ask for healing of my anger and unresolved hurts.

I realize that I am responsible for my own behavior, and I am accountable to You for my thoughts, words, and actions.

Thank You for the Holy Spirit who leads me into reality—the truth that makes me free. You have sent Your Word and healed me and delivered me from all my destructions.

Father, I am empowered through my union with You. I draw my strength from You—that strength which Your boundless might provides. Your strength causes me to be steadfast and trustworthy, gives me the capacity for perseverance and tolerance, and enables me to resist hypersensitivity, irritability, and touchiness.

I desire to be well-balanced (temperate, sober of mind), vigilant, and cautious at all times; for I recognize that enemy—the devil—who roams around like a lion roaring, seeking someone to seize upon and devour. In the name of Jesus, I withstand him, firm in faith against his onset—rooted, established, strong, immovable, and determined.

I am dwelling in the secret place of the Most High, and I shall remain stable and fixed under the shadow of the Almighty whose power no foe can withstand.

I purpose to walk in love toward my family members, my associates, and my neighbors with the help of the Holy Spirit. Whom the Son has set free is free indeed.

Thanks be to You, Lord, for You always cause me to triumph in Christ Jesus. I am an overcomer by the blood of the Lamb and by the word of my testimony. In Jesus' name, amen.

SCRIPTURE REFERENCES

1 John 1:9 • Ephesians 6:10 AMPC • Mark 11:24-25 • 1 Peter 5:8-9 AMPC
Matthew 12:36 • Psalm 91:1 AMPC • John 16:13 • John 8:36
John 8:32 • 2 Corinthians 2:14 • Psalm 107:20 • Revelation 12:11

50

Overcoming Chronic Fatigue Syndrome

Introduction

All fatigue does not fall into the category of Chronic Fatigue Syndrome. Most people at one time or another have feelings of apathy and energy loss—times when they go to bed tired and get up tired.

There are cases of fatigue that lasts for weeks, months, or even years. The medical profession has not determined the causes of Chronic Fatigue Syndrome and does not know its cure. In most individuals it simply runs its course.[6] Where there is no way, Jesus is the Way, the Truth, and the Life. God sent His Word to heal you and deliver you from all your destructions (see Ps. 107:20).

According to those who have shared their experience with this syndrome, they have flu-like symptoms—they feel achy with a low-grade fever. One person who suffers from it and for whom we pray is considered disabled and cannot work regularly.

You and I are created triune beings—spirit, soul, and body (see 1 Thess. 5:23). The apostle John wrote, "Beloved, I pray that you may prosper in all things and be in health, just as your soul prospers" (3 John 2 NKJV).

---

6 Editors of *Prevention* Magazine, *Symptoms, Their Causes & Cures* (Emmaus, PA: Rodale Press, 1994), 179,181.

God's Word is medicine to our flesh (see Prov. 4:20-22 AMPC). If any type of medication is to bring relief and a cure, it is necessary to follow the prescribed dosage. This is true with "spiritual" medicine. It is imperative to take doses of God's Word daily through reading, meditating, and listening to healing tapes. The spirit, soul, and body are interrelated; it is the Word of God that brings the entire being into harmony.

God made us and knows us inside and out. He sent His Word to heal us and to deliver us from all our destructions (see Ps. 107:20). Prayer prepares us to take action. Jesus said that if we pray in secret, our heavenly Father will reward us openly (see Matt. 6:6). Prayer includes praise, worship, and petition.

Prayer prepares us for change—it equips us for action. It puts us in tune and in harmony with the Spirit of God who is hovering over the face of the rivers of living waters, residing within us (see Gen. 1:2; John 7:38). He is waiting for us to speak, to move—to act out our faith. The ministry of the Holy Spirit is revealed in the names ascribed to Him—Comforter, Counselor, Helper, Advocate, Intercessor, Strengthener, Standby (see John 16:7 AMPC). He is with us and in us (see John 14:17).

Prayer

Father, in the name of Jesus, I come before Your throne of grace to receive mercy and to find grace to help in time of need. May blessing (praise, laudation, and eulogy) be to You, the God and Father of my Lord Jesus Christ the Messiah, for You have blessed me in Christ with every spiritual (given by the Holy Spirit) blessing in the heavenly realm!

Father, Chronic Fatigue Syndrome is a curse, not a blessing. Jesus became a curse and at the same time dissolved the curse. And now, because of that, the air is cleared and I can see that Abraham's blessing is present and available for me. I am able to receive Your life, Your Spirit, just the way Abraham received it.

Christ, the Messiah, purchased my freedom with His very own blood, and the law of the Spirit of life which is in Christ Jesus, the law of my new being, has freed me from the law of sin and of death.

Jesus Christ lives in me. Your Spirit who raised up Jesus from the dead dwells in me. You, Father, are restoring to life my mortal (short-lived, perishable) body through Your Spirit who dwells in me.

You, Sovereign Lord, have taught me what to say so that I can strengthen the weary. Every morning You make me eager to hear what You are going to teach me.

I have strength for all things in Christ who empowers me. I am ready for anything and equal to anything through Him who infuses inner strength into me. I am self-sufficient in Christ's sufficiency.

You are my Light and my Salvation—whom shall I fear or dread? You are the Refuge and Stronghold of my life—of whom shall I be afraid? You, Lord, are my Shield, my Glory, and the Lifter of my head. With my voice I cry to You, and You hear and answer me out of Your holy hill. I lie down and sleep, I awaken again, and You sustain me.

Father, I put on Your whole armor; and, having done all, I stand, knowing that You are watching over Your Word to perform it. Your Word will not return to You void—without producing any effect or useless. But it shall accomplish that which You please and purpose, and it shall prosper in the thing for which You sent it.

Lord Jesus, You carried our sins in Your body to the cross, so that we might die to sin and live for righteousness. It is by Your wounds that I have been healed.

Therefore, I throw off the spirit of heaviness and exchange it for a garment of praise. Thank You for the superhuman energy that You so mightily enkindle and work within me. In the name of Jesus, I pray, amen.

SCRIPTURE REFERENCES

Hebrews 4:16 • Psalm 27:1 AMPC • Ephesians 1:3 AMPC
Psalm 3:3-5 AMPC • Galatians 3:13-14 MSG • Ephesians 6:11,13
Acts 20:28 • Jeremiah 1:12 AMPC • Romans 8:2,10-11 AMPC
Isaiah 55:11 AMPC • 1 Peter 2:24 GNT • Isaiah 61:3
Isaiah 50:4 GNT • Colossians 1:29 AMPC • Philippians 4:13 AMPC

51

Forgiveness and Healing

FATHER, in the name of Jesus, I come before You asking You to heal me. It is written that the prayer of faith will save the sick, and the Lord will raise him up. And if I have committed sins, I will be forgiven. I let go of all unforgiveness, resentment, anger, and bad feelings toward anyone.

My body is the temple of the Holy Spirit, and I desire to be in good health. I seek truth that will make me free—both spiritual and natural (good eating habits, medications if necessary, and appropriate rest and exercise). You bought me at a price, and I desire to glorify You in my spirit and my body—they both belong to You.

Thank You, Father, for sending Your Word to heal me and deliver me from all my destructions. Jesus, You are the Word who became flesh and dwelt among us. You bore my griefs (pains) and carried my sorrows (sickness). You were pierced for my transgressions; You were crushed for my iniquities; upon You was the chastisement that brought me peace, and with Your wounds I am healed.

I will fill my thoughts with Your words until they penetrate deep into my spirit. Then, as I unwrap Your words, they will impart true life and radiant health into the very core of my being.

Because Your Spirit who raised Jesus from the dead dwells in me, He who raised Christ from the dead will also give life to my mortal body through Your Spirit who dwells in me.

Thank You, Father, that I will prosper and be in health, even as my soul prospers. Amen.

SCRIPTURE REFERENCES

James 5:15 NKJV • Proverbs 4:21-22 TPT • 1 Corinthians 6:19-20
Psalm 103:3-5 • Psalm 107:20 • Romans 8:11 NKJV • John 1:14
3 John 2 NKJV • Isaiah 53:4-5 ESV

52

Safety

FATHER, in the name of Jesus, I thank You that You watch over Your Word to perform it. I thank You that I dwell in the secret place of the Most High and that I remain stable and fixed under the shadow of the Almighty, whose power no foe can withstand.

Father, You are my Refuge and my Fortress. No evil shall befall me—no accident shall overtake me—nor any plague or calamity come near my home. You give Your angels special charge over me to accompany and defend and preserve me in all my ways. They are encamped around about me.

Father, You are my Confidence, firm and strong. You keep my foot from being caught in a trap or hidden danger. Father, You give me safety and ease me—*Jesus is my Safety!*

Traveling—As I go, I say, "Let me pass over to the other side," and I have what I say. I walk on my way, securely and in confident trust, for my heart and mind are firmly fixed and stayed on You, and I am kept in perfect peace.

Sleeping—Father, I sing for joy upon my bed because You sustain me. In peace I lie down and sleep, for You alone, Lord, make me dwell in safety. I lie down, and I am not afraid. My sleep is sweet, for You give blessings to me in sleep. Thank You, Father, in Jesus' name, amen.

SCRIPTURE REFERENCES

Jeremiah 1:12 • Proverbs 3:23 AMPC • Psalm 91:1-2 AMPC
Psalm 112:7 • Psalm 91:10 AMPC • Isaiah 26:3 • Psalm 91:11 AMPC
Psalm 149:5 • Psalm 34:7 • Psalm 3:5 • Proverbs 3:26 AMPC
Psalm 4:8 AMPC • Isaiah 49:25 • Proverbs 3:24 • Mark 4:35 • Psalm 127:2

53

Peaceful Sleep

FATHER, thank You for peaceful sleep, and for Your angels that encamp around us who fear You. You deliver us and keep us safe. The angels excel in strength, do Your word, and heed the voice of Your Word. You give Your angels charge over me, to keep me in all my ways.

I bring every thought, every imagination, and every dream into the captivity and obedience of Jesus Christ. Father, I thank You that, even as I sleep, my heart counsels me and reveals to me Your purpose and plan. Thank You for sweet sleep, for You promised Your beloved sweet sleep. Therefore, my heart is glad and my spirit rejoices. My body and soul rest and confidently dwell in safety. In Jesus' name, amen.

SCRIPTURE REFERENCES

Proverbs 3:24 • Psalm 91:11 • Psalm 34:7 • 2 Corinthians 10:5
Psalm 103:20

54

Knowing God's Will

FATHER, in Jesus' name, I thank You that You are instructing me in the way I should go, for all who are led by the Spirit of God are children of God.

Thank You for Your guidance concerning Your will, Your plan, and Your purpose for my life. I do hear the voice of the Good Shepherd, for I know You and follow You. You lead me in the paths of righteousness for Your name's sake.

In the name of Jesus, I will not imitate the ideals and opinions of the culture around me, but I will be inwardly transformed by the Holy Spirit through a total reformation of how I think. This will empower me to discern Your will as I live a beautiful life, satisfying and perfect in Your eyes.

Thank You, Father, that Your Word is a lamp to my feet and a light to my path. My path is growing brighter and brighter until it reaches the full light of day. As I follow You, Lord, I believe my path is becoming clearer each day.

Thank You, Father, that Jesus was made unto me wisdom. Confusion is not a part of my life. I am not confused about Your will for my life. I trust in You and lean not unto my own understanding. As I acknowledge You in all of my ways, You are directing my paths. I believe that as I trust in You completely, You will show me the path of life. In Jesus' name, amen.

SCRIPTURE REFERENCES

Romans 8:14 • Psalm 32:8 • Romans 12:2 TPT • 1 Corinthians 1:30
John 10:3-4 • 1 Corinthians 14:33 • Psalm 23:3 • Proverbs 3:5-6
Proverbs 4:18 • Psalm 16:11 • Ephesians 5:19

55

Godly Wisdom in the Affairs of Life

FATHER, You said if anyone lacks wisdom to guide him through a decision or circumstance, let him ask of You, our benevolent God, who gives to everyone generously and without rebuke or blame, and it will be given to him. Therefore, I ask in faith, nothing wavering, to be filled with the knowledge of Your will in all wisdom and spiritual understanding. Today I incline my ear unto wisdom, and I apply my heart to understanding so that I might receive that which has been freely given unto me.

In the name of Jesus, I receive skill and godly wisdom and instruction. I discern and comprehend the words of understanding and insight. I receive instruction in wise dealing and the discipline of wise thoughtfulness, righteousness, justice, and integrity. Prudence, knowledge, discretion, and discernment are given to me. I increase in knowledge. As a person of understanding, I acquire skill and attain to sound counsels so that I may be able to steer my course rightly.

Wisdom will keep, defend, and protect me; I love her and she guards me. I prize wisdom highly and exalt her; she will bring me to honor because I embrace her. She gives to my head a wreath of gracefulness; a crown of beauty and glory will she deliver to me. Length of days is in her right hand, and in her left hand are riches and honor.

Jesus has been made unto me wisdom, and in Him are all the treasures of divine wisdom, of comprehensive insight into the ways and purposes of God; and all the riches of spiritual knowledge and enlightenment are stored up and lie hidden. God has hidden away sound and godly wisdom and stored it up for me, for I am the righteousness of God in Christ Jesus.

Therefore, I will walk in paths of uprightness. When I walk, my steps shall not be hampered—my path will be clear and open; and when I run, I shall not stumble. I take fast hold of instruction and do not let her go; I guard her, for she is my life. I let my eyes look right on with fixed purpose, and my gaze is straight before me. I consider well the path of my feet, and I let all my ways be established and ordered aright.

Father, in the name of Jesus, I look carefully to how I walk! I have the mind of Christ. And I live purposefully and worthily and accurately, not as unwise and witless, but as a wise, sensible, and intelligent person, making the very most of my time—buying up every opportunity. In Jesus' name, amen.

SCRIPTURE REFERENCES

James 1:5-6 AMP • 1 Corinthians 1:30 • Colossians 1:9 • Colossians 2:3 AMPC
Proverbs 2:2 • Proverbs 2:7 AMPC • Proverbs 1:2-5 AMPC
2 Corinthians 5:21 • Proverbs 4:6,8-9 AMPC • Proverbs 4:11-13,25-26 AMPC
Proverbs 3:16 AMPC • Ephesians 5:15-16 AMPC • 1 Corinthians 2:16 NIV

56

Receiving a Discerning Heart

FATHER, thank You for creating within me a wise and discerning heart, so I am able to distinguish between right and wrong. I pray that my love may abound more and more in knowledge and depth of insight, so that I may be able to discern what is best and may be pure and blameless until the day of Christ, filled with the fruit of righteousness that comes through Jesus Christ—to Your glory and praise.

Father, I trust in You with all my heart and lean not on my own understanding; in all of my ways I acknowledge You, and You will make my paths straight. Through Your precepts I get understanding; therefore, I hate every false way. Your Word is a lamp to my feet and a light to my path.

Joseph, in Genesis 41:39-41, was described as a discerning and wise man who was put in charge of the entire land of Egypt. As You were with Joseph, so shall You be with me. You will cause me to find favor at my place of employment, at home, or wherever I may be.

I make special request, asking that I may be filled with the full (deep and clear) knowledge of Your will in all spiritual wisdom and in understanding and discernment of spiritual things. I pray that I may walk (live and conduct myself) in a manner worthy of You, Lord, fully pleasing to You and desiring to please You in all things. I pray that I am steadily growing and increasing in and by Your knowledge with fuller, deeper, and clearer insight, acquaintance, and recognition.

Because Jesus has been made unto me wisdom, I listen and add to my learning; I discern and get guidance, understanding Your will. In the name of Jesus, I pray, amen.

SCRIPTURE REFERENCES

1 Kings 3:9 NIV • Proverbs 3:1-4 • Philippians 1:9-11 NIV
Colossians 1:9-10 AMPC • Proverbs 3:5 NIV • 1 Corinthians 1:30
Psalm 119:104-105 AMPC • Proverbs 1:5 • Genesis 41:39-41 NIV
Ephesians 5:17 • Joshua 1:5

— 57 —

Developing Healthy Friendships

FATHER, help me to meet new friends—friends who will encourage me. May I find in these friendships the companionship and fellowship You have ordained for me. I know that You are my source of love, companionship, and friendship. Your love and friendship are expressed through my relationship with You and members of the Body of Christ.

As iron sharpens iron, so friends sharpen the minds of each other. As we learn from each other, may we find a worthy purpose in our relationship. Keep me well-balanced in my friendships so that I will always please You rather than pleasing other people.

I ask for divine connections—good friendships ordained by You. Thank You for the courage and grace to let go of detrimental friendships. By faith I ask and receive discernment for developing healthy relationships. Your Word says that two are better than one, because if one falls, there will be someone to lift up that person.

Father, You know the hearts of people, so I won't be deceived by outward appearances. Bad friendships corrupt good morals. Thank You for quality friends who help me build stronger character and draw me closer to You. Help me be a friend to others and to love my friends at all times. I will laugh with those who laugh, I will rejoice with those who rejoice, and I will weep with those who weep. Teach me what I need to know to be a quality friend.

Develop in me a fun personality and a good sense of humor. Help me to relax around people and to be myself—the person You created me to be. Instruct my heart and mold my character, that I may be faithful and trustworthy over the friendships You are sending into my life.

Father, Your Son, Jesus, is my best Friend. He is a Friend who sticks closer than a brother. He defined the standard when He said in John 15:13, "Greater love hath no man than this, than a man lay down his life for his friends."

Thank You, Lord, that I can entrust myself and my need for friends into Your keeping. I submit to the leadership of the Holy Spirit. In the name of Jesus. Amen.

SCRIPTURE REFERENCES

Proverbs 13:20 NIV • 1 Corinthians 15:33 AMPC • Ephesians 5:30 NIV
Proverbs 27:17 CEV • James 1:17 NIV • Philippians 2:2-3 NIV
Proverbs 17:17 • Proverbs 13:20 NIV • Romans 12:15 • Psalm 84:11 NIV
Proverbs 18:24 • Ecclesiastes 4:9-10 NIV • Psalm 37:4-5 NIV

58

Boldness

FATHER, in the name of Jesus, I am of good courage. I pray that You grant to me that with all *boldness* I speak forth Your Word. I pray that freedom of utterance be given me that I may open my mouth to proclaim *boldly* the mystery of the good news of the Gospel—that I may declare it *boldly* as I ought to do.

Father, I believe I receive that *boldness* now in the name of Jesus. Therefore, I have *boldness* to enter into the Holy of Holies by the blood of Jesus. Because of my faith in Him, I dare to have the *boldness* (courage and confidence) of free access—an unreserved approach to You with freedom and without fear. I can draw fearlessly and confidently and *boldly* near to Your throne of grace and receive mercy and find grace to help in good time for my every need. I am *bold* to pray. I come to the throne of God with my petitions and for others who do not know how to ascend to the throne.

I will be *bold* toward Satan, demons, evil spirits, sickness, disease, and poverty, for Jesus is the Head of all rule and authority—of every angelic principality and power. Disarming those who were ranged against us, Jesus made a *bold* display and public example of them, triumphing over them. I am *bold* to declare that Satan is a defeated foe. Let God arise and His enemies be scattered.

I take comfort and am encouraged and confidently and *boldly* say, "The Lord is my Helper; I will not be seized with alarm—I will not fear or dread or be terrified. What can man do to me?" I dare to proclaim the Word toward heaven, toward hell, and toward earth. I am *bold* as a lion, for I have been made the righteousness of God in Christ Jesus. I am complete in Him! Praise the name of Jesus! Amen.

SCRIPTURE REFERENCES

Psalm 27:14 • Hebrews 4:16 AMPC • Acts 4:29 • Colossians 2:10,15 AMPC
Ephesians 6:19-20 AMPC • Psalm 68:1 • Mark 11:23-24
Hebrews 13:6 AMPC • Hebrews 10:19 AMPC, KJV
Proverbs 28:1 • Ephesians 3:12 AMPC • 2 Corinthians 5:21

59

Being Equipped for Success

FATHER, thank You that the entrance of Your words gives light. Thank You that Your Word, which You speak (and which I speak), is alive and full of power—making it active, operative, energizing, and effective. Thank You, Father, that You have given me a spirit of power and of love and of a calm and well-balanced mind and discipline and self-control. I have Your power and ability and sufficiency, for You have qualified me (making me to be fit and worthy and sufficient) as a minister and dispenser of a new covenant of salvation through Christ.

In the name of Jesus, I walk out of the realm of failure into the arena of success, giving thanks to You, Father, for You have qualified and made me fit to share the portion that is the inheritance of the saints—God's holy people in the light.

Father, You have delivered and drawn me to Yourself out of the control and the dominion of darkness (failure, doubt, and fear) and have transferred me into the Kingdom of the Son of Your love, in whom there is good success and freedom from fears, agitating passions, and moral conflicts. I rejoice in Jesus who has come that I might have life and have it more abundantly.

Today I am a new creation, for I am engrafted in Christ, the Messiah. The old moral and spiritual condition has passed away. Behold, the fresh and new has come! I forget those things that are behind me and reach forth unto those things that are before me. I am crucified with Christ, nevertheless I live; yet not I, but Christ lives in me. And the life which I now live in the flesh I live by the faith of the Son of God, who loved me and gave Himself for me.

Today I attend to the Word of God. I consent and submit to Your sayings, Father. Your words shall not depart from my sight; I will keep them in the midst of my heart. For they are life and success to me, healing and health to all my flesh. I keep and guard my heart with all vigilance and above all I guard, for out of it flow the springs of life.

Today I will not let mercy and kindness and truth forsake me. I bind them about my neck; I write them upon the tablet of my heart. So, therefore, I will find favor, good understanding, and high esteem in the sight or judgment of God and man.

Today my delight and desire are in the law of the Lord, and on His law I habitually meditate (ponder and study) by day and by night. Therefore, I am like a tree firmly planted and tended by the streams of water, ready to bring forth my fruit in my season. My leaf also shall not fade or wither, and everything I do shall prosper and come to maturity.

Now thanks be to God, who always causes me to triumph in Christ! In His name I pray, amen.

SCRIPTURE REFERENCES

Psalm 119:130 • Philippians 3:13 • Hebrews 4:12 AMPC • Galatians 2:20
2 Timothy 1:7 AMPC • Proverbs 4:20-23 AMPC • 2 Corinthians 3:5-6 AMPC
Proverbs 3:3-4 AMPC • Colossians 1:12-13 AMPC • Psalm 1:2-3 AMPC
2 Corinthians 5:17 AMPC • 2 Corinthians 2:14 • John 10:10

60

Prayer for the Success of a Business

FATHER, Your Word says that I am a partaker of the inheritance and treasures of heaven. You have delivered me out of the authority of darkness and translated me into the Kingdom of Your dear Son. Your Word is a lamp that gives light wherever I walk, and it does not return to You void but always accomplishes what it is sent to do. I am a joint-heir with Jesus, and as Your son/daughter I accept that the communication of my faith is effectual by the acknowledging of every good work that is in me in Christ Jesus.

Father, I commit my works (the plans and cares of my business) to You, entrust them wholly to You. Because You are effectually at work in me, You cause my thoughts to become agreeable with Your will so that my business plans shall be established and succeed. In the name of Jesus, I submit to every kind of wisdom, practical insight, and prudence, which You have lavished upon me in accordance with the riches and generosity of Your gracious favor.

Father, I obey Your Word by making an honest living with my own hands so that I may be able to give to those in need. In Your strength and according to Your grace, I provide for myself and my own family. Thank You, Father, for making all grace, every favor and earthly blessing come to me in abundance so that having all sufficiency in all things at all times, I may abound in every good work.

Father, thank You for the ministering spirits that You have assigned to go forth to bring in consumers. Jesus said, "You are the light of the world." In His name my light shall so shine before all men that they may see my good works glorifying You, my heavenly Father.

Thank You for the grace to remain diligent in seeking knowledge and skill in areas where I am inexperienced. I ask You for wisdom and the ability to understand righteousness, justice, and fair dealing in every area and relationship. I affirm that I am faithful and committed to Your Word. My life and business are founded upon its principles.

Father, thank You for the success of my business! In Your name, amen.

SCRIPTURE REFERENCES

Romans 8:17 • 1 Timothy 5:8 • Colossians 1:12 • Psalm 119:105 CEV
2 Corinthians 9:8 AMPC • Hebrews 1:14 • Philemon 1:6
Matthew 5:14,16 • Proverbs 16:3 • Proverbs 22:29
Philippians 2:13 • Proverbs 2:9 • Ephesians 1:7-8 • Proverbs 4:20-22
Ephesians 4:28

61

Setting Proper Priorities

FATHER, too often I allow urgency to dictate my schedule, and I am asking You to help me establish priorities in my work. I confess my weakness[7] of procrastination and lack of organization. My desire is to live purposefully and worthily and accurately as a wise, sensible, intelligent person.

You have given me a seven-day week—six days to work and the seventh day to rest. I desire to make the most of the time, buying up each opportunity. Help me plan my day and stay focused on my assignments.

In the name of Jesus, I demolish and smash warped philosophies concerning time management, tear down barriers erected against the truth of God, and fit every loose thought, emotion, and impulse into the structure of life shaped by Christ. I clear my mind of every obstruction and build a life of obedience into maturity.

Father, You are in charge of my work and my plans. I plan the way I want to live, but You alone make me able to live it. Help me organize my efforts, schedule my activities, and budget my time.

Jesus, You want me to relax. It pleases You when I am not preoccupied with getting, so I can respond to God's giving. I know You, Father God, and how You work. I steep my life in God-reality, God-initiative, and God-provisions.

7 If you do not know your strengths and weaknesses, ask the Holy Spirit to reveal them to you. The Lord speaks to us: *"My grace is sufficient for you, for power is perfected in weakness"* (2 Cor. 12:9 NASB).

By the grace given me, I will not worry about missing out, and my everyday human concerns will be met. I purpose in my heart to seek (aim at and strive after) first of all Your Kingdom, Lord, and Your righteousness—Your way of doing and being right. And then all these things taken together will be given me besides.

Father, Your Word is my compass, and it helps me see my life as complete in Christ. I cast all my cares, worries, and concerns over on You, that I might be well-balanced, temperate, sober of mind, vigilant, and cautious at all times.

I tune my ears to the word of wisdom and set my heart on a life of understanding. I make insight my priority.

Father, You sent Jesus that I might have life and have it more abundantly. Help me remember that my relationships with You and with others are more important than anything else. Amen.

SCRIPTURE REFERENCES

Ephesians 5:15-16 AMPC • Genesis 2:2 NIV • 2 Corinthians 10:5-6 MSG
Proverbs 16:3,9 MSG • Matthew 11:29 MSG, AMPC • Colossians 2:10
1 Peter 5:7-8 AMPC • Proverbs 2:3 MSG • John 10:10

62

Maintaining Good Relations

FATHER, in the name of Jesus, I will not withhold good from those to whom it is due (its rightful owners) when it is in the power of my hand to do it. I will render to all men their dues. I will pay taxes to whom taxes are due, revenue to whom revenue is due, respect to whom respect is due, and honor to whom honor is due.

I will not lose heart and grow weary and faint in acting nobly and doing nobly and right, for in due season I shall reap if I do not loosen and relax my courage and faint. So then, as occasion and opportunity open up to me, I will do good morally to all people not only being useful or profitable to them, but also doing what is for their spiritual good and advantage. I am mindful to be a blessing, especially to those of the household of faith—those who belong to God's family with me, the believers.

I will not contend with a man for no reason when he has done me no wrong. If possible, as far as it depends on me, I purpose to live at peace with everyone. Amen.

SCRIPTURE REFERENCES (AMPC)

Proverbs 3:27 • Proverbs 3:30 • Romans 13:7 • Romans 12:18
Galatians 6:9-10

63

Overcoming Religious Bondage

Introduction

Most of the time when we are children, we believe that every family is the same as ours. We are surprised to discover this isn't true. Sometimes adults who grew up in strict religious environments are not prepared for the outside world. They don't fit in to the strange world where people are different and enjoying life on a level they had never known existed. They are faced with uncomfortable choices when their beliefs are questioned and even ridiculed. Some people might choose to become more dogmatic about their religious beliefs and try to convince "sinners" that they need to be like them; others find themselves on a search for truth. Others stay in the religious environment and even find the freedom to bring change. We are all unique, and we each have our own journey into the light of God's dear Son.

We cannot change others, so too often we try to fit in and get lost. We know we do not want to go back to what we once were, but where do we go from here?

On a glorious day, we cry out to God for help, and the light dawns. The Bible we had tried to read out of obligation and duty begins to make sense, and we embark on an adventure with God even though those religious ideas try to control us. Then we discover that we can pray the

Word and submit to the constant ministry of transformation by the Holy Spirit (see Rom. 12:1-2).

Prayer prepares us for change. Change produces change, which is often uncomfortable. If we will move through the discomfort, God will work with us, leading us out of our self-developed defense mechanisms into a place of victory. He heals our brokenness. He opens our blind eyes, and we choose to submit to the Champion of our salvation. We continue to make this new life fully manifested as we live in the holy awe of God (see Phil. 2:12 TPT).

Adults who grew up in religious, judgmental, and critical homes, where they were never allowed to express themselves, sometimes carry much hurt and anger into their relationships. Often, they were not permitted to have their own feelings without being condemned; they were not permitted to explore any ideas different from their parents or caregivers. There was an eye watching their every move. Any punishment they received was justified. Their parents were incapable of making a mistake.

Adult children of religiously rigid environments were led to believe that any slip, error in judgment, or mistake was a sin that would send them straight to hell; the parents' religious doctrine was the only way to heaven and to deviate from it would lead to destruction. Forgiveness could be attained only after much sorrow, penance, and retribution. Death before the completion of repentance led to an eternity in hell.

People raised in such oppressive home environments were never allowed to find themselves or to travel their own individual spiritual journeys leading to the truth of Jesus Christ. The head of the home, usually the father, was considered God in the flesh. Conflict resolution was never taught or practiced. Whatever the head of the household said was law—and disobedience to his law was not discussed but beaten out of the child. The wife was subservient and was not allowed to question the dictates of the husband.

When these adults marry, they often feel that they have finally found a platform from which to express themselves. They have escaped a place of abiding fear, constant condemnation, and continual criticism. Having no communication skills, they often have difficulty expressing themselves properly. When anyone disagrees with them, they tend to react as they were taught.

Only now, the marriage partner or friend does not submit to dogmatic, manipulative words. Frustration develops. The adult child seeks to make himself or herself understood, resulting in more frustration. Anger is fed, and the individual continues to be in bondage to the idea that he or she should never have been born. The person either retreats to a silent corner, refusing to talk, or uses words to build walls of defense—shutting others out. He or she resides inside emotional isolation, attempting to remove himself or herself from more hurt and criticism.

There is a way of escape. God sent His Word to heal us and to deliver us from all our destructions (see Ps. 107:20). God has not given us a spirit of fear, but power, love, and a sound mind. We can choose to listen, to learn, to grow, and to achieve with the help of the Holy Spirit—our Teacher, our Guide, and our Intercessor. The anointing is upon Jesus to bind up and heal our emotional wounds (see Luke 4:18). His anointing destroys every yoke of bondage (see Isa. 10:27), setting the captives free.

Prayer

Father, thank You for opening my blind eyes and giving me sight so I can see and know who Jesus is! When I embraced Him and took hold of His name, You gave me the authority to become Your child. I am Your child, and I know that if I pray to You in secret, You will reward me openly.

Father, I desire with all my heart to walk in love as it is defined in 1 Corinthians 13, but I am ever sabotaging my own efforts and failing in my relationships. I know that without faith it is impossible to please You. I worship You because I have been crucified with Christ. It is no longer I who live, but Christ who lives in me. The life that I now live in the flesh, I live by faith in the Son of God who loved me and gave Himself for me.

Father, expose the man-made religious thought patterns contrary to Your Word. Uncover me—bring everything to the light. When anything is exposed and reproved by the light, it is made visible and clear; and where everything is visible and clear, there is light.

Heal the past wounds and hurts that have controlled my behavior and my speech. Teach me to guard my heart with all diligence, for out of it flow the very issues of life. Teach me to speak the truth in love in my home, in my church, with my friends, and in all my relationships. Also, help me to realize that others have a right to express themselves. Help me to make room for their ideas and their opinions, even when they are different than mine.

Words are powerful. The power of life and death is in the tongue, and You said that I would eat the fruit of it.

Father, I realize that words can be creative or destructive. A word out of my mouth may seem of no account, but it can accomplish nearly anything—or destroy it! A careless or wrongly placed word out of my mouth can set off a forest fire. By my speech I can ruin the world, turn harmony to chaos, throw mud on a reputation, send the whole world up in smoke, and go up in smoke with it—smoke right from the pit of hell. This is scary!

Father, forgive me for speaking curses. I reacted out of past hurts and unresolved anger. At times I am dogmatic, even boasting that I am wise; sometimes unknowingly I have twisted the truth to make myself sound wise; at times I have tried to look better than others or get the better of another; my words have contributed to things falling apart. My human anger is misdirected and works unrighteousness.

Father, forgive me. I cannot change myself, but I am willing to change and walk in the wisdom that is from above.

Father, I submit to that wisdom from above that begins with a holy life and is characterized by getting along with others. It is gentle and reasonable, overflowing with mercy and blessings, not hot one day and cold the next, not two-faced. Use me as Your instrument to develop a healthy, robust community that lives right with You. I will enjoy its results only if I do the hard work of getting along with others, treating them with dignity and honor.

With the help of the Holy Spirit and by Your grace, I will not let any unwholesome talk come out of my mouth, but only what is helpful for building others up according to their needs, that it may benefit those who listen.

My heart overflows with a goodly theme; I address my psalm to You, the King. My tongue is like the pen of a ready writer. Mercy and kindness shut out all hatred and selfishness, and truth shuts out all deliberate hypocrisy or falsehood; and I bind them about my neck, write them upon the tablet of my heart.

I speak excellent and princely things; and the opening of my lips shall be for right things. My mouth shall utter truth, and wrongdoing is detestable and loathsome to my lips. All the words of my mouth are righteous (upright and in right standing with You, Lord); there is nothing contrary to truth or crooked in them. My tongue is as choice silver, and my lips feed and guide many. I open my mouth in skillful and godly wisdom, and on my tongue is the law of kindness giving counsel and instruction.

Father, thank You for loving me unconditionally. I thank You for sending Your Son, Jesus, to be my Friend and elder Brother and for giving me Your Holy Spirit to teach me and to bring all things to my remembrance. I am an overcomer by the blood of the Lamb and by the word of my testimony. In the name of Jesus I pray, amen.

SCRIPTURE REFERENCES

1 John 3:1 • Ephesians 4:29 NIV • Matthew 6:6 • Psalm 45:1 AMPC
Hebrews 11:6 AMPC • Proverbs 3:3 AMPC • Ephesians 5:13 AMPC
Proverbs 8:6-8 AMPC • Proverbs 4:23 • Proverbs 10:20-21 AMPC
Ephesians 4:15 • Galatians 2:19-20 ESV • Proverbs 31:26 AMPC
Proverbs 18:21 • Romans 8:31-39 NIV • James 3:5-10 MSG
Hebrews 2:11 NIV • James 3:9-16 MSG • John 15:15 NIV
James 3:17 • John 14:26 • James 3:17-18 MSG • Revelation 12:11

64

Trusting God in Financial Situations

FATHER, I come to You in the name of Jesus concerning my financial situation. You are a very present help in trouble, and You are more than enough. Your Word declares that You shall supply all my need according to Your riches in glory by Christ Jesus.

Holy Spirit, You are my Counselor and my Teacher. By grace I will be a doer of the Word of God. I choose to set my gaze deeply into the perfecting law of liberty and respond to the truth that I am hearing. Then I will be strengthened and experience Your blessing in all that I do.

Forgive me for robbing You in tithes and offerings. I repent and purpose to bring all my tithes into the storehouse that there may be food in Your house. Thank You for wise financial counselors and teachers who are teaching me the principles of good stewardship.

Lord of hosts, You said, "Try Me now in this, and I will open the windows of heaven and pour out for you such a blessing that there will not be room enough to receive it." You will rebuke the devourer for my sake, and my heart is filled with thanksgiving.

Lord, my God, I shall remember that it is You who gives me the power to get wealth, that You may establish Your covenant. In the name of Jesus, I worship You only, and I will have no other gods before You.

You are able to make all grace—every favor and earthly blessing—come to me in abundance, so that I am always, and in all circumstances, furnished in abundance for every good work and charitable donation. In Jesus' name, amen.

SCRIPTURE REFERENCES

Psalm 56:1 • Deuteronomy 8:18-19 • Philippians 4:19
2 Corinthians 9:8 AMPC • Malachi 3:8-12 • James 1:22-23 TPT

65

Dedication of Your Tithes

FATHER, I profess this day that I have come into the inheritance that You promised me, and I am in the land that You have provided for me in Jesus Christ. I was a sinner serving Satan; he was my god. But I called upon the name of Jesus, and You heard my cry and delivered me into the Kingdom of Your dear Son.

Jesus, as my Lord and High Priest, I bring the firstfruits of my income to You and worship the Lord my God with it.

Father, thank You for Your Word that says, "Try Me now in this, and I will open the windows of heaven and pour out for you such a blessing that there will not be room enough to receive it" (Mal. 3:10). You will rebuke the devourer for my sake. My heart is filled with thanksgiving!

Father, I rejoice in all the good which You have given to me and my household. Thank You for supplying every need of mine according to Your riches in glory in Christ Jesus. You so generously provide all I need that I will always have everything I need and plenty left over to share with others. Thank you, Father, in Jesus' name, amen.

SCRIPTURE REFERENCES

Malachi 3:8-12 • Colossians 1:13 • Hebrews 3:1,7-8
Ephesians 2:1-5 • Philippians 4:19 • 2 Corinthians 9:8 AMPC
Deuteronomy 26:1,3, 10-11,14-15 AMPC

66

Selling Real Estate

FATHER, I thank You for the skillful and godly wisdom needed in offering my house (or other real estate) to be sold. I am preparing my house or property in excellence that it may be beautiful and desirable, as though I am preparing it for Your habitation. I am asking a fair and competitive market price and will not take advantage of a potential buyer.

Father, I ask that You prepare and send a ready, willing, and able buyer to purchase my house or property—a person who has the funds available to pay the fair market value, pre-qualified and approved by a lending institution; one who has perfect timing of possession that fits into my need and his/hers.

Thank You for going before me and preparing the way. In the name of Jesus, I seek and pursue peace, thanking You that the spirit of truth shall prevail in our deliberations. I declare and decree that everyone involved speaks truly, deals truly, and lives truly.

Should there be anything that is hidden, I ask that it be revealed and brought to the light. Truth and mercy are written upon the tablets of my heart, and I have favor, good understanding, and high esteem in Your sight and in the sight of the potential buyer. In the name of Jesus, amen.

SCRIPTURE REFERENCES

Proverbs 2:6,9,12,15 AMPC • 1 Corinthians 4:5 AMPC • 1 Corinthians 2:9
Proverbs 3:3-4 AMPC • Ephesians 4:15 AMPC

67

In Court Cases

FATHER, in the name of Jesus, it is written in Your Word to call on You, and You will answer me and show me great and mighty things. I put You in remembrance of Your Word and thank You that You watch over it to perform it.

In Jesus' name, no weapon formed against me shall prosper. Any false accuser who takes me to court will be dismissed as a liar. This is what Your servants can expect, for You said that You would see to it that everything works out for the best. That is Your decree. Peace, security, and triumph over opposition is my inheritance as Your child. This is the righteousness I obtain from You, Father, which You impart to me as my justification. I am far from even the thought of destruction; for I shall not fear, and terror shall not come near me.

Father, You say You will establish me to the end—keep me steadfast, give me strength, and guarantee my vindication; that is, be my warrant against all accusation or indictment. Father, You contend with those who contend with me, and You perfect that which concerns me. I dwell in the secret place of the Most High, and this secret place hides me from the strife of tongues, for a false witness who breathes out lies is an abomination to You.

I am a true witness, and all my words are upright and in right standing with You, Father. By my long forbearing and calmness of spirit the judge is persuaded, and my soft speech breaks down the most bone-like resistance. Therefore, I am not anxious beforehand how I shall reply in defense or what I am to say, for the Holy Spirit teaches me *in that very hour* and moment what I ought to say to those in the outside world. My speech is seasoned with salt.

As a child of the light, I enforce the triumphant victory of my Lord Jesus Christ in this situation, knowing that all of heaven is backing me. I am strong in You, Lord, and in the power of Your might. Thank You for the shield of faith that quenches every fiery dart of the enemy. I am increasing in wisdom and in stature and in years, and in favor with You, Father, and with man. Praise the Lord! Amen.

SCRIPTURE REFERENCES

Jeremiah 33:3 • Proverbs 6:19 • Jeremiah 1:12 AMPC • Proverbs 14:25
Isaiah 43:26 AMPC • Proverbs 8:8 AMPC • Isaiah 54:17 MSG
Proverbs 25:15 AMPC • Isaiah 54:14 AMPC • Luke 12:11-12 AMPC
1 Corinthians 1:8 AMPC • Colossians 4:6 • Isaiah 49:25
Matthew 18:18 • Psalm 138:8 • Ephesians 6:10,16 • Psalm 91:1
Luke 2:52 AMPC • Psalm 31:20

68

Protection for Travel

FATHER, today, in Jesus' name, I confess Your Word over my travel plans and know that Your Word does not go out and return to You void, but it accomplishes what You say it will do. I give You thanks for moving quickly to perform Your Word and fulfill its promises.

As I prepare to travel, I rejoice in the promises that Your Word holds for protection and safety of the righteous. Only You, Father, make me live in safety. I trust in You and dwell in Your protection. Father, if I face any problems or trouble, I will run to You, my Strong Tower and Shelter in time of need. Believing in the written Word of God, I speak peace, safety, and success over my travel plans in Jesus' name.

As a child of God, my path of travel is made safe. God, You command Your angels to protect me wherever I go, and You surround my car/airplane/train/ship/bus. I have the peace of God wherever and however I travel and allow fear no place in my life.

Thank You, Father, that in every situation You are there to protect me. You have redeemed me, and You will protect me. Through my faith in You, dear heavenly Father, I have the power to tread on serpents and have all power over the enemy. No food or water will harm me when I arrive at my destination.

Father, I give You the glory in this situation. Your mercy is upon me and my family, and our travels will be safe. Not a hair on our heads shall perish. Thank You, Father, for Your guidance and safety—You are worthy of all praise! Amen.

SCRIPTURE REFERENCES

Isaiah 55:11 • Isaiah 43:1-3 • Jeremiah 1:12 • 2 Timothy 4:18
Psalm 4:8 • Hosea 2:18 • Psalm 91:1 • Luke 10:19 • Proverbs 18:10
Psalm 91:13 • Proverbs 29:25 • Luke 21:18 • Mark 11:23-24
Mark 16:18 • Proverbs 2:8 • Matthew 18:18 • Psalm 91:11-12
John 14:13 • 2 Timothy 4:18 • Daniel 9:18 • Philippians 4:7 • Luke 1:50
2 Timothy 1:7

PRAYERS for the Needs and Concerns of the Single, Divorced, and Widowed

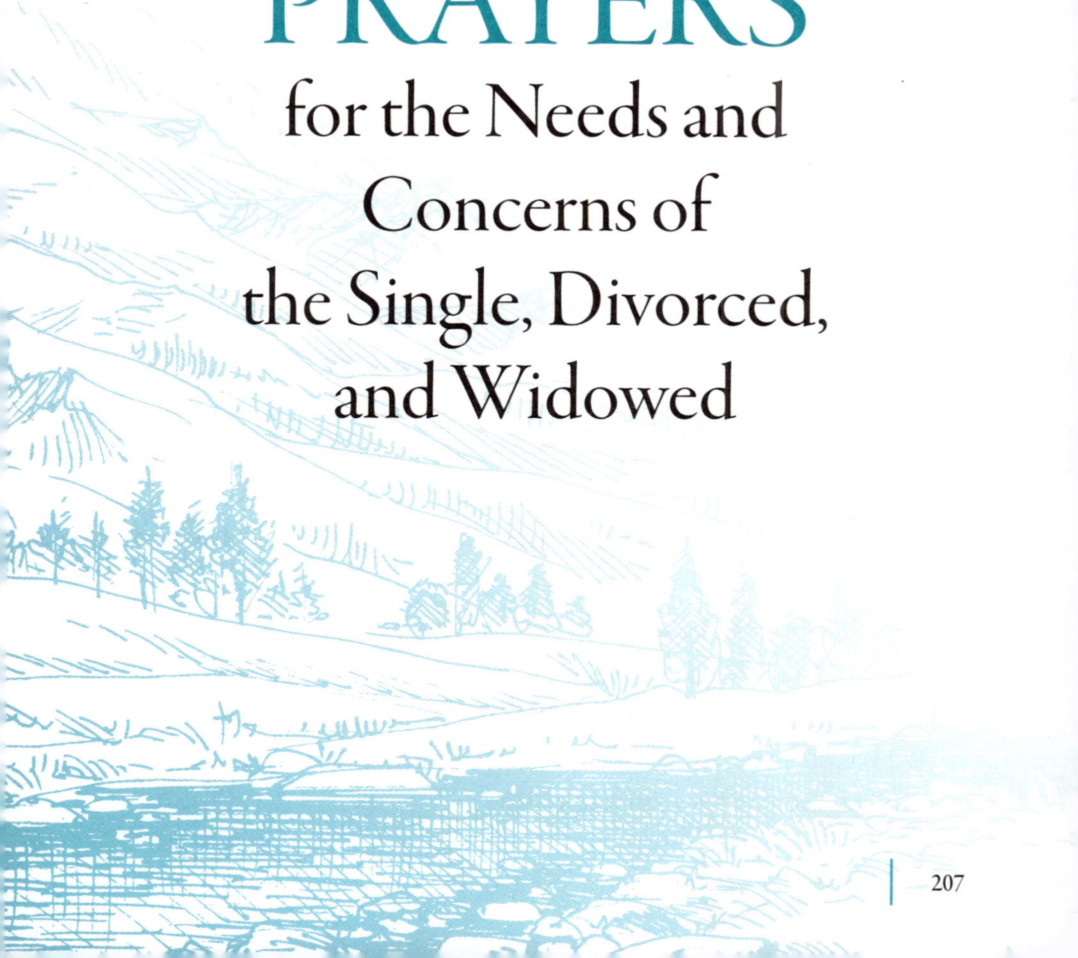

69

Overcoming Temptation

Introduction

Let no one say when he is tempted, I am tempted from God; for God is incapable of being tempted by [what is] evil and He Himself tempts no one.

But every person is tempted when he is drawn away, enticed and baited by his own evil desire (lust, passions).

Then the evil desire, when it has conceived, gives birth to sin, and sin, when it is fully matured, brings forth death (James 1:13-15 AMPC).

Single people sometimes express the difficulty of keeping themselves pure. (See the following prayers on purity.) Some have asked, "Doesn't God understand that we are only human? Why did He create us with desires? Surely He understands and excuses us when we fall into temptation. If He wants me to avoid sexual temptation, then why doesn't He send me the spouse I have asked Him to give me?"

The Scriptures condemn premarital sex, fornication, adultery, and all forms of sexual perversion (see Matt. 15:19; Mark 7:21 AMPC; Gal. 5:19-21; Col. 3:5-6). Although sexual desires are not a sin, if not properly controlled, those desires can lead to sin.

According to James 1:13-15, sin begins with a thought conceived from lust. Lust is not limited to sex. It is possible to lust after many things that can cause sin. That's why it is so important to take control over the mind and heart to keep them pure and holy—in spite of temptation.

One of the myths that has ensnared many single people is the mistaken idea that marriage will automatically release them from the temptation to sin. Without repentance and the renewing of the mind, those who have a problem with lustful thoughts before they are married will have the same problem after they are married, just as those who have a problem with sexual perversion before marriage will continue to have the same problem after marriage.

One married man shared his testimony of deliverance from pornography. He was having to continually guard himself from mental images that kept reappearing. Marriage is not a cure-all for sexual sins or any other sin.

Yes, God does understand. That is why with every temptation He has provided a way of escape (see 1 Cor. 10:13).

Yes, there is forgiveness for sin (see 1 John 1:9)—through God's abounding grace (see Rom. 5:20). The question is: "Are we to remain in sin in order that God's grace (favor and mercy) may multiply and overflow? Certainly not! How can we who died to sin live in it any longer?" (Rom. 6:1-2 AMPC).

We who are in Christ desire to bring glory to the Father. We cannot do so in our own strength. It is abiding in union with Jesus and loving as Jesus loves that ensures answered prayers (see John 15:7-9). If our prayers are not being answered, it is time to check our love walk. We must ask ourselves, "Are we keeping ourselves in the love of God—remaining vitally united with Jesus?"

> *We know [absolutely] that anyone born of God does not [deliberately and knowingly] practice committing sin, but*

the One Who was begotten of God carefully watches over and protects him [Christ's divine presence within him preserves him against the evil], and the wicked one does not lay hold (get a grip) on him or touch [him] (1 John 5:18 AMPC).

This verse says that the wicked one cannot touch us. What is the condition? Having Christ's presence within, staying united with Him—abiding in Him and allowing His Word to abide in us.

If you want to abide in Christ and have His Word abide in you, pray the following prayer with a sincere and believing heart.

Prayer

Lord, I choose to abide in Your Word and hold fast to Your teachings. As I align my mind with Your thoughts, I will live in accordance with them. I desire to be Your true disciple, vitally united to the Vine—Jesus. I cannot bear fruit unless I abide in You. Lord, because You are the Vine and I am a branch living in You, I bear much (abundant) fruit. Apart from You, cut off from vital union with You, I can do nothing.

Father, Your Son Jesus said, "If you live in life-union with me and if my words live powerfully within you—then you can ask whatever you desire and it will be done" (John 15:7 TPT). Thank You, God, for continually revitalizing me, implanting within me the passion to accomplish the good things You desire to do in and through me.

When I bear abundant fruit, I demonstrate that I am a mature disciple who glorifies my Father. And I do so honor and glorify You, dear Father. By Your grace that I have received, I will show and prove myself to be a true follower of Your Son, Jesus. Jesus has said that He loves me with the same love that You have loved Him, and I am abiding in that love. Jesus said it would continually nourish my heart.

Jesus has said if I keep His commands, I will live in His love, just as He kept Your commands, Father, and continually lives nourished and empowered by Your love. Jesus told me these things so that I would experience the same joy He experienced and fill my heart with overflowing gladness.

Father, thank You for Your Word—it is the truth that makes me free. I am born (begotten) of You, Lord, and I do not deliberately, knowingly, and habitually practice sin. Your nature abides in me, and Your principle of life remains permanently within me. I cannot practice sinning because I am born (begotten) of You. I have hidden Your Word in my heart that I might not sin against You.

May Jesus Christ through my faith actually dwell (settle down, abide, make His permanent home) in my heart! It is my desire to be rooted deep in love and founded securely on love, that I may have the power and be strong to apprehend and grasp with all the saints—Your devoted people—the experience of that love, what is the breadth and length and height and depth of it.

I pray, in the name of Jesus, that I may know this love that surpasses knowledge—that I may be filled to the measure of all Your fullness. Now to You who is able to do immeasurably more than all I ask or imagine, according to Your power that is at work within me, to You be glory in the Church and in Christ Jesus throughout all generations, forever and ever! Amen.

SCRIPTURE REFERENCES

John 8:31 AMPC • 1 John 3:9 AMPC • John 15:4-5 AMPC
Psalm 119:11 • John 15:7-12 AMPC • Ephesians 3:17-18 AMPC
John 8:32 • Ephesians 3:19-21 NIV • John 17:17 • Philippians 2:13 TPT

70

Knowing God's Plan for Marriage

DEAR Father, I bring You my life. I trust in, lean on, rely on, and am confident in You. I trust You to direct me throughout my journey so I can experience Your plans for my life. Reveal the life-paths that are pleasing to You. Escort me along the way; take me by the hand and teach me. For You, Father, are my increasing salvation; I have wrapped my heart into Yours!

It is written, "For I know the thoughts and plans that I have for you, says the Lord, thoughts and plans for welfare and peace and not for evil, to give you hope in your final outcome. Then you will call upon Me, and you will come and pray to Me, and I will hear and heed you. Then you will seek Me, inquire for, and require Me [as a vital necessity] and find Me when you search for Me with all your heart. I will be found by you, says the Lord" (Jer. 29:11-14 AMPC).

Father, I am looking for Your plan, Your answer for my life. It is my desire to be married. But I must be sure in my decision that I am living as You intend. According to Your Word, marriage will bring extra problems that I may not need to face at this time in my life.

All the ways of a man or woman are pure in his or her own eyes, but You, Lord, weigh the spirits (the thoughts and intents of the heart). Therefore, I roll my works upon You—commit and trust them wholly to You. You will cause my thoughts to become agreeable to Your will, and so shall my plans be established and succeed.

Because You, Lord, are my Shepherd, I have everything I need! You let me rest in the meadow grass and lead me beside the quiet streams. You give me new strength. You help me do what honors You the most.

Even when walking through the dark valley of death, I will not be afraid, for You are close beside me, guarding and guiding me all the way.

You provide delicious food for me in the presence of my enemies. You have welcomed me as Your guest; my blessings overflow!

Your goodness and unfailing kindness shall be with me all of my life, and afterward I will live with You forever in Your home. In Jesus' name I pray, amen.

SCRIPTURE REFERENCES

Psalm 25:1-5 AMPC, TPT • Proverbs 16:2-3 AMPC • Luke 18:1 AMPC
Psalm 23:1-6 TLB • Psalm 37:3-5 • 1 Corinthians 7:1-2 TLB

71

Preparing for a Healthy Marriage

Introduction

If you are single and desire to be married, do not skip over this important message. I pray this will challenge you to develop a more intimate relationship with your heavenly Father who chose you before the foundation of the world. You are made whole and complete in Christ Jesus. Do not believe that you have to be married to be complete as some have taught. The apostle Paul wrote to the unmarried and those who have lost their spouses, saying, "It is fine for you to remain single as I am." However, he does not condemn anyone who desires to be married (1 Cor. 7:8 TPT).

For the Christian, the foundation of all healthy relationships begins with God. His love is unconditional, and we are His workmanship created in Christ Jesus. Jesus gave us a new commandment: "Love each other just as much as I have loved you" (John 13:34 TPT).

The marriage relationship, which is intended to be a representation of Jesus and His Church, is a unique testing ground for spiritual development. One definition of love is "to extend one's self for the purpose of nurturing one's own or another's spiritual growth."[8]

Everyone is unique; we all think, feel, and choose differently. Everyone brings a hidden box of expectations to the marriage relationship based

8 M. Scott Peck, *The Road Less Traveled* (New York: Touchstone, 2003).

on their past experiences and/or observations. Throughout my years of witnessing and listening to the painful stories of both men and women, I believe we simply have not understood the importance of preparing ourselves for marriage. After all, we prepare for college or a trade school; we prepare for a career.

After marriage, there are gaps between your expectations and your experiences. This might bring up a trust challenge. I dare say that we all have trust issues because of past hurts whether in the family we grew up in or a disappointment in a former relationship. I encourage you to memorize and meditate on 1 Corinthians 13 long before you say, "I do." Do you know what it means to defer to someone? Are you always ready to believe the best of the other person? Love is not a feeling; it is a decision!

Trying to force anyone to live in your box of expectations will not work! Knowing the reality of your completeness in Christ Jesus will enable you to enter into a healthy relationship, one in which both you and your partner will grow together spiritually and in every other area of life. Seeking first the Kingdom of God and His righteousness (see Matt. 6:33) and doing those things that are pleasing in His sight (see 1 John 3:22) will prepare you to be the person designed by Him to fulfill the role of husband or wife.

This prayer is written for your own growth and benefit.

Prayer

Father, I come before You in the name of Jesus, asking for Your will to be done in my life as I look to You for a marriage partner. I submit to the constant ministry of transformation by the Holy Spirit, making my petition known to You.

Prepare me for marriage by bringing everything to light that has been hidden—wounded emotions, walls of denial, emotional isolation, silence or excessive talking, anger, or rigidity (name any wall that separates you from healthy relationships and God's love and grace). The weapons of my warfare are not carnal, but mighty through You, Lord, to the pulling down of strongholds.

I know the One in whom I have placed my confidence, and I am perfectly certain that the work, whether I remain unmarried or marry, is safe in Your hands until that day.

Because I love You, Lord, and because I am called according to Your plan, everything that happens to me fits into a pattern for good. In Your foreknowledge, You chose me to bear the family likeness of Your Son. You chose me long ago; when the time came You called me, You made me righteous in Your sight, and then You lifted me to the splendor of life as Your child.

I lay aside every weight, and the sins that so easily ensnare me, and run with endurance the race that is set before me, looking unto Jesus, the Author and Finisher of my faith, who for the joy that was set before Him endured the cross, despising the shame, and has sat down at the right hand of the throne of God. I consider Him who endured such hostility from sinners against Himself, lest I become weary and discouraged in my soul. He makes intercession for me.

I turn my back on the turbulent desires of youth and give my positive attention to goodness, integrity, love, and peace in company with all those who approach You, Lord, in sincerity. I have nothing to do with silly and ill-informed controversies, which lead inevitably to strife. As Your servant, I am not a person of strife. I seek to be kind to all, ready and able to teach. I seek to be tolerant and have the ability to gently correct those who oppose Your message.

Father, I desire and earnestly seek (aim at and strive after) first of all Your Kingdom and Your righteousness (Your way of doing and being right), and then all these things taken together will be given me besides. So I do not worry and will not be anxious about tomorrow.

I am persuaded that I can trust You because You first loved me. You chose me in Christ before the foundation of the world. In Him the whole fullness of Deity (the Godhead) continues to dwell in bodily form giving complete expression of the divine nature; and I am in Him, made full and have come to the fullness of life in Christ.

I am filled with the Godhead—Father, Son, and Holy Spirit—and I reach toward full spiritual stature. And He (Christ) is the Head of all rule and authority of every angelic principality and power. So, because of Jesus, I am complete. Jesus is my Lord.

I come before You, Father, expressing my desire for a Christian mate. I petition that Your will be done in my life. Now I enter into that blessed rest by adhering to, trusting in, and relying on You. In Jesus' name, amen.

SCRIPTURE REFERENCES

Matthew 6:10 • Matthew 6:33-34 AMPC • 1 Corinthians 4:5
1 John 4:19 • 2 Corinthians 10:4 • Ephesians 1:4 • 2 Timothy 1:12 PHI
Colossians 2:9-10 AMPC • Romans 8:28-30 PHI • Matthew 6:10
Hebrews 12:1-3 NKJV • Hebrews 4:10 • Romans 8:34 • John 14:1 AMPC
2 Timothy 2:22-25 PHI

72

Developing Patience

FATHER, I come before You in the name of Jesus. I desire to meditate, consider, and inquire in Your presence. Waiting patiently for a marriage partner has become a challenge—a trial, sometimes leading to temptation. I am asking for Your help in developing patience, quietly entrusting my future to Your will. It is to You that I submit my desire to be married.

Love is *large and incredibly* patient! Word of God, I ask You to penetrate to the very core of my being where soul and spirit, bone and marrow meet. Interpret and reveal the true thoughts and secret motives of my heart.

By Your grace I surrender my life—all my desires, all that I am, and all that I am not—to the control of the Holy Spirit who produces this kind of fruit in me—love, joy, peace, *patience,* kindness, goodness, faithfulness, gentleness, and self-control; and here there is no conflict. I belong to Jesus Christ, and I seek to live by the Holy Spirit's power and to follow the Holy Spirit's leading in every part of my life. In exercising self-control, I develop steadfastness (patience, endurance), and in exercising steadfastness, I develop godliness (piety).

By faith, I consider it wholly joyful whenever I am enveloped in, or encounter, trials of any sort or fall into various temptations. It is then that I am reminded to rest assured and understand that the trial and proving of my faith brings out endurance and steadfastness and patience. I purpose to let endurance and steadfastness and patience have full play and do a thorough work so that I may be perfectly and fully developed, with no defects, lacking in nothing.

Father, fill me with the knowledge of Your will through all spiritual wisdom and understanding, that I may live a life worthy of You and may please You in every way—bearing fruit in every good work, growing in the knowledge of You, being strengthened with all power according to Your glorious might, so that I may have great endurance and patience and joyfully give thanks to You who qualified me to share in the inheritance of the saints in the Kingdom of light.

Father, I strip off everything that hinders me, as well as the sin which dogs my feet, and I run my race with patience, my eyes fixed on Jesus the source and the goal of my faith.

With patience I am able to persevere through the difficult times—times of anxiety and worry—and overcome the fear that I may never be married. I am an overcomer by the blood of the Lamb and by the word of my testimony. In Jesus' name, amen.

SCRIPTURE REFERENCES

1 Corinthians 13:4 TPT • Hebrews 4:12 TPT • Psalm 3:4 AMPC
James 1:2-4 AMPC • Psalm 37:4-5 • Colossians 1:9-12 NIV
Galatians 5:22-25 TLB • Hebrews 12:1-2 PHI • 2 Peter 1:6 AMPC
Revelation 12:11

73

Comfort in Times of Loneliness

FATHER, sometimes being single can be so lonely, so painful. Seeing people in pairs, laughing and having fun, makes me feel even more alone and different. Fear and dread overwhelm me, and if I could, I would fly away from all of this. I would run far away where no one could find me, escape to a wilderness retreat. O God, search me and know my heart, test me and know my anxious thoughts. Point out anything in me that offends You and lead me along the path of everlasting life.

Lord, You know everything there is to know about me. You perceive every movement of my heart and soul, and You understand my every thought before it even enters my mind. You are so intimately aware of me, Lord. You read my heart like an open book, and you know all the words I'm about to speak before I even start a sentence. You know every step I will take before my journey even begins. You've gone into my future to prepare the way, and in kindness You follow behind me to spare me from the harm of my past. With Your hand of love upon my life, You impart a blessing to me.

You have given me a spirit of power, of love, and of a sound mind. I have the power to think, feel, and choose in my own unique way. I choose to love and accept myself as You created me to be. I choose to align my mind with Your Word.

Today, I choose wisdom and discernment as my goals for my life, and I will not forget how they empower me. They strengthen me inside and out and inspire me to do what's right. I am energized and refreshed by the healing they bring. They give me living hope to guide me, and not one of life's tests will cause me to stumble. At night I will sleep like a baby, safe and sound; rest with You will be sweet and secure.

My Father, I surrender myself to You to be Your sacred, living sacrifice. I choose to live in holiness, experiencing all that delights Your heart, which is my genuine expression of worship. I choose to stop imitating the ideals and opinions of the culture around me and be inwardly transformed by the Holy Spirit through a total reformation of how I think. This empowers me to discern God's will as I live a beautiful life, satisfying and perfect in Your eyes.

I pray that You will keep my foot from being caught in a hidden trap of danger. I cast the care of this decision on You, knowing that You will cause my thoughts to come in line with Your will so that my plans will be established and succeed. In Jesus' name I pray, amen.

SCRIPTURE REFERENCES

Psalm 55:5-7 TPT • Psalm 139 TPT • 2 Timothy 1:7
Proverbs 3:21-24 TPT • Romans 12:1-2 TPT • Proverbs 16:3 AMPC
Proverbs 3:26 AMPC

74

Committing to a Life of Purity

FATHER, I come before Your throne of grace in the name of Jesus. At one time I walked habitually following the course and fashion of this world under the sway of the tendency of this present age. I lived and conducted myself in the passions of my flesh, my behavior governed by my corrupt and sensual nature. I obeyed the impulses of the flesh and the thoughts of my mind—my cravings dictated by my senses and my dark imaginings.

But, God, You are so rich in Your mercy! Even when I was dead (slain) by my own shortcomings and trespasses, You made me alive together in union with Christ, and it is by Your grace (Your favor and mercy that I did not deserve) that I am saved (delivered from judgment and made a partaker of Christ's salvation). You raised me up together with Him and made us sit down together, giving me joint seating with Him in the heavenly sphere in Christ Jesus (the Messiah, the Anointed One).

You are my Father; I am Your child. Because I am in Christ, I am a new creature; old things have passed away, and behold, all things have become new.

In accordance with Your Word, I rid myself of all malice and all deceit, hypocrisy, envy, and slander of every kind. Like a newborn baby, I crave pure spiritual milk so that by it I may grow up in my salvation now that I have tasted that You, Lord, are good.

Father, forgive me for the years of watching, reading, and listening to vile things. I submit to Jesus Christ, who loves me and gave Himself up for me, to make me holy and pure, cleansing me through the showering of the pure water of the Word of God. All You do, Father, is designed to make me—all Your children—a mature church for Your pleasure, until we all become a source of praise to You—glorious and radiant, beautiful and holy, without fault or flaw.

Thank You for the blood of Christ, who through the eternal Spirit offered Himself unblemished to You, which cleanses my conscience from acts that lead to death so that I may serve You, the living God! Thank You for the Holy Spirit who indwells me. He is holy (chaste, pure).

Father, I ask for and receive an impartation of the wisdom that comes from heaven—it is first of all pure, then peace-loving, considerate, submissive, full of mercy and good fruit, impartial, and sincere.

I will watch the way I talk and let nothing foul—dirty, abusive, ugly, or hateful—come out of my mouth. Instead, I will let my words become beautiful gifts that encourage others; I do this by speaking words of grace to help them.

Father, I will stop imitating the ideals and opinions of the culture around me, but I will be transformed by the renewal of my mind—a total transformation of how I think. I capture, like prisoners of war, every thought of mine and insist it bow in obedience to Your Word. I fix my thoughts on all that is authentic and real, honorable and admirable, beautiful and respectful, pure and holy, merciful and kind. I fasten my thoughts on every glorious work of Yours, praising You always. And, above all, I guard my heart for it determines the course of my life.

My Father, I look with wonder at the depth of Your marvelous love You have lavished on me! You have called me and made me Your very own beloved child. I am Your child right now; however, it is not yet apparent what I will become. But when Jesus comes and is manifested, I will be just like Him, for I will see Him as He truly is. I focus my hope on Him and will always be purifying myself just as Jesus is pure.

Through the power of the Holy Spirit given to me, I am an overcomer by the blood of the Lamb and by the word of my testimony! In Jesus' name I pray, amen.

SCRIPTURE REFERENCES

Ephesians 2:2-6 AMPC • Proverbs 15:16 AMPC • 2 Corinthians 5:17
Zephaniah 3:9 AMPC • 1 Peter 2:1-2 NIV • Romans 12:2 TPT
Psalm 101:3 NIV • 2 Corinthians 10:5 TPT • Ephesians 5:25-27 TPT
Philippians 4:8 TPT • Hebrews 9:14 NIV • Proverbs 4:23 NLT
1 Thessalonians 4:8 AMPC • 1 John 3:1-3 TPT • James 3:17 NIV
Ephesians 4:29 TPT • Revelation 12:11

I. A Man of Purity

Father, I attend to Your Word. I hide it in my heart that I might not sin against You. It is not wrong to have sexual desires. You made me, You know me, and You bought me—I belong to You. I commit myself and all my natural affections to You, Father, and acknowledge the power of the Holy Spirit in my life. I give You control and submit to Your will.

Forgive me for sinning against You, against myself, and against others. Thank You for Your grace that enables me to leave my gift at the altar when I remember that someone has a grievance against me. I will go and make peace with that person whenever possible and then come back and present my gift to You.

In the name of Jesus, I thank You for the power to shun immorality and all sexual looseness. I flee from impurity in thought, word, or deed. My body is the temple (the very sanctuary) of the Holy Spirit who lives within me, whom I have received as a gift from You. I am not my own. I was bought with a price—purchased with a preciousness and paid for, made Your own. So then, I will honor You, Father, and bring glory to You in my body.

When I read Your Word, I receive the truth that makes me free. I have won my battle with Satan. I have learned to know You as my Father. I am strong with Your Word in my heart. I no longer love this evil world and all that it offers me, for when I love these things I show that I do not really love You, Lord; for all these worldly things, these evil desires—the craze for sex, the ambition to buy everything that appeals to me, and the pride that comes from wealth and importance—are not from You, Father. They are from this evil world itself. This world is fading away, and these evil, forbidden things will go with it; but whoever keeps doing Your will, Lord, will live forever.

Thank You, Father, that I have been anointed by (I hold a sacred appointment from, and I have been given an unction from) the Holy One, and I know the truth. I have received the Holy Spirit, and He lives within me, in my heart, so that I don't need anyone to teach me what is right. For He teaches me all things, and He is the Truth and no liar; and so, just as He has said, I must live in Christ, never to depart from Him.

Father, I stay in happy fellowship with You, so that when Your Son, Jesus, comes, I will be sure that all is well and will not have to be ashamed and shrink back from meeting Him. I know that You are always good and do only right, and I seek to be an imitator of You and do what is good and right. In Jesus' name, amen.

SCRIPTURE REFERENCES

Proverbs 4:20 • 1 John 2:12-17 TLB • Psalm 119:11 • 1 John 2:20,27-29 TLB
Matthew 5:23-24 AMPC • Matthew 6:33 AMPC
1 Corinthians 6:18-20 AMPC • Ephesians 5:1 AMPC • John 8:32 AMPC

II. A Woman of Purity

Father, on the authority of Your Word, I declare and decree that I am a new creation in Christ. I repent of my former sins, receive Your forgiveness, and renew my mind—replacing old thought patterns and habits with Your thoughts and plans for me.

I was a sinner, separated, living apart from Christ. But now in Christ Jesus, my Lord, I have been brought near through the blood of Christ. Father, I confess that Jesus is my Lord and believe in my heart that You raised Him from the dead. In Christ, I have become a new person altogether—a new creation. The past is finished and gone, everything has become fresh and new. My old life is gone; my new life has begun!

Father, I cling tightly to the hope that lives within me, knowing that You always keep Your promises. I pray that You will give me creative ways to encourage others and to motivate them toward acts of compassion, beautiful works as expressions of love. I will not pull away and neglect meeting with fellow believers because we need each other. Father, create within our hearts the desire to come together even more frequently. May we be eager to encourage and urge each other onward as we should anticipate that day of Jesus' return dawning.

Father, I am Your daughter—Your handmaiden. You have poured out Your Spirit upon me, and I shall prophesy as You have said. I seek (aim at and strive after) first of all Your Kingdom and Your righteousness (Your way of doing and being right). All the less important things will be given to me abundantly. I refuse to worry about tomorrow but deal with each challenge that comes my way, one day at a time. Tomorrow will take care of itself.

As Your daughter, I thank You for enduing me with Your grace (free, spontaneous, absolute favor, and lovingkindness). With You, Father, nothing is ever impossible, and not one word of Your good promise has ever failed to come to pass.

Father, I submit to Your will for my life. Your ways are higher than my ways; Your thoughts higher than my thoughts. I commit my way to You, and You will cause my thoughts to become agreeable to Your will, and so shall my plans be established and succeed. I am Your handmaid; let it be done to me according to Your Word.

Because I have such a huge crowd of men and women of faith watching me from the grandstands, I strip off anything that slows me down or holds me back, and especially those sins that wrap themselves so tightly around my feet and trip me up; and I run with patience the particular race that You have set before me. I keep my eyes on Jesus, my Leader and Instructor.

To those who are pure, You show yourself pure; but You destroy those who are evil.

You will save those in trouble, but You bring down the haughty. You watch their every move. Lord, You are my light! You make my darkness bright. By your power I can crush an army; by your strength I leap over a wall. Your way is perfect; Your Word is true. You shield all who hide behind You. I trust and take refuge in You.

Father, that I might ascend into the presence of the Lord with the privilege of entering into Your Holy Place, I come clean—with works and ways that are pure, a heart that is true and sealed by the truth. I never deceive, and my words are sure. Therefore, I receive Your own goodness as a blessing from You, planted in my life by You, dear Father. In Jesus' name I pray, amen.

SCRIPTURE REFERENCES

2 Corinthians 5:17 • Luke 1:28,30,37 AMPC • 1 Kings 8:56 ESV
Romans 12:1-2 AMPC • Isaiah 55:9 AMPC • Jeremiah 29:11 AMPC
Proverbs 16:3 AMPC • Ephesians 2:12-13 AMPC • Luke 1:38 AMPC
Romans 10:9 • Hebrews 12:1-2 TLB • 2 Corinthians 5:17 PHI
2 Samuel 22:27-31 TLB • Hebrews 10: 23-25 TPT • Psalm 24:3-5 TPT, TLB
Acts 2:17 AMPC • Matthew 6:33-34 AMPC

— 75 —

Letting Go of Bitterness

Introduction

During interviews with divorced men and women, I have been encouraged to write a prayer on overcoming bitterness. Often the injustice of the situation in which divorced people find themselves creates deep hurts, wounds in the spirit, and anger so near the surface that the individuals involved risk sinking into the trap of bitterness and revenge. Their thoughts may turn inward as they consider the unfairness of their situation and dwell on how badly they have been treated.

In a family divorce situation, bitterness sometimes distorts ideas of what is best for the child/children involved. One parent (and sometimes both parents) will use the child/children against the other.

Unresolved anger often moves the divorced person to hurt the ex-spouse, holding him or her responsible for the hurt and sense of betrayal that is felt. The pain is so great that the passion of emotions may lead to sin.

Yet God has given a spirit of power, love, and a sound mind. You have the power to choose the way of love! You have the power to choose to forgive. Negative feelings often attempt to linger, but forgiveness will enable you to choose the way of escape by submitting to the Healer, obeying Him and trusting Him. "Don't let anger control you *or be fuel for revenge*, not for even a day" (Eph. 4:26 TPT).

Prayer

Father, life seems so unjust, so unfair. The pain of rejection is almost more than I can bear. My past relationships have ended in strife, anger, rejection, and separation.

Lord, I repent for giving place to bitterness, which is causing trouble for many. I choose to let go of all bitterness and indignation and wrath (passion, rage, bad temper) and resentment (anger, animosity). I resist revenge; I will not let *anger* control me *or be fuel for revenge*, not for even a day (see Eph. 4:26 TPT).

You are the One who binds up and heals the broken-hearted. I receive Your anointing that destroys every yoke of bondage. I receive emotional healing by faith and thank You for giving me the grace to stand firm until the process is complete.

Thank You for wise counselors. I acknowledge the Holy Spirit as my wonderful Counselor.

Thank you for helping me work out my salvation with fear and trembling, for it is You, Father, who works in me to will and to act according to Your good purpose.

In the name of Jesus, I choose to forgive those who have wronged me. Whenever I stand praying, if I have anything against anyone, I forgive him or her. I let it drop (leave it, let it go), in order that my Father who is in heaven may also forgive me of my own failings and shortcomings and let them drop.

I purpose to live a life of forgiveness because You have forgiven me. With the help of the Holy Spirit, I get rid of all bitterness, rage, anger, brawling, and slander, along with every form of malice. I desire to be kind and compassionate to others, forgiving them just as in Christ You forgave me.

With the help of the Holy Spirit, I make every effort to live in peace with all people and to be holy, for I know that without holiness no one will see You, Lord. I purpose to see to it that I do not miss Your grace and that no bitter root grows up within me to cause trouble. I will watch and pray that I enter not into temptation or cause others to stumble.

Thank You, Father, that You watch over Your Word to perform it and that whom the Son has set free is free indeed. I declare that I have overcome resentment and bitterness by the blood of the Lamb and by the word of my testimony. In Jesus' name, amen.

SCRIPTURE REFERENCES

Ephesians 4:31 AMPC • Ephesians 4:31-32 NIV • Luke 4:18
Hebrews 12:14-15 NIV • Isaiah 10:27 • Matthew 26:41
Proverbs 11:14 • Romans 14:21 • John 15:26 AMPC
Jeremiah 1:12 AMPC • Philippians 2:12-13 NIV • John 8:36
Matthew 5:44 • Revelation 12:11 • Mark 11:25 AMPC

76

Complete in Him as a Single

FATHER, thank You for loving me and choosing me in Christ to be holy and without fault in Your eyes. Thank You for adopting me into Your own family. My first priority in life is to seek Your Kingdom and live righteously, and You will give me everything I need.

Jesus is my Lord and in Him lives all the fullness of God in a human body. So I am also complete through my union with Christ, who is the head over every ruler and authority.

I come before You, Father, praying for a marriage partner who also seeks first Your Kingdom and lives righteously. May Your will be done in my life. Now I choose to enter into that blessed rest by adhering, trusting in, and relying on You, in the name of Jesus. Amen.

SCRIPTURE REFERENCES

Ephesians 1:4-5 NLT • Matthew 6:33 • Hebrews 4:10 AMPC
Colossians 2:9-10 NLT

77

Single Female Trusting God for a Mate

FATHER, in the name of Jesus, I believe that You are at work in me, energizing and creating in me the power and desire to do Your will for Your good pleasure. You are preparing me to receive my future mate who will provide leadership to me the way You do to Your church, not by being domineering but by cherishing me.

Out of respect for Christ, we will be courteously reverent to one another.

Prepare me to understand and support my future husband in ways that show my support for You, the Christ.

Father, I believe, because he has been divinely chosen by You, my future mate is full of Your wisdom, which is straightforward, gentle, reasonable, and overflowing with mercy and blessings. He speaks the truth in love.

Father, I believe that everything not of You shall be removed from my life. Forgive me for my past mistakes and heal the broken places. Your grace is sufficient as I prepare my heart to honor my future mate. Today, I purpose to always believe the best and to speak truly, live truly, and deal truly with marriage issues. I thank You that every word that You give to me will come true. Father, I praise You for performing Your Word! Amen.

SCRIPTURE REFERENCES

Isaiah 62:5 NCV • Proverbs 8:8 NCV • Ephesians 5:25
Jeremiah 1:12 MSG • James 3:17 MSG

78

Single Male Trusting God for a Mate

FATHER, in the name of Jesus, I believe that You are providing a wonderful woman who will understand and support me. I pray that we will walk together with like faith and in agreement. Prepare me to provide leadership to my future wife the way You do to Your church, not by being domineering but by cherishing her.

Father, a wise wife is a gift from the Lord, and he who finds a wife finds what is good and receives favor from You.

Father, forgive me for my past sins and help me to always believe the best about my future wife. Teach me to be quick to listen and slow to speak. Father, I have written mercy and truth on the tablets of my heart and bind them about my mind. I will receive favor and good understanding from You and from others.

May Your will be done in my life, even as it is in heaven. Amen.

SCRIPTURE REFERENCES

Ephesians 5:22-23 MSG • Philippians 2:2 MSG
Proverbs 18:22 NIV • Jeremiah 1:12 NLT • Proverbs 19:14

PRAYERS
for the Needs and Concerns of Marriage Partners and Heads of Household

79

Husbands

FATHER, in the beginning, You said it's not good for man to be alone, and You provided Adam a partner—a companion, a complement, a helper that was just right for him. Now, I have found a wife to be my partner, and You have given me a treasure. For she is a gift from You to bring me joy and pleasure. Your Word says, "Find a good spouse, you find a good life—and even more: the favor of God!" (Prov. 18:22 MSG). Thank You, Father, for blessing me!

In the name of Jesus, I purpose to provide leadership to my wife the way Christ does to His Church, not by domineering but by cherishing. I will go all out in my love for her, exactly as Christ did for the Church—a love marked by giving, not getting. We are the Body of Christ, and when I love my wife, I love myself.

It is my desire to give my wife what is due her, and I purpose to share my personal rights with her. Father, I am neither anxious nor intimidated, but I am a good husband to my wife. I honor her and delight in her. In the new life of God's grace, we are equals. I purpose to treat my wife as an equal so that our prayers will be answered.

Lord, I delight greatly in Your commandments, and my descendants will be mighty on earth, and the generation of the upright will be blessed. Wealth and riches will be in our house, and my righteousness will endure forever. In the name of Jesus, amen.

SCRIPTURE REFERENCES

Matthew 18:18 • Ephesians 5:22-23 MSG • Genesis 2:18 NEB
1 Corinthians 7:3-5 PHI • Proverbs 18:22 NKJV • 1 Peter 3:7-9 MSG
Proverbs 3:3-4 NKJV • Psalm 112:1-4 NKJV • Proverbs 31:28-31 NLB

80

Wives

FATHER, I cultivate inner beauty—the gentle, gracious kind that delights You. In Jesus' name, I choose to be a good, loyal wife to my husband and address him with respect. I will not be overanxious and intimidated. By Your grace, Father, I purpose to be agreeable, sympathetic, loving, compassionate, and humble. I will be a blessing to my husband!

By the grace of God, I yield to the constant ministry of transformation by the Holy Spirit. I am being transformed into a gracious woman who retains honor, and a virtuous woman who is a crown to my husband. I purpose to walk wisely that I may build my house. Houses and riches are the inheritance of fathers, and a prudent wife is from the Lord. In Christ I have redemption through His blood, the forgiveness of sins, according to the riches of His grace, which He made to abound toward me in all wisdom and prudence.

Holy Spirit, I ask You to help me understand and support my husband in ways that show my support for Christ.[9] Teach me to function so that I preserve my own personality while responding to his desires. We are one flesh, and I realize that this unity of persons that preserves individuality is a mystery, but that is how it is when we are united to Christ. So I will keep on loving my husband and let the miracle keep happening!

Just as my husband gives me what is due me, I seek to be fair to my husband. I share my rights with my husband.

9 Ben Campbell Johnson, *The Heart of Paul* (Waco, TX: Word Books, 1976).

Strength and dignity are my clothing as I smile at the future. I have no fear of old age. My shining light will not be extinguished. When I speak I have something worthwhile to say, and I always say it kindly. I keep an eye on everyone in my household and keep them all busy and productive. Charm can be misleading and beauty is vain and so quickly fades, but I desire to be the virtuous woman who lives in the wonder, awe, and fear of the Lord. Father, I choose to be the radiant woman Your Word describes in Proverbs 31. In Jesus' name, amen.

SCRIPTURE REFERENCES

Proverbs 19:14 • 1 Peter 3:1-5,8-9 MSG • Ephesians 1:7-8 NKJV
Psalm 51:10 NKJV • Ephesians 5:22,33 MSG • 2 Corinthians 3:18
1 Corinthians 7:2-5 PHI • Proverbs 11:6 • Proverbs 31:25-27
Proverbs 12:4 • James 3:17-18 NKJV • Proverbs 14:1
Proverbs 31 MSG, TPT, TLB • James 3:17-18 NKJV

81

Loving in Marriage

FATHER, I desire to walk in love surrendered to the extravagant love of Christ in my home. This great love is like an aroma of adoration—a sweet healing fragrance for everyone.

My mission in life is to live as a child flooded with revelation-light! And the supernatural fruits of Your light will be seen in me—goodness, righteousness, and truth. Then I will learn to choose what is beautiful to You, my Lord.

Our home is a spiritual training ground where the revelation-light is exposing wrong perceptions about marriage and correcting me. Forgive me when I forget my mission and place all my energy in self-protection and trying to change the other person.

Father, I ask You to deliver me from the sin of pride. I choose to let go of self-promotion, which creates a false image of my importance. Help me to honestly assess my worth by using my God-given faith as the standard of measurement, and then I will see my true value with an appropriate self-esteem.

Even in times of trouble, I have a joyful confidence, knowing that pressure will develop in me patient endurance. And patient endurance will refine my character and proven character leads me back to hope. My hope is not a disappointing fantasy, because I can now experience the endless love of God cascading into my heart through the Holy Spirit who lives in me!

I am learning to be incredibly patient. I choose to be gentle and consistently kind to all. I choose to be pleasant rather than irritated, and I purpose to believe the best of my spouse.

Above all, there remains faith, hope, and love—yet love surpasses them all. So, above all else, I choose to let love be the beautiful prize for which I run. In the name of Jesus, amen.

SCRIPTURE REFERENCES

Ephesians 5:1-2 TPT • Romans 12:3 TPT • Romans 5:3-5 TPT
1 Corinthians 13:12 TPT

— 82 —

New Creation Marriage

The following prayer was given to me by the Holy Spirit for my husband and me.

Husband: you may pray the part for the wife in the third person.

Wife: you may pray the part for the husband in the third person.

Find time to pray together if both parties are willing and receptive.

Prayer

The couple prays together:

May our family be seen as bright lights—stars or beacons shining out clearly—in the dark world. We are willing to receive suggestions from each other. Our relationships in our individual families can benefit from the analogy of the family of God in Ephesians 5. In this relationship we are learning to function so that each preserves his or her own personality while responding to the desires of each other. This unity of persons that preserves individuality is a mystery, but that is how it is when we are united to Christ. So we love each other and let the miracle keep happening!

Father, in the name of Jesus, we rejoice and delight ourselves in one another. We are in Christ, enfolded in Him, and we have become an entirely new creation. The old life is gone; a new life has begun. Behold, the fresh and new has come!

We will walk in agreement on the authority of Your Word and seek to understand one another. That is more important than being understood. We will be quick to listen, slow to speak, and slow to anger in the name of Jesus.

The husband prays:

Father, I take responsibility for my family just as Christ does for the Church. I am a provider for my family. Marriage calls for reciprocal giving, so I love my wife with the self-giving love that Christ showed for His family, the Church.[10]

You are helping me provide leadership to my wife the way Christ does to His Church, not by domineering but by cherishing. I will go all out in my love for her, exactly as Christ did for the Church—a love marked by giving, not getting.

Christ's love makes the Church whole. His words evoke her beauty. Everything He does and says is designed to bring the best out of her, dressing her in dazzling white silk, radiant with holiness. And that is how I want to love my wife. I realize that I am doing myself a favor because we are already "one" in marriage. Christ feeds and pampers the Church because we are part of His Body. And this is why I left my father and mother and cherish my wife. We are no longer two, but we have become "one flesh." This is a huge mystery, and I don't pretend to understand it all. What is clearest to me is the way Christ treats the Church. And this provides a good picture of how I am to treat my wife, loving myself in loving her.

The wife prays:

Father, in the name of Jesus, I purpose to understand and support my husband in ways that show my support for Christ. As the Church is

10 Based on *The Heart of Paul* by Ben Campbell Johnson, published by A Great Love, Inc., Toccoa, GA.

totally responsive to Christ, I respond to my husband in every aspect of our relationship.[11]

I am being transformed by the entire renewing of my mind. I am a good wife to my husband and choose to always believe the best about him and extend myself for the purpose of our mutual spiritual growth. I'm tenderly devoted to my husband, and I respect and honor him. I don't put others before him, and I'm responsive to his needs. I honor him, love him, and admire him exceedingly.

Father, thank You for my inner disposition that reflects the glory of God. I cultivate inner beauty—the gentle, gracious kind that God delights in. The holy women of old were beautiful before God that way and were good, loyal wives to their husbands. I resist the temptation to become anxious and intimidated. When I speak, I have something worthwhile to say, and I say it with kindness. In Jesus' name, amen.

SCRIPTURE REFERENCES

2 Corinthians 5:17 AMPC • 2 Corinthians 5:18 • Philippians 2:15 AMPC
Ephesians 1:4,6,8 AMPC • Ephesians 5:25-30 AMPC
Ephesians 5:22,33 AMPC, TPT, MSG • 1 Peter 2:6 AMPC
1 Corinthians 11:7 AMPC • 1 Peter 2:23 AMPC • Proverbs 31:11-12 AMPC
2 Corinthians 3:6 • Matthew 19:5-6 AMPC

11 Based on *The Heart of Paul* by Ben Campbell Johnson, published by A Great Love, Inc., Toccoa, GA.

83

Harmonious Christian Marriage

FATHER, we believe that love is displayed in full expression, enfolding and knitting us together in truth, making us perfect for every good work to do Your will, working in us that which is pleasing in Your sight.

In the name of Jesus, it is written in Your Word that we can now experience the endless love of God cascading into our hearts through the Holy Spirit who lives in us. Your love reigns supreme in our marriage.

We live and conduct ourselves and our marriage honorably and becomingly. We esteem it as precious, worthy, and of great price. *We commit ourselves to live in mutual harmony and accord with one another,* delighting in each other, being of the same mind and united in spirit.

Father, we believe and say that we are gentle, compassionate, courteous, tenderhearted, and humble-minded. We seek peace, and it keeps our hearts in quietness and assurance. Because we follow after love and dwell in peace, our prayers are not hindered in any way, in the name of Jesus. We are heirs together of the grace of God.

Our marriage grows stronger day by day in the bond of unity because it is founded on Your Word and rooted and grounded in Your love. Father, we thank You for the performance of it, in Jesus' name, amen.

SCRIPTURE REFERENCES

Romans 5:5 TPT • Ephesians 4:32 • Philippians 1:9
Isaiah 32:17 • Colossians 3:14 • Philippians 4:7 • Colossians 1:10
1 Peter 3:7 • Philippians 2:13 • Ephesians 3:17-18 • Philippians 2:2
Jeremiah 1:12

— 84 —

God's Provision for a Childless Couple

OUR Father, dwelling in the heavenly realms, may the glory of Your name be the center on which our lives turn. We kneel humbly in awe before You—the perfect Father of every father and child in heaven and on the earth. We ask You to unveil within us the unlimited riches of Your glory and favor until supernatural strength floods our innermost being with Your divine might and explosive power. Together, as husband and wife, we ask You to release the life of Christ deep inside us. This life is the resting place of His Love which is the very source and root of our life.

Father, You see and understand our desire to have children. We choose to keep trusting in You, and we purpose to do what is right in Your eyes. By God's grace our hearts are fixed on Your promises and we are secure, feasting on Your faithfulness. You are our utmost delight and the pleasure of our life together, and You will provide for what we desire the most. We give You the right to direct our life, and we trust You to fulfill Your promise.

You are our God whose grace provides us a joyful home with children so that we become a family. You make us happy parents surrounded by our pride and joy. You are the God we praise, so we give it all to You!

Father, Your mighty power is working in us and will accomplish all this. You will achieve infinitely more than our greatest request, our most unbelievable dream, and exceed our wildest imagination! You will outdo them all, for Your miraculous power constantly energizes us.

Now we offer up to You all the glorious praise that rises from every church in every generation through Jesus Christ—and all that will yet be manifest through time and eternity. Amen!

SCRIPTURE REFERENCES

Matthew 6:9 TPT • Ephesians 3:14-21 TPT • Psalm 113:9 • Psalm 37:3-5

85

The Unborn Child

FATHER, in Jesus' name, I thank You for my unborn child. I treasure this child as a gift from You. My child was created in Your image, perfectly healthy and complete. You have known my child since conception and know the path he/she will take with his/her life. I ask Your blessing upon him/her and stand and believe in his/her salvation through Jesus Christ.

When You created man and woman, You called them blessed and crowned them with glory and honor. It is in You, Father, that my child will live and move and have his/her being. He/she is Your offspring and will come to worship and praise You.

Heavenly Father, I thank and praise You for the great things You have done and are continuing to do. I am in awe at the miracle of life You have placed inside of me. Thank You! Amen.

SCRIPTURE REFERENCES

Psalm 127:3 • Matthew 18:18 • Genesis 1:26 • John 14:13 • Jeremiah 1:5
Galatians 3:13 • 2 Peter 3:9 • 1 John 3:8 • Psalm 8:5 • Psalm 91:1
Acts 17:28-29

86

Godly Order in Pregnancy and Childbirth

FATHER, in Jesus' name, I confess Your Word this day over my pregnancy and the birth of my child. I ask You to quickly perform Your Word, trusting that it will not go out from You and return to You void, but rather that it will accomplish that which pleases You. Your Word is powerful, alive, and active and pierces more sharply than a two-edged sword.

Right now, I put on the whole armor of God so that I may be able to stand against the tricks and traps of the devil. I recognize that my fight is not with flesh and blood, but against principalities, powers, and the rulers of darkness and spiritual wickedness in high places. God, I stand above all, taking the shield of faith and being able to quench the attacks of the devil with Your mighty power. I stand in faith during this pregnancy and birth, not giving any room to fear, but possessing power, love, and a sound mind, as Your Word promises in 2 Timothy 1:7.

Heavenly Father, I confess that You are my Refuge; I trust You during this pregnancy and childbirth. I am thankful that You have assigned angels to watch over me and my unborn child. I cast all the care and burden of this pregnancy on You, Lord. Your grace is sufficient for me through this pregnancy; You strengthen my weaknesses.

Father, Your Word declares that my unborn child was created in Your image, fearfully and wonderfully made to praise You. You have made me a joyful mother, and I am blessed with a heritage from You as my reward.

I commit this child to You, Father, and pray that he/she will grow and call me blessed.

I am not afraid of pregnancy or childbirth because I am fixed and trusting upon You, Father. I thank You that my pregnancy will be successful and all decisions regarding my pregnancy and delivery will be directed by the Holy Spirit. Lord, You are my Dwelling Place, and I rest in the knowledge that evil will not come near me and no sickness or infirmity will strike me or my unborn child. I know that Jesus died on the cross to take away my sickness and pain.

Having accepted Your Son, Jesus, as my Savior, I confess that my child will be born healthy and completely whole. Thank You, Father, for the law of the Spirit of life in Christ Jesus that has made me and my child free from the law of sin and death!

Father, thank You for protecting me and my baby and for our good health. Thank You for hearing and answering my prayers. In Jesus' name, amen.

SCRIPTURE REFERENCES

Jeremiah 1:12 • Proverbs 31:28 • Isaiah 55:11 • Psalm 112:7
Hebrews 4:12 PHI, TPT • Psalm 91: 1-2, 10-11 • Ephesians 6:11-12,16
Matthew 8:17 • Romans 8:2 • 1 Peter 5:7 • James 4:7
2 Corinthians 12:9 • Ephesians 6:12 • Genesis 1:26 • John 4:13
Psalm 139:14 • Matthew 18:18 • Psalm 113:9 • Psalm 127:3 • Jeremiah 33:3

87

Adopting a Child

FATHER, in Jesus' name, we come boldly before Your throne of grace, that we may receive mercy and find grace to help in our time of need. We are trusting You and fixing our hearts on Your promises, so we will be secure, feasting on Your faithfulness.

We delight ourselves in You, and You give us the desires and secret petitions of our hearts. We believe our desire to adopt a child is from You, and we are willing to assume the responsibility of rearing this child in the ways of the Master.

Father, we commit our way to You and thank You for Your promise: "Make God the utmost delight and pleasure of your life, and he will provide for you what you desire the most. Give God the right to direct your life, and as you trust him along the way you'll find he pulled it off perfectly!" (Ps. 37:4-5 TPT). Our confidence is in You, and You will bring this adoption to pass according to Your purpose and plan.

Lord, Your Son, Jesus, demonstrated Your love for children when He said, "Let the children alone, don't prevent them from coming to me. God's kingdom is made up of people like these" (Matt. 19:14 MSG). Then He laid hands on them and blessed them.

Use us as Your instruments of peace and righteousness to bless this child. We purpose in our hearts to train this child in the way that he/she should go.

Lord, we are embracing this child (Your best gift) as our very own with Your love, as Jesus said, "Whoever embraces one of these children as I do embraces me, and far more than me—God who sent me" (Mark 9:37 MSG).

Father, we will be a father and mother to him/her, extending our hands and our hearts to embrace him/her. Thank You for the blood of Jesus that gives protection to this one we love.

We thank You for the man and woman who conceived this child, and we pray that You will bless them. If they do not know Jesus, we ask You, the Lord of the harvest, to send forth laborers to share truth with them that they may come out of the snare of the devil.

Mercy and truth are written upon the tablets of our hearts, and You cause us to find favor and good understanding with You and with man—the adoption agency staff, the judges, and all those who are involved in this decision-making process. May all be careful that they do not despise one of these little ones over whom they have jurisdiction—for they have angels who see Your face continually in heaven.

We believe that all our words are righteous, upright, and in right standing with You, Father. By our long forbearing and calmness of spirit those in authority are persuaded, and our soft speech breaks down the most bone-like resistance.

Lord, we are looking to You as our Great Counselor and Mighty Advocate. We ask for Your wisdom for us and our attorneys.

Father, contend with those who contend with us, and give safety to our child and ease him/her day by day. We are calling on You in the name of Jesus, and You will answer us and show us great and mighty things. No weapon formed against us and this adoption shall prosper, and any tongue that rises against us in judgment we shall show to be in the wrong. This peace, righteousness, security, and triumph over opposition is our inheritance as Your children.

Father, we believe; therefore, we have spoken. May it be done unto us according to Your Word. In Jesus' name, amen.

SCRIPTURE REFERENCES

Hebrews 4:16 • Matthew 18:10 PHI • Psalm 37:3-5 TPT • Proverbs 8:8 AMPC
Psalm 37:6-7 TPT • Proverbs 25:15 AMPC • Ephesians 6:4 MSG
James 1:5 • Isaiah 49:25 • Proverbs 22:6 • Jeremiah 33:3 • Psalm 67:1
Isaiah 54:17 AMPC • Matthew 9:38 • Psalm 116:10 • 2 Timothy 2:26
Luke 1:38 • Proverbs 3:3-4 • Matthew 9:38

88

The Home

FATHER, I thank You that You have blessed me with all spiritual blessings in Christ Jesus.

Through skillful and godly wisdom is my house (my life, my home, my family) built, and by understanding it is established on a sound and good foundation. By knowledge shall the chambers of its every area be filled with all precious and pleasant riches—great priceless treasure. The house of the uncompromisingly righteous shall stand. Prosperity and welfare are in my house in the name of Jesus.

My house is securely built. It is founded on a rock—revelation knowledge of Your Word, Father. Jesus is Lord of my household, and my Cornerstone. Jesus is my Lord—spirit, soul, and body.

Whatever may be our task, we work at it heartily as something done for You, Lord, and not for men. We love each other with the God-kind of love, and we dwell in peace. My home is deposited into Your charge, entrusted to Your protection and care.

Father, as for me and my house, we shall serve the Lord, in Jesus' name. Hallelujah! Amen.

SCRIPTURE REFERENCES

Ephesians 1:3 • Acts 16:31 • Proverbs 24:3-4 AMPC • Philippians 2:10-11
Proverbs 15:6 • Colossians 3:23 • Proverbs 12:7 AMPC • Colossians 3:14-15
Psalm 112:3 • Acts 20:32 • Luke 6:48 • Joshua 24:15 • Acts 4:11 ESV

89

Blessing the Household

Introduction

As the head of the family, it is your privilege and duty to pray for the household in your charge and those under your care and authority.

The following prayer was written to be prayed by a man or a woman. So often in today's society, the woman finds herself having to assume the responsibility and position of the head of the household.

I. Prayer of Blessing for the Household

Father, as the priest and head of this household, I declare and decree, "As for me and my house, we shall serve the Lord" (Josh. 24:15 NKJV). As I believe on the Lord Jesus Christ and am saved, so it is with everyone in my household. Everyone is unique, created in Your image, and we dedicate our children to You and point them in the way that they should go. The values they learn from us will be with them for life.

Praise be to You, the God and Father of our Lord Jesus Christ, for You have blessed us in the heavenly realms with every spiritual blessing in Christ. We reverence You and worship You in spirit and in truth.

Lord, we acknowledge and welcome the presence of Your Holy Spirit here in our home. We thank You, Father, that Your Son, Jesus, is here with us because we are gathered together in His name.

Lord God, Your divine power has given us everything we need for life and godliness through our knowledge of You who called us by Your own glory and goodness.

As spiritual leader of this home, I declare on the authority of Your Word that my family will be mighty in the land; this generation of the upright will be blessed.

Father, You delight in the prosperity of Your people, and we thank You that wealth and riches are in our house and that our righteousness endures forever. In the name of Jesus, amen.

SCRIPTURE REFERENCES

Revelation 1:6 • Matthew 18:20 • Joshua 24:15 • Acts 16:31 • 2 Peter 1:3 NIV
Ephesians 1:3 NIV • Psalm 112:2 NIV • John 4:23 • Psalm 112:3

II. Prayer of Blessing at the Table

Introduction

This prayer was written for the head of the household to pray not only to thank and praise God for His blessings but also to cleanse and consecrate the food received and to sanctify the family members who partake of it.

Prayer

Father, thank You for giving to us our daily bread. We receive this food with thanksgiving and praise. You bless our bread and our water and take sickness out of the midst of us.

In the name of Jesus, we call this food clean, wholesome, and pure nourishment to our bodies. Should there be any deadly thing herein, it shall not harm us, for the Spirit of life in Christ Jesus makes us free from the law of sin and death. In the name of Jesus, amen.

SCRIPTURE REFERENCES

Matthew 6:11 • Mark 16:18 • 1 Timothy 4:4 NIV • Romans 8:2
Exodus 23:25

III. Husband's Prayer of Blessing for His Wife

Introduction

It is positive reinforcement, validation, and affirmation for children to hear their father pray, blessing his wife and their mother. This is a method of honoring her and reaffirming her position in the home. Words are powerful, and the blessings for the wife in front of the children will promote appropriate self-esteem necessary for success in life.

Sometimes a wife will feel that she has failed because she is not fulfilling all the roles expressed in Proverbs 31. I believe that God had this passage written to encourage a woman to be all that He created her to be. Out of her "being"—knowing herself, both her strengths and her weaknesses, developing her talents, seeing herself as God sees her, and looking to Christ for her completeness (wholeness)—comes the "doing."

> The woman described in this chapter has outstanding abilities. Her family's social position is high. In fact, she may not be one woman at all—she may be a composite portrait of ideal womanhood. Do not see her as a model to imitate in every detail; your days are not long enough to do everything she does! See her instead as an inspiration to be all you can be. We can't be just like her, but we can learn from her industry, integrity, and resourcefulness.[12]

Prayer

Father, I thank You for my wife who is a capable, intelligent, and virtuous woman. Her worth is far more precious than jewels, and her value is far above rubies or pearls.

I thank You that she is a woman of strong character, great wisdom, many skills, and great compassion. Strength and dignity are her clothing, and her position is strong and secure. She opens her mouth with skillful and godly wisdom, and on her tongue is the law of kindness giving counsel and instruction. Our children rise up and call her blessed (happy, fortunate, and to be envied). I boast of and praise her, saying, "Many daughters have done virtuously, nobly, and well [with the strength of character that is steadfast in goodness], but you excel them all" (Prov. 31:29 AMPC). Father, my wife reverently and worshipfully fears You; she shall be praised! Give her of the fruit of her hands, and let her own works praise her in the gates of the city. I respect, value, and honor my wife before our children. In the name of Jesus, amen.

---

12 *Life Application Bible,* New International Version edition (Wheaton, IL: Tyndale House Publishers, 1988, 1989, 1990, 1991), commentary at 1131.

Scripture References (AMPC)

Proverbs 31:10 • Proverbs 31:28-29 • Proverbs 31:25-26 • Proverbs 31:30-31

IV. Parent's Prayer of Blessing for Children

Introduction

> The [Hebrew] father's place in the [traditional Jewish] home is fittingly shown by the beautiful custom of blessing the children, a custom which dates back to Isaac and Jacob. To this day, in many homes, the father blesses his children on Friday nights, on Rosh Hashanah eve and on Yom Kippur before leaving for the synagogue....
>
> In very ancient times, the father or patriarch was the ruler of home and family. He made laws and enforced them. Later, however, laws were instituted by teachers, parents, judges, and kings. The father, as the master of the house, was looked up to for support and depended on for guidance.[13]

The following prayer, based on a translation of the traditional Hebrew father's blessing upon his children, may be used by the head of the household, whether male or female.

13 Ben M. Edidin, *Jewish Customs and Ceremonies* (New York: Hebrew Publishing Company, 1941), 23.

Prayer

Father, I receive, welcome, and acknowledge each of my children as a delightful blessing from You. I speak Your blessings upon them and over them.

Children, I bless you in the name of Jesus, proclaiming the blessings of God, my Redeemer, upon you. May He give you wisdom, a reverential fear of God, and a heart of love.

May He create in you the desire to attend to His words, a willing and obedient heart that you may consent and submit to His sayings and walk in His ways. May your eyes look straight ahead with purpose for the future. May your tongue be as the pen of a ready writer, writing mercy and kindness upon the tablets of your heart. May you speak the truth in love. May your hands do the works of the Father; may your feet walk the paths which He has foreordained for you.

I have no greater joy than this—to hear that my children are living their lives in the truth.

May the Lord prepare you and your future mate to love and honor one another, and may He grant to your union upright sons and daughters who will live in accordance with His Word. May your source of livelihood be honorable and secure, so that you will earn a living with your own hands. May you always worship God in spirit and in truth.

I pray above all things that you may always prosper and be in health, even as your soul prospers. "I know the thoughts and plans that I have for you, says the Lord, thoughts and plans for welfare and peace and not for evil, to give you hope in your final outcome" (Jer. 29:11 AMPC). In the name of Jesus, amen.

SCRIPTURE REFERENCES

Psalm 127:3 AMPC • Ephesians 2:10 AMPC • Philippians 2:13 AMPC
3 John 4 AMPC • Proverbs 4:20 • 1 Thessalonians 4:11-12 NIV
Psalm 45:1 • John 4:23 • Proverbs 3:3 • AMPC 3 John 2 • Ephesians 4:15

90

Prayer for a Troubled Marriage

NOTE: I encourage you to pray all or parts of this prayer. The Holy Spirit is present to help you during these painful times. Consider finding a Christian marriage counselor and go for counseling even if you have to go alone.

PRAYER

Lord, I'm fading away. I'm discouraged and lying in the dust; revive me by Your Word, just like You promised. Lord, hear me as I pray; pay attention to my groaning. Listen to my cry for help, my King and my God, for I pray to You only. I am broken, I am hurting, and I need help!

Holy Spirit, I ask You to come to my aid and bear me up in my weakness, for I do not know what prayer to offer nor how to offer it worthily as I ought. You go to meet my supplication and plead on my behalf with unspeakable yearnings and groanings too deep for utterance. You search not only my heart, but also the heart of my mate. You know what is in the mind of the Spirit because You intercede on our behalf according to and in harmony with God's will.

Lord, I expected my marriage to last until death do us part. Right now, it seems as though I am facing nothing but difficulties, and I'm trying to count it all joy. You and I know that I do not feel joyful. But I choose to believe Your Word that says when my faith is tested, it stirs up power within me to endure all things. I don't know what to do, but right now, I ask You for wisdom knowing that You will give it! Thank You for letting me know that You don't see my lack of wisdom as an opportunity to scold me over my failures, but You are here to overwhelm my failures with Your generous grace.

Forgive me for rushing ahead and making all the plans I wanted. I have tried compromise, manipulation, and even tried to live out Ephesians 5 in my desperate desire to save my marriage, but it's You who will ultimately direct my steps. Too often I have been in love with my own opinions, convinced that I was correct. Lord, even during this time of trouble You are here, testing and probing my every motive. Before I do anything, I choose to put my trust totally in You and not in myself.

By faith, I choose the privilege of living with You, my Father, every moment in Your house that I might find the sweet loveliness of Your face. Here in my brokenness, I am filled with awe and choose to delight in Your glory and grace. I want to live so close to You that You take pleasure in my every prayer.

SCRIPTURE REFERENCES

Psalm 119:25 TPT • Psalm 5:1-3 NLT • Psalm 5:1-3 • Romans 8:26-27 AMPC
James 1:2-5 TPT • Proverbs 16:1-4 TPT • Psalm 27:4-5 TPT

91

When Marriage Vows Are Broken

Introduction

This prayer was originally written for a wife whose husband had been unfaithful. If you are a husband who has been betrayed, simply change this prayer to fit your situation.

Prayer

Lord, You made us one when we became husband and wife. You made us one in body and spirit, and You intended for us to have godly children. My husband has dishonored me; we are no longer equal partners of life, and our prayers have been disturbed. The rejection and betrayal is very painful.

Father, forgive us for speaking our marriage vows so casually and without understanding. I have covered Your altar with tears because our prayers have been hindered. You witnessed the vows we made to each other on our wedding day when we were young. Our marriage vows are broken, and I am abandoned. Father, I cannot encourage my husband's wayward behavior and become a partaker of his evil work.

Jesus was wounded for our transgressions and bruised for our iniquities; the chastisement of our peace was upon Him, and by His stripes we are healed (see Isa. 53:5). I ask You to forgive my shortcomings and failures concerning my marriage. Help me learn and grow spiritually and receive emotional wholeness, as I grow more intimately acquainted with You. Father, give me the grace to forgive my husband's infidelity.

You hate divorce, but You allow it when a spouse is unfaithful. You know my husband's heart and the decisions he will make concerning his future, and I am responsible to You and my children. ________ has behaved as an unbeliever in this situation, and if he desires to go, give me the grace to let him go.

Lord, I trust in You with all of my heart and lean not unto my own understanding. In all of my ways I acknowledge You, and You shall direct my path. Father, You promised to never leave me, abandon me, or leave me without support. I know that the preparations of the heart belong to man, but I desire the wise answer of the tongue that comes from You. In Jesus' name I pray, amen.

SCRIPTURE REFERENCES (AMPC)

Titus 2:4-6 • Ephesians 5:21 • Proverbs 5:15-19 • Jeremiah 1:12
Hebrews 9:14 • Hebrews 13:5 • 1 Corinthians 11:3

92

Overcoming Rejection in Marriage

FATHER, in the name of Jesus, __________ and __________ are delivered from this present evil age by the Son of the Living God, and whom the Son has set free is free indeed. Therefore, they are delivered from a spirit of rejection and accepted in the Beloved to be holy and blameless in Your sight. They forgive all those who have wronged them, and their hurts from the past are healed, for Jesus came to heal the brokenhearted.

Father, they are Your chosen people, holy, and dearly loved. They clothe themselves with compassion, kindness, humility, gentleness, and patience. They bear with each other and forgive whatever grievances they may have against one another. They forgive as You forgave them. Over all these virtues, they put on love, which binds them together in perfect unity.

Father, when they were children, they talked like children, thought like children, and reasoned like children; but now they have become husband and wife, and they are done with childish ways and have put them aside. The blood of Christ, who through the eternal Spirit offered Himself without spot to You, purges their consciences from dead works of selfishness, agitating passions, and moral conflicts so they can serve You, the Living God. They touch not any unclean thing, for they are Your son and daughter. Satan's power over them is broken, and his strongholds are torn down. Sin no longer has dominion over them and their household.

Your love reigns supreme in their home, and Your peace acts as an umpire in all situations. Jesus is their Lord—spirit, soul, and body. Amen.

SCRIPTURE REFERENCES (AMPC)

Galatians 1:4 • Colossians 3:12-15 NIV • John 8:36
1 Corinthians 13:11 AMPC • Ephesians 1:16 • 1 Thessalonians 5:23
Luke 4:18 • Colossians 3:15 AMPC • Romans 6:18

93

Peace in the Christian Family

FATHER, thank You that You have poured out Your Spirit on our family from heaven. Our wilderness has become a fertile field, and the fertile field yields bountiful crops. Justice rules in the wilderness and righteousness in our fertile field. This righteousness brings peace—quietness and confidence forever.

Our family dwells in a peaceable habitation, in safe dwellings, and in quiet resting places. And there is stability in our times, abundance of salvation, wisdom, and knowledge. There, reverent fear and worship of the Lord is our treasure and Yours.

Lord, You are gracious to us; we have waited expectantly for You. You are the Arm of Your servants—our Strength and Defense—every morning, our Salvation in the time of trouble.

Father, we thank You for our peace, our safety, and our welfare this day. Hallelujah! Amen.

SCRIPTURE REFERENCES

Isaiah 32:15-18 NLT • Isaiah 33:2,6 AMPC

— 94 —

Handling Household Finances

Introduction

THE following prayers may be prayed individually or as a couple. In preparation for marriage it is great wisdom for the couple to discuss finances. Each party comes with an individual view of how to handle money—spending and/or saving. It is wise to set up a budget that is agreeable to both.

There is a danger in the tendency to assume that the other party has the same opinions and ideas about money or, in case of disagreement, that one's own way is right and the other person's is wrong. Financial differences are one of Satan's greatest weapons for introducing strife and bringing pressure to bear on a marriage. Spending money can quickly evolve into an emotional experience, causing many other problems.

God is *El-Shaddai,* God Almighty (see Exod. 6:3 AMPC)—the God who is more than enough—and His intention is that His children enjoy good health and that all may go well with them, even as their souls are getting along well (see 3 John 2 NIV). Two people coming into agreement with God's financial plan will offset the enemy's schemes to divide and conquer.

If you and your beloved are planning to marry or to establish a financial plan in your existing marriage, listen to one another. Understand what each other is saying. Realize that there are differences in viewpoints about money and allow for those differences. Determine who is more astute in financial matters—balancing the checkbook, paying the bills on time, and making wise investments. Set aside time in your schedules to keep each other informed, review goals, and make plans. Wisdom from above is willing to yield to reason; cooperate one with the other (see James 3:17 AMPC).

Prayer

Father, we come before You in the name of Jesus. Thank You for the Holy Spirit who is present with us as we discuss our financial future together. We thank You for bringing us to this place in our lives. You have started a good work in us and will perform it until the day of Jesus Christ. We welcome You as we prepare to set up a budget that is pleasing to You and to each of us.

Jesus is our Lord and our High Priest, and we purpose to bring Him the firstfruits of our income and worship You, the Lord our God, with them.

Father, You are Lord over our marriage—over this union that has been ordained by You. We confess Your Word over our life together and our finances. As we do so, we say that Your Word will not return to You void but will accomplish what it says it will do.

Therefore, we believe in the name of Jesus that all of our needs are met, according to Your riches in glory. We acknowledge You as Lord over our finances by giving tithes and offerings to further Your cause.

Father, as we choose to give generously, generous gifts will be given back to us, shaken down to make room for more. Abundant gifts will pour out upon us with such an overflowing measure that it will run over the top! Our measurement of generosity becomes the measurement of our return.

We remember that it is written in Your Word that he who sows sparingly and grudgingly will also reap sparingly and grudgingly. He who sows generously—that blessings may come to someone—will also reap generously and with blessings.

Lord, remind us always, and we purpose to remember, that it is You who give us power to become rich, and You do it to fulfill Your promise to our ancestors. We will never feel that it was our own power and might that made us wealthy.

Father, not only do we give tithes and offerings to You, but we choose also to give to those around us who are in need. Every time we give to the poor, we make a loan to You, our Lord, without worry. We are repaid in full for all the good we do.

Thank You, Father, that as You bless us and we bless others, they will praise You and give You thanks and bless others and the circle of Your love and blessing will go on and on into eternity. In the name of Jesus, we pray, amen.

SCRIPTURE REFERENCES

John 14:17 • Luke 6:38 TPT • Philippians 1:6 • 2 Corinthians 9:6 AMPC
Hebrews 3:1 • Deuteronomy 8:17-18 TLB • Deuteronomy 26:10-11
Proverbs 19:17 TPT • Isaiah 55:11 • 2 Corinthians 9:12-15 AMPC, NIV, PHI
Philippians 4:19

I. Setting Aside the Tithe

Father, Your Word states, "Be sure to set aside a tenth of all that your fields produce each year...so that you may learn to revere the Lord Your God always" (Deut. 14:22-23 NIV). We purpose to set aside the tithe because it belongs to You, dear Father.

It is our delight to bring all the tithes (the whole tenth of our income) into the storehouse, that there may be food in Your house. Lord of hosts, in accordance with Your Word, we prove You now by paying You the tithe. You are opening the windows of heaven for us and pouring us out such a blessing that there shall not be room enough to receive it.

Thank You, Father, for rebuking the devourer for our sakes; he shall not destroy the fruits of our ground, neither shall our vine drop its fruit before the time in the field.

We praise You, Lord, for recording our names in Your book of remembrance of those who reverence and worshipfully fear You and who think on Your name so that we may be Yours in the day when You publicly recognize and openly declare us to be Your jewels—Your special possession, Your peculiar treasure.

Thank You for bringing us out of the authority of darkness and translating us into the Kingdom of Your dear Son, Jesus Christ, our Lord. In His name we pray, amen.

SCRIPTURE REFERENCES

Malachi 3:10-11 AMPC • Colossians 1:13 • Malachi 3:16-17 AMPC

II. Giving the Offering

Father, we give offerings at the direction of the Holy Spirit. We are ever ready with a generous and willing gift. At Your instructions we remember this: A stingy planter gets a stingy crop; a lavish planter gets a lavish crop.

We choose to allow our giving to flow from our hearts, not from a sense of religious duty. We let it spring up freely from the joy of giving—all because God loves hilarious generosity!

Father, we thank You that You are able to make all grace (every favor and earthly blessing) come to us in abundance, so that we may always, under all circumstances and whatever the need, be self-sufficient, possessing enough to require no aid or support and furnished in abundance for every good work and charitable donation.

Father, You are generous to supply abundant seed for the farmer, which becomes bread for our meals, but You are even more extravagant toward us. First, You supply every need, plus more. Then You multiply the seed we sow so that the harvest of our generosity will grow. You abundantly enrich us in every way as we give generously on every occasion, for when we take gifts to those in need, it causes many to give thanks to You.

We confess with the psalmist David—we have not seen the righteous forsaken, nor his seed begging bread.

We thank You for food, clothing, and shelter. In the name of Jesus, we determine to stop being perpetually uneasy (anxious and worried) about our life together, what we shall eat and what we shall drink or about our bodies and what we shall put on. Our life—individually and together—is greater in quality than food, and our bodies far above and more excellent than clothing.

The bread of idleness—gossip, discontent, and self-pity—we will not eat. We declare on the authority of Your Word that our family will be mighty in the land; this generation of the upright will be blessed.

Father, You delight in the prosperity of Your people; we thank You that wealth and riches are in our house and our righteousness endures forever.

Good comes to us for we are generous and lend freely and conduct our affairs with justice. When we lack wisdom, we will ask of You, and You will give generously without finding fault with us. In the name of Jesus, amen.

SCRIPTURE REFERENCES

2 Corinthians 9:5-11 MSG, TPT, AMPC • Psalm 112:2-3 • Psalm 37:25 NIV
Psalm 37:26 NIV • Matthew 6:25 AMPC • 2 Corinthians 9:9 AMPC
Proverbs 31:27 AMPC • James 1:5 NIV • Psalm 35:27

96

Moving to a New Location

FATHER, Your Word says that You will perfect that which concerns us. Your mercy and loving-kindness endure forever. We bring to You our apprehensions concerning our relocation. We ask You to go before us to make the crooked places straight in finding a new home.

Give us wisdom to make wise decisions in choosing the movers and packers best suited to handle our possessions. We have favor, good understanding, and high esteem in the sight of You and man—with the utility companies, with the school systems, and with the banks—with everyone involved in this move.

Father, we thank You for supplying and preparing the new friends that You want us to have. We are trusting You to direct us to a church where we can fellowship with like believers, in one accord, where we are free to worship and praise You and sing to You a new song.

Father, in the name of Jesus, we commit this move to You, knowing that You provide for Your children. We trust You and delight ourselves in You, and You will give us the desires of our hearts.

We make all these requests known unto You with thanksgiving, and the peace that passes all understanding shall guard our hearts and minds. You will keep us in perfect peace because our minds are stayed on You.

We trust in You, Father, with all of our hearts. We lean not unto our own understanding, but in all of our ways we acknowledge You, and You shall direct our paths.

Thank You, Father, for Your blessing on this move. In the name of Jesus, amen.

SCRIPTURE REFERENCES

Psalm 138:8 • Psalm 40:3 • Isaiah 45:2 • Psalm 96:1 • James 1:5
Psalm 98:1 • Proverbs 3:4 • Psalm 149:1 • Hebrews 10:25 • Psalm 37:4-5
Acts 2:1,46 • Philippians 4:6-7 • Acts 4:34 • Isaiah 26:3
Philippians 2:2 • Proverbs 3:5-6 • Isaiah 42:10

97

Seeking Safety in a Place of Violence

FATHER, Thank You that I have been redeemed by the blood of the Lamb. I come before You today as Your child and the head of my household asking for Your protection for my family. Give safety to my children and ease them day by day. We have had more than our fill of the scoffing of the proud and the contempt of the arrogant.

Lord, You see the violence that is in the streets and in our schools. The drug dealers and the gang members living in our neighborhoods are waiting to snare our children. I am calling upon You, Lord, confident that You will save me and my household as well.

Confuse my enemies, Lord! Upset their plans. Cruelty and violence are all I see in the city, and they are like guards on patrol day and night. The city is full of trouble, evil, and corruption.

Troublemakers and liars freely roam the streets. I ask for Your help, Lord God, and thank You for keeping my family safe.

Father, in the name of Jesus, You, and You alone, are our safety and our protection. My household and I are looking to You, for our strength comes from You—the God who made heaven and earth. You will not let us stumble. You are our Guardian God who will not fall asleep. You are right at our side to protect us. You guard us from every evil, You guard our very lives. You guard us when we leave and when we return. You guard us now; You guard us always.

My household was chosen and foreknown by You, Father, and consecrated (sanctified, made holy) by the Spirit to be obedient to Jesus Christ the Messiah and to be sprinkled with His blood. We receive grace (spiritual blessing) and peace in ever-increasing abundance—that spiritual peace to be realized in and through Christ, freedom from fears, agitating passions, and moral conflicts.

With thanksgiving we are looking to Jesus who became our Passover by shedding His own precious blood. He is the Mediator (the Go-between, Agent) of a new covenant, and His sprinkled blood speaks of mercy. On the authority of Your Word, I proclaim that the blood of Jesus is our protection, as it is written: "when I see the blood, I will pass over you" (Exod. 12:13). I declare and decree that I am drawing a bloodline around my children, and the evil one cannot cross it.

I know that none of the God-begotten make a practice of sin—fatal sin. The God-begotten are also the God-protected. The evil one can't lay a hand on my household. I know that we are held firm by You, Lord. Father, thank You for Your divine protection. In the name of Jesus, I pray, amen.[14]

SCRIPTURE REFERENCES

1 John 3:1 • Psalm 121:1-8 MSG • 1 Peter 1:18-19 • 1 Peter 1:2 AMPC
1 John 2:12 • Hebrews 12:24 AMPC • Psalm 123:4 NLT
1 John 5:18-19 MSG • Psalm 55:9-11,16 CEV

14 In addition to praying this prayer above, I encourage you to read Psalm 91 aloud over your family each day.

98

Dealing with an Abusive Family Situation

Introduction

In our ministry, we receive letters from women who are living in abusive situations. Because many of them do not feel or believe that they can leave, they request that we write prayers to cover this area of need. They are fearful of practicing tough love. A need for security plays a big role in their decision to remain where they are. Or, in certain cases, they fear increased or even more severe abuse should they try to leave. Others have asked the abuser to leave or have moved out themselves; yet, their request is for prayer for deliverance for the abuser and other family members.

When I am traveling, I often meet women who feel that it is safe to talk with me. At the close of a meeting a few years ago, I was approached by an attractive woman whom I recognized by her manner of dress as belonging to a certain denomination. As she shared her agony and emotional pain, I moaned inwardly. I took her in my arms, encouraging her to go to her pastor for counseling. Her answer grieved me. She had been told by both her husband and her pastor that the beatings were because of her "rebellious nature."

"I don't know what else I can do to stop the abuse," she confided. "I've tried to please my husband. Scripturally, I cannot leave him. What can I do but stay with him? I don't want to disobey God, but I want the abuse to stop."

When we turn to the Scriptures, we find that God is much more merciful than we human beings. Jesus is our Example, and in one incident He turned around and walked away from the crowd who would have thrown Him off a cliff (see Luke 4:28-30). There are times to take action; change brings change. Often we want God to do something when all the time He is waiting for us to do something: "Trust God from the bottom of your heart; don't try to figure out everything on your own. Listen for God's voice in everything you do, everywhere you go; he's the one who will keep you on track" (Prov. 3:5-6 MSG).

A testimony of deliverance from abusive behavior was shared by a young husband who had been born again for only a short time. His mother had given him a copy of *The Living Bible.* One day he picked it up and read Malachi 2:15-16: "You were united to your wife by the Lord. In God's wise plan, when you married, the two of you became one person in his sight. And what does he want? Godly children from your union. Therefore, guard your passions! Keep faith with the wife of your youth. For the Lord, the God of Israel, says he hates divorce and cruel men. Therefore, control your passions—let there be no divorcing of your wives."

The young man said, "When I read these verses, I realized that I was treating my wife cruelly and admitted to myself that the addictions in my life were controlling me. It wasn't so much that I wanted to stop doing drugs, but I did want to change the way that I was treating my wife. I cried out to God, and He heard me and delivered me."

The following prayer was written for Christian women who want to know how to pray prayers that avail much while in an abusive family situation.

Prayer

Father, Your Word says that You loved me and my family so much that You sent Your very own Son, Jesus, to die for our sin so we could live with

You forever. You said that You would give us a new life that is wonderful and rich. I pray that I may become like You, for I am Your child and You love me.

By Your grace, Father, I will live my life in love. Your love in me is not a feeling, but a decision requiring more than mere words. As a Christian I am "light," and I will live as a child of the Light. The Light produces in me all that is good and right and true.

Lord, lead me in paths of righteousness for Your name's sake. I purpose to live with a due sense of responsibility, not as others who do not know the meaning of life, but as one who does. Direct me by Your Holy Spirit that I may make the best use of my time, despite all the evils of these days.

Father, there was a time when You looked for an intercessor. I am willing to stand in the gap and make up the hedge so that my family will not suffer judgment. Send Your Holy Spirit to convict, convince, and demonstrate to us about sin, righteousness, and judgment. Give us a heart of flesh and send a laborer of the harvest to share with us the Gospel of the glory of Christ the Messiah.

I thank You, Father, that each family member who is lost receives and confesses that Jesus is his/her Lord, and I ask that Your will be done in his/her life. It is You who rescues him/her from the dominion of darkness, and You translate him/her into the Kingdom of the Son of Your love. In the name of Jesus, I ask that You help him/her to grow in grace, that he/she may experience Your love and trust You to be his/her Father.

Lord, reveal the steps that I should take to break what appears to be a generational curse. The sins of the fathers are being repeated in our household, and I do not want this curse passed down to my children.

Father, Your Word says that we are overcomers by the blood of the Lamb and by the word of our testimony. In the name of Jesus, I am committing my life to You—to obey You. Show me the path of life for me and my family.

Uncontrollable, irrational anger, rage, and abuse are a curse. Your Son, Jesus, was made a curse for us; therefore, I put on Your whole armor that I may be able to successfully stand against all the strategies and the deceits of the devil.

In the name of Jesus, I am the redeemed, and I plead the blood of Jesus over my family. I thank You that the evil power of abuse is broken, overthrown, and cast down out of my family. The abuse is exposed and reproved by the light—it is made visible and clear; and where everything is visible and clear, there is light.

You sent Jesus to bind up our heartaches and to heal our pain. The Bible says that You have sent Your Word to heal us and to deliver us from our own destructions. Give us the grace and faith to receive healing and to forgive those who have abused us; thank You for the courage to make amends to those whom we have harmed.

Teach us how to guard our hearts with all diligence. I declare and decree that we are growing in grace and the knowledge of You, developing the trust we need to receive Your transforming power to change. I make my petitions known to You with thanksgiving, in the name of Jesus. Amen.

SCRIPTURE REFERENCES

John 3:16 • 1 Peter 3:18 • John 10:10 • Revelation 12:11
Ephesians 5:1 PHI • Psalm 16:11 • 1 John 3:18 AMPC
Galatians 3:13 • Ephesians 5:8-9 PNT • Ephesians 6:11 AMPC
Psalm 23:3 • Ephesians 5:13 AMPC • Ephesians 5:15-16 PHI
Luke 4:18 • Ezekiel 22:30 • Psalm 107:20 • John 16:8 AMPC
Matthew 5:44 • Ezekiel 11:19 • Proverbs 4:23 • Matthew 9:38
Romans 12:2 • Matthew 6:10 • Philippians 4:6 NIV • Colossians 1:13

99

Overcoming Weariness

THIS prayer is for everyone who is experiencing weariness. It is not limited to the unmarried who are awaiting a life partner. Many spouses become weary with heartaches that they did not expect to encounter in marriage. Their expected marital bliss has turned into disappointment, additional wounds, and frustration. They are weary with waiting for the healing of the marriage relationship or the deliverance of a spouse, children, or other loved ones from various addictions or negative, destructive behaviors. They long for someone who will heal their wounds without judging them—someone who will love them unconditionally.

Each individual brings baggage into marriage, hoping for a miracle—each partner looking to the other for acceptance and approval.

According to the letters and comments we have received in our ministry, unmarried people experience weariness in matters that married couples may not encounter. Hopefully, we who are married share responsibilities—household chores. Married homeowners may divide the work up into inside and outside labor. Sometimes one spouse neglects his/her responsibility, and the other finds himself/herself doing the work of two. The single person is responsible at all times for "the work of two."

We who are married have another individual involved in the decision-making process, which can lead to conflict. Conflict is not always bad. Out of this conflict can come intimacy. We are not alone in financial decisions, in planning for the future. We may feel alone, but there is another with whom we can talk, with whom we can explore possibilities.

We have another human being from whom we can draw strength. Ideally, we grow together.

Sometimes a married person may experience feelings of "aloneness," but there is another person in the house, someone who is going to return, someone whose presence—although in certain marriages noncommunicative—is experienced.

The unmarried often feel such weariness and dread going home to emptiness—to nothingness. They look for that individual who will be their soul mate, a life partner, someone who will be present and available in good times and bad, someone who will love them unconditionally.

We must all ask ourselves, "Am I ready and willing to love another person unconditionally?"

If you have grown weary and are disappointed in your expectations, I encourage you to seek God for His plan for your life. Ask the Holy Spirit to help you trust God and not be afraid.

Prayer

Father, You see my weariness, my uneasiness, proceeding from continual waiting and disappointed expectation. It seems that my patience is exhausted, and I am discouraged. I am weary of asking and waiting for ________.

My soul is weary with sorrow; strengthen me according to Your Word.

Lord, I come to You, and You give me rest. I take Your yoke upon me and learn of You, for You are gentle and humble in heart, and I will find rest for my soul. Your yoke is easy, and Your burden is light.

I look to You, Lord, and Your strength; I seek Your face always. You are my Refuge and Strength, an ever-present help in trouble. I'm ever aware that my strength is found when I wait upon You. Watch over me, Father, for You are my mountain fortress; You set me on high! You are the

God of passionate love, and You meet with me. You will empower me to rise in triumph over my foes.

You, God, don't come and go. You *last.* You are Creator of all we can see or imagine. You don't get tired out, and You don't pause to catch Your breath. You know *everything,* inside and out. Thank You, Father, that You energize me when I get tired, give fresh strength to dropouts. For even young people tire and drop out; young folk in their prime stumble and fall. But those who wait upon You get fresh strength. They spread their wings and soar like eagles, they run and don't get tired, they walk and don't lag behind. Father, I choose to wait on You because You empower me! In Jesus' name, I will soar like an eagle. I will run and not get tired. I will not lag behind.

You are my Strength and my Song; You have become my Salvation. You are my God, and I will praise You, my father's God, and I will exalt You. In Your unfailing love You will lead the people You have redeemed. In Your strength You will guide them to Your holy dwelling.

You, Sovereign Lord, have given me an instructed tongue to know the word that sustains the weary. You waken me morning by morning, waken my ear to listen like one being taught.

You are my Light and my Salvation—whom shall I fear or dread? You are the Refuge and Stronghold of my life—of whom shall I be afraid? You are a shield for me, my Glory, and the Lifter of my head. With my voice I cry to You, Lord, and You hear and answer me out of Your holy hill. Lord, You sustain me.

Father, when it seems as though I'm facing nothing but difficulties, I see it as an invaluable opportunity to experience the greatest joy that I can! For I know that when my faith is tested, it stirs up power within me to endure all things. And then as my endurance grows even stronger, it will release perfection into every part of my being until there is nothing missing and nothing lacking. I praise You with my whole heart, Lord. Your joy is my strength.

Today, I choose to consider Jesus who endured such opposition from sinful men so that I will not grow weary and lose heart.

Father, Your grace is sufficient, and I will not grow weary in doing good, for at the proper time I will reap a harvest if I do not give up. I am strong in You, Lord, and in Your mighty power. In the name of Jesus I pray, amen.[15]

SCRIPTURE REFERENCES

Psalm 119:28 NIV • Psalm 27:1 AMPC • Matthew 11:28-30 NIV
Psalm 3:3-4 AMPC • 1 Chronicles 16:11 NIV • James 1:2-4 TPT
Psalm 46:1 NIV • Psalm 9:1 • Psalm 59:9,17 TPT • Nehemiah 8:10
Isaiah 40:29-31 MSG • Hebrews 12:3 NIV • Psalm 27:14 NIV
2 Corinthians 12:9 • Exodus 15:2,13 NIV • Galatians 6:9 NIV
Isaiah 50:4 NIV • Ephesians 6:10 NIV

15 For additional strength and guidance, I suggest reading and meditating on the following passages: Psalm 6, Psalm 18, Psalm 27, Psalm 28, Psalm 38, and Psalm 71.

PRAYERS
for Children

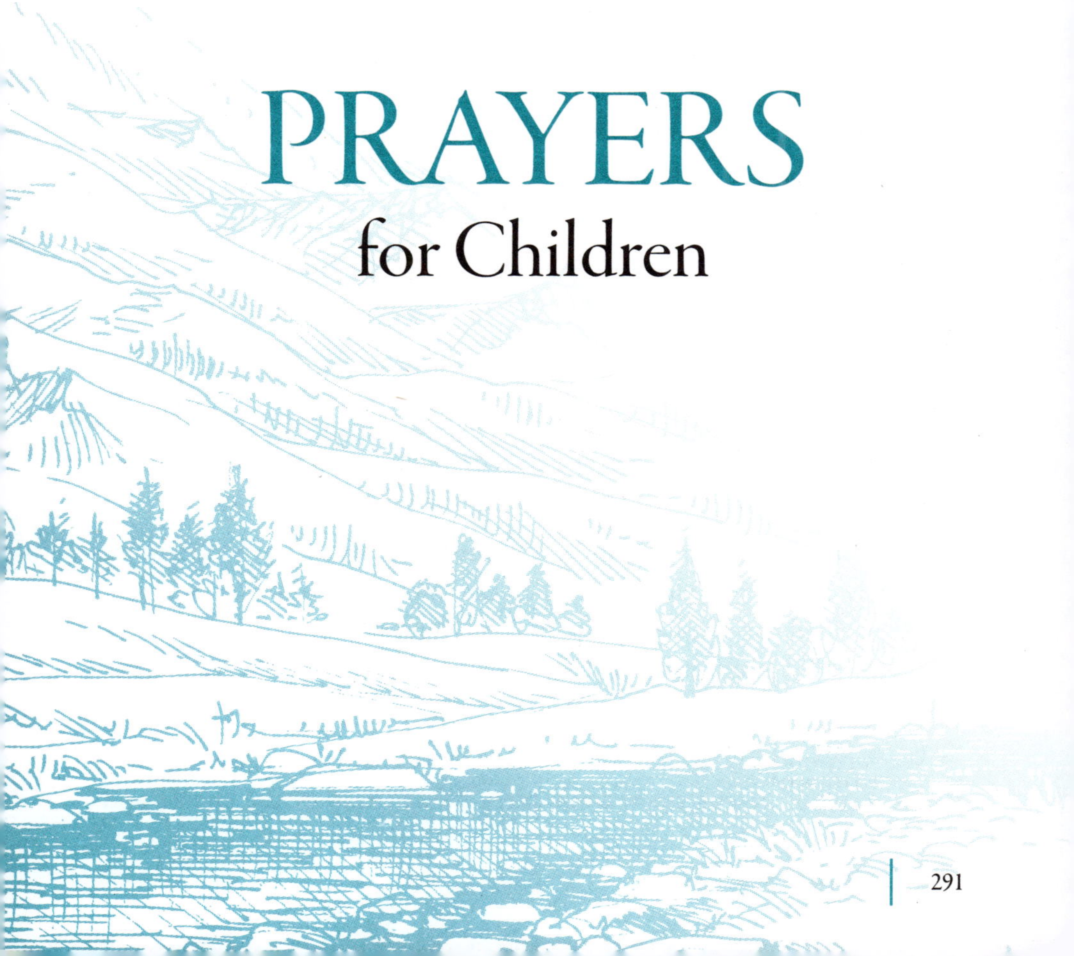

100

A Prayer for Your Children

FATHER, we come before You to repair the wall and stand in the gap on behalf of our children. We love You and desire to assume the responsibility of teaching them sound biblical doctrine. Day by day, we choose to instruct our children to keep the "way of the Lord" by doing what is right and just. Create in the heart of each child the desire to listen and learn, to pay attention so they may gain discernment. Together, as we memorize Your precepts, You will write them on our hearts to keep us from committing sin's treason against You.

Holy Spirit, I ask You to give me creative ways for our family devotions. Help me teach my children the meaning of true repentance leading to salvation. We are here to take our children by the hand in wisdom's way, pointing them to the path of integrity. You are faithful, and we pray their progress will have no limits when they walk in paths of righteousness. We ask You to give them the courage to receive correction no matter how hard it is to swallow, for wisdom will snap them back into place.

Our children are like arrows in the hand of a warrior. When they are older, may each one be victorious when they face those who oppose them. I pray they will have influence and honor to prevail on our behalf and for Your glory! No greater joy do I have than hearing that my children are living according to the truth.

We surround our children with faith in You and the power of Your Word. You will rescue them from every hidden trap of the enemy and protect them from false accusations and any deadly curse. Your massive arms are wrapped around them, protecting them wherever they may be. Wherever they go, Your hand will guide them; Your strength will empower them. It is impossible for them to disappear from You or to ask the darkness to hide them, for Your presence is everywhere, bringing light into their night.

Lord, Your name is so great and powerful! People everywhere see Your splendor. Your glorious majesty streams from the heavens, filling the earth with the fame of Your name! You have built a stronghold by the songs of babies. Strength rises up with the chorus of singing children. This kind of praise has the power to shut Satan's mouth. Child-like worship will silence the madness of those who oppose You. We are in awe of Your majesty! We are in awe of such great power and might!

The enemy is turned back from my children in the name of Jesus! They increase in wisdom and in favor with God and man. In Jesus' name, amen.

SCRIPTURE REFERENCES

Ezekiel 22:30 • Proverbs 4:1-15 TPT • Genesis 18:19 • Psalm 119:11 TPT
Psalm 127:4-5 TPT • 3 John 4 • Psalm 91:3-4 TPT • Psalm 139:10-11 TPT
Psalm 8:1-1-2 TPT • Psalm 29:2 TPT

101

Dealing with a Child with ADD/ADHD

Introduction

In these last days, Satan is working harder than ever to destroy our children. One of the areas of his attack is what psychologists and educators call Attention Deficit Disorder/Attention Deficit Hyperactivity Disorder. These disorders are tools of the enemy to disrupt households—causing confusion, frustration, division, and every evil work. Their effects are far reaching.

Children and adults with ADD/ADHD are thought of as bullies, unruly, destructive, overbearing, impulsive, defiant—and the list goes on. It has been estimated that about two to five percent of school-aged children are now diagnosed with the disorder, and many adults who have it have never been diagnosed. Many who might be helped if properly diagnosed are in mental institutions, jails, and prisons.[16]

Although working with children diagnosed with ADD/ADHD can sometimes be frustrating and discouraging, as believers we know that God's Word, prayer, understanding caretakers, Christian counseling, medication, and their peers can all help them become overcomers.

16 For additional information on ADD/ADHD, including instructional practices for use in dealing with this disorder, see "101 Ways To Help Children with ADD Learn, Tips from Successful Teachers," published by Division of Innovation and Development, Office of Special Education Programs, Office of Special Education and Rehabilitative Services, U.S. Department of Education.

In our ministry to these special children, we must remember that, according to 2 Corinthians 10:4, "the weapons of our warfare are not carnal, but mighty through God to the pulling down of strong holds." Psalm 107:20 says of the Lord's intervention on behalf of those in need, "He sends forth His word and heals them and rescues them from the pit and destruction" (AMPC). Prayer, according to the Word of God, will avail much (see James 5:16).

Declare and decree victory for the child as you teach and direct him/her through the following prayers.

The first two were written by a grandmother, one of our associates at Word Ministries, whose grandson has been diagnosed with ADD/ADHD. They pray together each morning before he leaves for school.

The third prayer and the following series of daily prayers were based on conversations and prayer times that I have had with this young man. He and I have cried and laughed together in my office, where we talk privately and confidentially.

At times, he asks to sit in a class where I am teaching, and later we discuss the subject matter. For instance, we may talk about abandonment issues and how Jesus felt when He was on the cross. He is not shy about asking for prayer when he is having a problem.

If you use any of these prayers, I encourage you when necessary to explain in simple language the meaning of the terms found in them. Remember, the child's imagination is creating pictures with the words he or she speaks and hears.

As the child prays, listen carefully, allowing him/her to express his/her feelings, fears, thoughts, and ideas. Ask the Holy Spirit for discernment—it can be difficult to separate seriousness from horseplay. If you give the child time, he/she will let you know the difference.

I. Coming Against ADD/ADHD

Father, in the name of Jesus, I come against ADD/ADHD and say that I have the mind of Christ the Messiah and hold the thoughts, feelings, and purposes of His heart; I am able to concentrate and stay focused on each task.

I am a disciple (taught by You, Lord, and obedient to Your will), and great is my peace and undisturbed composure. I do not have a spirit of fear, but You have given me a spirit of power and of love and of a calm, well-balanced mind and discipline and self-control.

In the name of Jesus, I come against my defiant behavior and tantrums and hyperactivity and speak peace and love to the situations in which I find myself. I cast down imaginations and every high thing that would exalt itself against the knowledge of You, Lord, and bring into captivity every thought to the obedience of Christ.

Father, I ask for Your wisdom to reside in me each day as I learn new techniques for handling stressful incidents.

Father, Your Word says not to worry about anything but to pray and ask You for everything I need and to give thanks when I pray, and Your peace will keep my heart and mind in Christ Jesus. The peace You give me is so great that I cannot understand it.

Thank You for keeping my mind quiet and at peace. I declare that I am an overcomer; I am in control. In the name of Jesus, amen.

SCRIPTURE REFERENCES

1 Corinthians 2:16 AMPC • Philippians 4:6-7 ICB • Isaiah 54:13 AMPC
Isaiah 26:3 • 2 Timothy 1:7 AMPC • Revelation 12:11 • 2 Corinthians 10:5

II. Making New Friends

Father, I am asking You to supply me with good friends I can relate to, spend time with, and enjoy as You intended. I desire to develop relationships that will be lasting and helpful to both me and my friends.

Father, I will be sound-minded, self-restrained, and alert. Above all things, I purpose to have intense and unfailing love for others, for I know love covers a multitude of sins and forgives and disregards the offenses of others.

I ask You to help me manage my behavior and attitude so others will want to be around me. I purpose to bridle my tongue and speak words of kindness. I will not insist on having my own way, and I will not act unbecomingly. When someone is unkind and falsely accuses me, help me to maintain a cool spirit and be slow to anger. I commit to plant seeds of love, and I thank You for preparing hearts ahead of time to receive me as a friend and as a blessing to their lives.

Father, thank You for causing me to find favor, compassion, and loving-kindness with others.

Thank You, Lord, for my new friends. In Jesus' name, amen.

SCRIPTURE REFERENCES

1 Peter 4:7-8 AMPC • James 1:19 AMPC • Proverbs 21:23
1 Corinthians 3:6 • 1 Corinthians 13:4-5 • Daniel 1:9 AMPC
Proverbs 18:24 AMPC

III. Having a Bad Day

Father, this was not a good day. My scores were low. It was a hard day for me at school and at home. I feel that I messed up a lot. Because I know that You love me unconditionally and You are not holding anything against me, I come to talk with You.

Father, You expect me to be accountable to You, my teachers, and my parents for my behavior.[17] I ask Your forgiveness for acting mean and disrespectful to _______________. I acknowledge my misbehavior, and I ask You to forgive me for _______________.

Thank You, Lord, for helping me as I learn good social skills and how to do unto others as I want them to do unto me.

Father, I release my disappointment to You, and I believe that tomorrow will be a great day! I look forward to the new day with its new beginnings. In the name of Jesus, amen.

17 Note to parent: Effective reprimands should be brief and directed at the child's behavior, not at the character of the child. Direct him/her in assuming responsibility for his/her actions, acknowledging and asking forgiveness when appropriate.

SCRIPTURE REFERENCES

Romans 8:33-39 NIV • Matthew 15:4 NIV • 2 Corinthians 5:18 TLB
1 John 1:9 TLB • Matthew 12:36 NIV • Luke 6:31 NIV
Romans 13:1-5 NIV • Proverbs 4:18

IV. Living Each Day

Monday:

Father, in the name of Jesus, I thank You for giving me life. You picked me out for Your very own even before the foundation of the world—before I was ever born. You saw me while I was being formed in my mother's womb, and You know all about ADD/ADHD.

Lord, You see the weird things I do, and You know all my weird thoughts even before I think them. Thank You for loving me and helping me replace bad thoughts with good thoughts.

Help my parents, teachers—and, especially, the bus driver—to help me do right things. Help me to be kind to others. In the name of Jesus, amen.

SCRIPTURE REFERENCES

Ephesians 1:4 AMPC • Psalm 139:2 TLB • Psalm 139:13-16 TLB
Ephesians 4:32 TLB

Tuesday:

Father, Psalm 91 says that You have assigned angels to me—guarding me wherever I go.

Lord, I need Your help. Sometimes my weird thoughts scare me, and I don't like the way I behave. I become so frightened and confused that I have to do something—run, make noises, even scream or try to hurt someone. These actions separate me from playmates, and when they don't want to be my friends, I am hurt, disappointed, and angry.

I am asking You, Father, to help me form new behavior patterns and successfully overcome the disobedience and defiance that cause my parents and teachers anguish. I don't like to see them all upset, even though I laugh about it sometimes.

Thank You for helping me overcome obsessive, compulsive actions that create confusion for me and others around me. Even when others don't want me around, You will never abandon me. You will always be with me to help me and give me support. In the name of Jesus, amen.

SCRIPTURE REFERENCES

Psalm 91:11 MSG • Psalm 27:10 TLB • Romans 7:21-25 TLB
Hebrews 13:5 AMPC

Wednesday:

Father, thank You for my parents, grandparents, wise counselors, and teachers who understand me and are helping me learn good behavior patterns. Help me to listen and develop good relationships with others—especially other children.

Thank You for giving me the ability to learn how to express my anger appropriately; I rejoice every time I have a victory. Your Son, Jesus, said that He has given me power to overcome all the obstacles that ADD/ADHD causes in my life. In Jesus' name I pray, amen.

SCRIPTURE REFERENCES

Ephesians 4:26 TLB • Luke 10:19 NIV

Thursday:

Father, Your Son, Jesus, is my Lord and Master, and He lives in my heart. Thank You for giving me the mind of Christ the Messiah, His thoughts, feelings, and purposes.

Lord, You are with me when my thoughts get jumbled up, and You have sent the Holy Spirit to help me concentrate and stay focused on each task at home and at school. I am a disciple taught by You, Lord, and obedient to Your will, and great is my peace and undisturbed composure. Thank You for giving me Your helmet of salvation to protect my thought life. In the name of Jesus, amen.

SCRIPTURE REFERENCES

Romans 10:9-10 NIV • Isaiah 54:13 AMPC • 1 Corinthians 2:16 AMPC
1 Thessalonians 5:8 NIV • John 16:13 NIV

Friday:

Father, You have not given me a spirit of fear, but You have given me a spirit of power and of love and a calm, well-balanced mind and discipline and self-control. Thank You that as I grow in the grace and knowledge of Jesus Christ, You are creating in me a willing heart to be obedient.

Forgive me for throwing tantrums and help me recognize and control the destructive ideas that cause them. The Holy Spirit is my Helper. Thank You for giving me the ability to channel hyperactivity in constructive, productive ways.

I choose to speak peace and love into the situations that confront me and make me feel uncomfortable and out of control. In the name of Jesus, amen.

SCRIPTURE REFERENCES

2 Timothy 1:7 AMPC • Philippians 2:13 • 2 Peter 3:18
John 14:16 AMPC • Exodus 35:5

Saturday:

Father, sometimes awful thoughts come to me, and I command the voices that tell me bad things to be quiet and leave me in the name of Jesus.

Lord, in Your Word You said that I can make choices. I choose to cast down imaginations that cause me to feel afraid and angry; these thoughts are not Your thoughts. You love me, and I will think on good things.

Father, I ask for Your wisdom to reside in me each day as I learn new techniques for handling stressful incidents. In the name of Jesus, amen.

SCRIPTURE REFERENCES

Deuteronomy 30:19-20 TLB • Isaiah 55:8 TLB
2 Corinthians 10:5 • Philippians 4:8 TLB

Sunday:

Father, there are so many everyday things that worry and torment me. I feel so different from other people.

Lord, Your Word says not to worry about anything but to pray and ask You for everything I need and to give thanks when I pray, and Your peace will keep my heart and mind in Christ Jesus. The peace You give me is so great that I cannot understand it.

Thank You for keeping my mind quiet and at peace. I declare that I am an overcomer, and by submitting to Your control, I am learning self-control.

Father, thank You for teaching me how to be a good friend to those You are sending to be my friends. In the name of Jesus, amen.

SCRIPTURE REFERENCES

Philippians 4:6-7 ICB • Revelation 12:11 • Isaiah 26:3 AMPC
Galatians 5:23 AMPC

Prayer to Be Prayed by the Caregiver

Introduction

Caregivers of ADD/ADHD children often find themselves in situations that far exceed their parenting skills.

Much prayer and faith are required to see the ADD/ADHD child as God sees him/her. The emotional turmoil and disruption to the household often become overwhelming, and caregivers sometimes discover that the challenges are greater than themselves.

Responsible adults involved in the life of an ADD/ADHD child need godly wisdom, spiritual discernment, and mental and emotional alertness to overcome weariness, bewilderment, and anxiety. Often, they second-guess themselves, processing confusing emotions and scenes of great conflict. Words spoken to the child and over him/her can comfort, giving him/her hope—or they can reinforce his/her belief that he/she is bad and that something terrible is wrong with him/her. Words can heal or words can wound.

The prayers of the ADD/ADHD child must be reinforced by those who love him/her. Often our image of another individual—even our children—can only be changed as we pray according to God's will and purpose for him/her. The following personal prayer for the caregiver is a composite of things the Holy Spirit has directed me to pray for my friend and associate and her husband who are raising their ADD/ADHD grandson. I have observed in them the heartache, the delight, the exasperation—the full gamut of emotions involved in this challenging experience. But through it all, God is faithful!

Prayer

Father, in the name of Jesus, I thank You for this very special child. You see my confusion, anxiety, frustration, and bewilderment as I attempt to rear ______________ tenderly in the training and discipline and counsel and admonition of the Lord. Forgive me for times when I knowingly or unknowingly irritate and provoke him/her to anger, exasperating him/her to resentment.

You see my intense pain when I observe the rejection this child suffers by adults who speak harsh words against him/her and our family. Children refuse to play with him/her, and it hurts even though I understand. I know that those who have never walked in our shoes cannot fully understand us.

But, Lord, where others are unmerciful and unkind, You are merciful and kind. Surely, goodness and mercy shall follow us all the days of our lives, and we shall dwell in Your house forever. What a stack of blessing You have piled up for those of us who worship You! You are ready and waiting for us to run to You to escape an unkind world. You hide us safely away from the opposition.

Lord, perfect the fruit of my lips that I may offer to You effective praise and thanksgiving for this child who is a blessing from You. His/her intellect astounds me, and his/her wit is a delight. I ask You for divine intervention and guidance as I train him/her up in the way that he/she should go. I thank You for the awesomeness of Your handiwork and the techniques that You have given him/her to survive—to overcome emotional turmoil—and the ability to function in this world around us. Truly, this child is fearfully and wonderfully made. I plead the blood of Jesus over him/her to protect him/her in every situation.

You have a divine purpose for this child. You have foreordained steps that he/she is to walk in, works that he/she is to do. Help me to look at his/her strengths and weaknesses realistically, that I may know how to help him/her develop and demonstrate self-control techniques. Forgive me for times when I lose patience and berate him/her for his/her behavior. Sometimes, I lose sight of who he/she really is. Anoint my eyes to see him/her as You see him/her.

Father, help me to speak works of grace; anoint my lips to speak excellent and princely things over him/her, about him/her, and to him/her. Help me to give him/her healthy doses of unconditional love, administer to him/her appropriate discipline for misbehavior, and reward him/her for his/her good behavior. Anoint my lips with coals of fire from Your altar that I may speak words that comfort, encourage, strengthen, and honor him/her. Keep watch at the door of my lips and forgive me when my patience has come to an end.

Father, You are my Comforter, Counselor, Helper, Intercessor, Advocate, Strengthener, and Standby. Whatever comes my way, help me to consider it wholly joyful, allowing endurance and steadfastness and patience to have full play and do a thorough work, so that I may be perfectly and fully developed, with no defects, lacking in nothing. When I am deficient in wisdom, I will ask of You, and You will give wisdom to me liberally and ungrudgingly, without reproaching or finding fault in me.

I pray that I may be invigorated and strengthened with all power according to the might of Your glory, to exercise every kind of endurance and patience (perseverance and forbearance) with joy.

Father, You have seen the tears in the night season, and I know that I shall experience the joy that comes in the morning times. You are my Exceeding Joy! You are my Wisdom, Righteousness, Sanctification, and Redemption. Thank You for being a constant companion.

Lord, I see my child, ____________, growing and becoming strong in spirit, increasing in wisdom, in broad and full understanding, and in stature and years and in favor with You and with man. In the name of Jesus, I pray. Amen.

SCRIPTURE REFERENCES

Ephesians 6:4 AMPC • Isaiah 6:6-7 • Psalm 117:2
Psalm 141:3 AMPC • Psalm 23:6 • John 14:16 AMPC
Psalm 31:19-24 MSG • James 1:2,4-5 AMPC • Hebrews 13:15
Colossians 1:11 AMPC • Psalm 127:3 AMPC • Psalm 22:2
Proverbs 22:6 • Psalm 30:5 • Psalm 139:14 • Psalm 43:4 • Ephesians 2:10
1 Corinthians 1:30 • Proverbs 8:6 AMPC • Luke 1:80; 2:52 AMPC

Daily Affirmations for Use by the Caregiver

Introduction

Often it is very difficult for ADD/ADHD children to learn, to develop new learning techniques in their lives, and to change their negative behavior patterns. When working with them, it is so important that we love them with the God-kind of love and praise them for their accomplishments.

Following are examples of the kinds of positive daily affirmations that can be said to the ADD/ADHD child to help him/her develop a good self-image and to become all that God intends for him/her in this life.

Affirmations

Great job • Well done • I'm very proud of you • Good for you • Neat • Outstanding • That was a smart decision • You are smart • God loves you • I love you • I knew you could do it • I believe in you • I know you are trying • Super-duper • You are a good boy/girl • Way to go • What an imagination • You are growing up • Good memory • Amazing • Nice work • What a wise choice • You are a blessing to me • You are special to me • You are valuable • You are a gem, a precious jewel • You are more precious than gold • You are incredible • You are important • Outstanding performance • You are a winner • Remarkable • Nothing can stop you • Now you've got it • Excellent • You are catching on great • Wonderful • Good • Terrific • Beautiful • Now you are cooking • You are fantastic • Beautiful work • Outstanding • You are spectacular • You are a real trooper • You are unique • Great discovery • You try so hard • Good try • Good effort • Magnificent • You've got it • Super work • Phenomenal • Marvelous • Dynamite • You mean so much to me • You make me laugh • You brighten my day • Hurray for you • You are beautiful • You are handsome • You are a good friend • You are a loving son/daughter [grandson/granddaughter] • You light up my life • You belong • You are an important part of our family • We are family • You mean the world to me • That's right • You are correct • You are a success • Hurray • You are growing in wisdom every day • You are a beautiful creation • You are loved • I love you • Wow! • You are a success • You are an overcomer • You are a child of my love • You are victorious • You are a ray of sunshine • You are patient • You have a good attitude • You are a doer • You know how to get the job done • You are a chosen one • You give good hugs • Thank you for being a part of my life

You are deserving of praise!

Scripture Passages for Meditation

- A good report: Proverbs 15:30; Philippians 4:8
- A soft answer: Proverbs 15:1
- Perfect love: 1 John 4:18

102

Children at School

FATHER, in Jesus' name, I confess Your Word this day concerning my children as they pursue their education and training at school. You are effectually at work in them, creating within them the power and desire to please You. They are the head and not the tail, above and not beneath.

I pray that my children will find favor, good understanding, and high esteem in the sight of God and their teachers and classmates. I ask You to give my children wisdom and understanding as knowledge is presented to them in all fields of study and endeavor.

Father, thank You for giving my children an appreciation for education and helping them to understand that the Source and beginning of all knowledge is You. They have the appetite of the diligent, and they are abundantly supplied with educational resources; their thoughts are those of the steadily diligent, which tend only to achievement. Thank You that they are growing in wisdom and knowledge. I will not cease to pray for them, asking that they be filled with the knowledge of Your will, bearing fruit in every good work.

Father, I thank You that my children have divine protection because they dwell in the secret place of the Most High. My children trust and find their refuge in You and stand rooted and grounded in Your love. They shall not be led astray by philosophies of men and teaching that is contrary to truth. You are their Shield and Buckler, protecting them from attacks or threats. Thank You for the angels whom You have assigned to them to accompany, defend, and preserve them in all their ways of obedience and service. My children are established in Your love, which drives all fear out of doors.

I pray that the teachers of my children will be godly men and women of integrity. Give our teachers understanding hearts and wisdom in order that they may walk in the ways of piety and virtue, revering Your holy name. Amen.

SCRIPTURE REFERENCES

Philippians 2:13 • Psalm 91:1-2 • Deuteronomy 28:1-2,13
Ephesians 4:14 • Proverbs 3:4 AMPC • Psalm 91:3-11 • 1 Kings 4:29
Ephesians 1:17 • Daniel 1:4 • Psalm 112:8 • Proverbs 1:4,7
Ephesians 3:17 • Proverbs 3:13 • Matthew 18:18 • Proverbs 4:5
James 1:5 • Colossians 1:9-10

103

Praying for Your Child's Future

Note: The personal pronoun *we* may be changed to *I* when appropriate. The Holy Spirit may lead you to pray every word—or—He may add to this prayer. Sometimes, He will impress you to pause and meditate after one sentence or paragraph. Always, remember the Holy Spirit helps you pray!

FATHER, Your Word declares that children are an inheritance from You and promises peace when they are taught in Your ways. We dedicate ______________ to You today, that he/she may be raised as You would desire and will follow the path You would choose. As we pray Your Word, it goes out and will not return unto You void but will accomplish what it says it will do.

Heavenly Father, as parents we choose to train ___________ in the way he/she should go, trusting in the promise that he/she will not depart from Your ways but will grow and prosper in them. We choose to parent according to Your Word, turning the care and burden of raising him/her over to You. Father, we stand together and ask You to help us during trying experiences to raise them up with loving discipline and counsel that will bring the revelation of Jesus our Lord before them. We pray that we will not exasperate _________. We choose to teach our children to do all to the glory of God. Your grace is sufficient to overcome my mistakes as a parent.

I ask You to create within the heart of my child, ___________, a desire to be obedient and honor both his/her parents, being able to accept the abundant promises of Your Word of long life and prosperity. You have not given him/her a spirit of fear, but of power, of love, and a sound mind. I pray that __________ will choose to walk in pathways of righteousness, unafraid to honor and keep Your Word. May our children keep trusting You and do what is right in Your eyes and fix their hearts on Your promises so they will be secure, feasting on Your faithfulness.

We surround them with faith in You and Your Word praying they will always stand convinced that You are the Almighty God. I am thankful that as __________ grows, he/she will remember You and not pass by the opportunity of a relationship with Your Son, Jesus. Your great blessings will be upon __________ for keeping Your ways. I thank You for Your blessings over every area of __________'s life, that You will see to the salvation and obedience of his/her life to Your ways.

Heavenly Father, we thank You now that laborers will be sent into __________'s path, preparing the way for salvation, as it is written in Your Word, through Your Son, Jesus. We are thankful that __________ will recognize the traps of the devil and will be delivered to salvation through the purity of Your Son. With hearts of thanksgiving, we believe that our children have become Your poetry, re-created in Christ Jesus to fulfill their destiny that You have given to each one. Even before ______ was born You created and planned in advance for their destiny and the good works they will do to fulfill it!

We pray that just as Jesus increased in wisdom and stature, You would bless _______ with the same wisdom and pour out Your favor and wisdom openly to him/her.

We praise You in advance for ____________'s future spouse. Father, Your Word declares that you desire for children to be pure and honorable, waiting upon marriage. We speak blessings to the future union and believe that ____________ will be well-suited to his/her partner and their household will be in godly order, holding fast to the love of Jesus Christ. Continue to prepare ____________ to be the man/woman of God that You desire him/her to be.

We ask You to grant the grace to ____________ to be diligent and hardworking, never being lazy or undisciplined. Your Word promises great blessing to his/her house, and he/she shall always be satisfied and will always increase. Godliness is profitable unto his/her house, and __________ shall receive the promise of life and all that is to come.

Father, thank You for protecting and guiding my child. In Jesus' name I pray, amen.

SCRIPTURE REFERENCES

Psalm 127:3 • Matthew 7:14 • Isaiah 54:13 • Luke 2:52
Isaiah 55:11 • Hebrews 13:4 • Proverbs 22:6 • 1 Thessalonians 4:3
1 Peter 5:7 • Ephesians 5:22-25 • Ephesians 6:4 • 2 Timothy 1:13
Deuteronomy 6:7 • Proverbs 13:11 • 2 Corinthians 12:9
Proverbs 20:13 • Ephesians 6:1-3 • Romans 12:11 • 2 Timothy 1:12
1 Timothy 4:8 • Proverbs 8:17,32 • 1 John 3:8 • Luke 19:10
John 10:10 • Matthew 9:38 • Psalm 37:3 TPT • Ephesians 2:10 TPT
Matthew 18:18 • 2 Corinthians 2:11 • John 14:13 • 2 Timothy 2:26
Psalm 91:1,11 • Job 22:30

104

Praying for Your Teenager

FATHER, in the name of Jesus, I affirm Your Word over my son/daughter. I commit ______________ to You and delight myself also in You. I thank You that You deliver ______________ out of rebellion into right relationship with us, his/her parents.

Father, the first commandment with a promise is to the child who obeys his/her parents in the Lord. You said that all will be well with him/her and he/she will live long on the earth. I affirm this promise on behalf of my child, asking You to give ___________ an obedient spirit that he/she may honor, esteem, and value as precious his/her father and mother.

Father, forgive me for mistakes made out of my own unresolved hurts or selfishness, which may have caused __________ hurt. I release the anointing that is upon Jesus to bind up and heal our broken hearts (both parents' and child's). Give us the ability to understand and forgive one another, as God for Christ's sake has forgiven us. Thank You for the Holy Spirit who leads us into all truth and corrects erroneous perceptions about past or present situations.

Thank You for teaching us to listen to each other and giving ___________ an ear that hears admonition, for then he/she will be called wise. I affirm that I will speak excellent and princely things, and the opening of my lips shall be for right things. Father, I commit to train and teach ______________ in the way that he/she is to go, and when ____________ is old, he/she will not depart from sound doctrine and teaching but will follow it all the days of his/her life. In the name of Jesus, I command rebellion to be far from the heart of my child and confess that he/she is willing and obedient, free to enjoy the reward of Your promises. ____________ shall be peaceful, bringing peace to others.

Father, according to Your Word, we have been given the ministry of reconciliation, and I release this ministry and the word of reconciliation into this family situation. I refuse to provoke or irritate or fret my child; I will not be hard on him/her lest he/she becomes discouraged, feeling inferior and frustrated. I will not break his/her spirit, in the name of Jesus and by the power of the Holy Spirit. Father, I forgive my child for the wrongs he/she has done and stand in the gap until he/she comes to his/her senses and escapes out of the snare of the enemy (rebellion). Thank You for watching over Your Word to perform it, turning and reconciling the heart of the rebellious child to the parents and the hearts of the parents to the child. Thank You for bringing my child back into a healthy relationship with You and with me, that our lives might glorify You! Amen.

SCRIPTURE REFERENCES

Psalm 55:12-14 • Proverbs 8:6-7 • 1 Peter 5:7 • Proverbs 22:6
Psalm 37:4 • Isaiah 1:19 • John 14:6 • Isaiah 54:13 • Ephesians 6:1-3
2 Corinthians 5:18-19 • 1 John 1:9 • Colossians 3:21 • Isaiah 61:1
John 20:23 • John 16:13 • Ezekiel 22:30 • Proverbs 15:31
Jeremiah 1:12 • Proverbs 13:1 • Malachi 4:6

PART II

Group Prayers

An INTERCESSORY Prayer Group

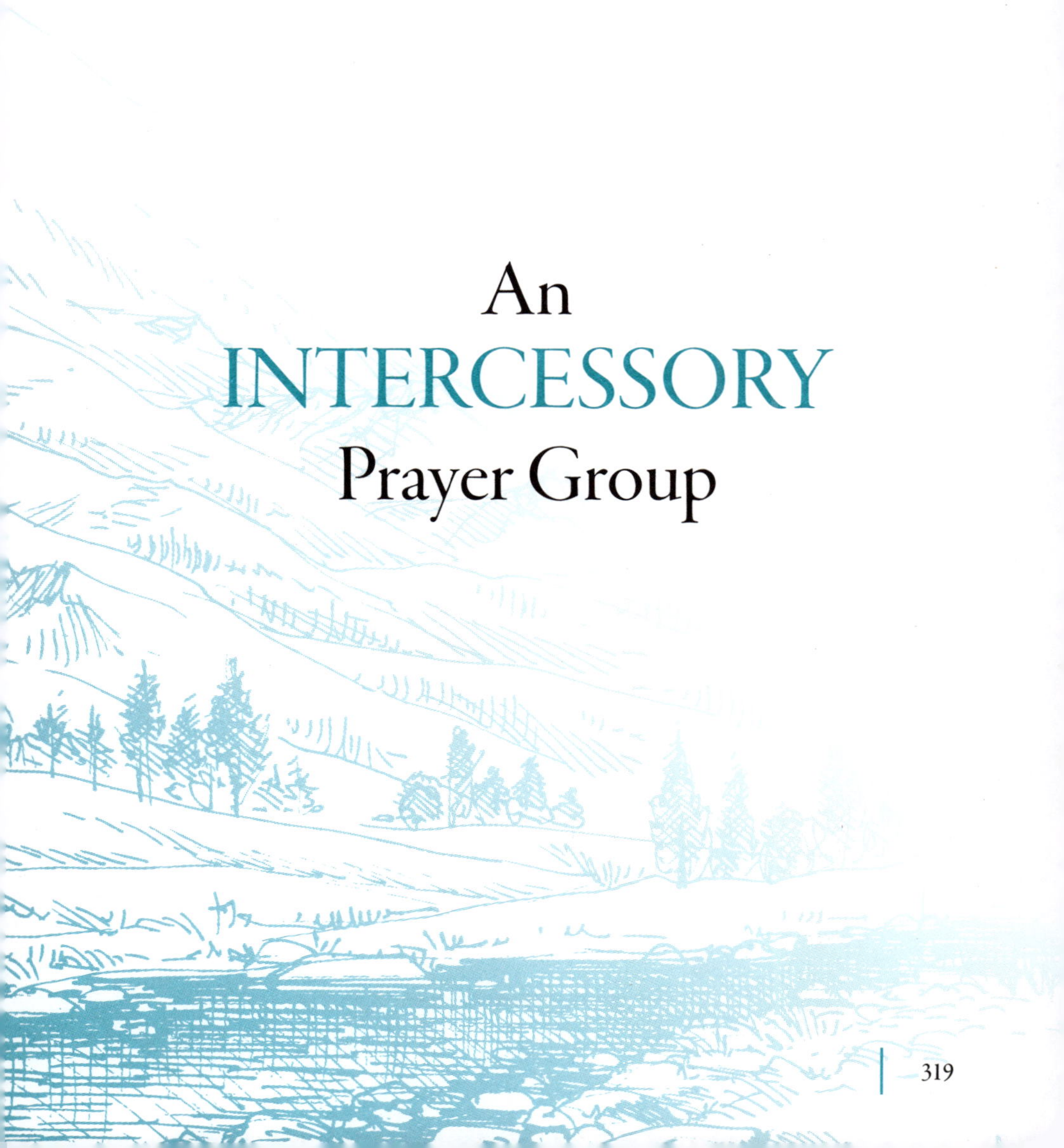

105

Individual Growth

FATHER, in the name of Jesus, we in our prayer group desire that our prayers avail much. We've been mingled into one body in Christ, which means we are vitally joined to one another—each contributing to the others. We can all draw close to Him with the veil removed from our faces so that we become like mirrors who brightly reflect the glory of the Lord Jesus. We are being transfigured into His very image as we move from one brighter level of glory to another. This glorious transfiguration comes from the Lord, who is the Spirit.

Father, we realize that You know what we have need of before we ask and that we are not all growing in the same manner or on the same time schedule, but we are growing in the grace and knowledge of our Lord and Savior Jesus Christ.

We give each other space to grow, for we are becoming a patient people, bearing with one another and making allowances because we love one another. We are faithful to guard the sweet harmony of the Holy Spirit among us in the bonds of peace, being one body and one spirit, as we were all called into the same glorious hope of divine destiny. In Jesus' name, amen.

SCRIPTURE REFERENCES

James 5:16 • 2 Peter 3:18 • Romans 12:5-6 TPT • 2 Corinthians 1:24 AMPC
2 Corinthians 3:18 NIV • Ephesians 4:20 • Ephesians 4:3-4 TPT
Matthew 6:32

106

A Group Member Experiencing Grief or Loss

FATHER, in the name of Jesus, we approach Your throne of grace, bringing ________ before You. We recognize that grieving is a human emotional process, and we give him/her the space that he/she needs to enter into the rest that You have for him/her.

Father, Jesus bore _____________'s griefs (sicknesses, weaknesses, and distresses) and carried his/her sorrows and pains; we know that Your Spirit is upon Jesus to bind up and heal ________'s broken heart. May he/she be gentle with himself/herself, knowing that he/she is not alone in his/her grief. You are with him/her, and You will never leave him/her without support.

Give us, ________________'s friends and prayer partners, discernment, sympathy, and understanding so that we may bear (endure, carry) his/her burden of loss. We trust You to guide him/her, and we respect his/her decisions awaiting the manifestation of Your healing.

Father, we desire to be doers of Your Word, and not hearers only. Therefore, we commit to share the happiness of those who are happy and the sorrow of those who are sad and grieve. And we pray that our love impacts _______________ with joy and encouragement.

We also thank You, Father, for sending the Holy Spirit to comfort, counsel, help, intercede, defend, strengthen, and stand by ____________ as only He can in this time of grief and sorrow. In Jesus' name, amen.

SCRIPTURE REFERENCES

Isaiah 53:4 AMPC • James 1:22 • Isaiah 61:1 AMPC • Romans 12:15 TPT
Hebrews 13:5 AMPC • Philemon 7 TPT • Galatians 6:2 AMPC
John 14:26 AMPC

107

Loving and Caring for Self

FATHER, I realize that before I can love others as You have instructed, I must love myself. Help me to speak truly, deal truly, and live truly in harmony with You, myself, and others in my prayer group.

I am Your workmanship, created in Christ Jesus. I am fearfully and wonderfully made. Help me to remember that others do not always know what is best for me. I trust You with all my heart and do not depend on my own understanding. I always let You lead me, knowing that You will show me which path to take and clear the road for me to follow.

I look to You to cause my thoughts to be agreeable to Your will that I may make healthy choices. Give me the courage to say no when it is in my best interest according to Your purpose and plan for my life.

You are my confidence, and You keep my heart at rest in every situation. I walk along Your paths of integrity, and therefore You have said I will never lack one thing I need. You provide it all! You wrap Yourself around me like a shield, and You are brighter than the brilliance of a sunrise.

I take responsibility for myself and allow others in our prayer group to take responsibility for themselves in the name of Jesus. This frees me so that I am not merely concerned with my own interests, but also with the interests of others.

I desire to do unto others as I would have them do unto me. Because Your endless love cascades into my heart through the Holy Spirit, I will love my neighbor as myself. In Jesus' name, amen.

SCRIPTURE REFERENCES

Romans 13:9 • Philippians 2:4 AMPC • Ephesians 4:15 AMPC
Matthew 7:12 • Ephesians 2:10 • Proverbs 21:29 AMPC
Psalm 139:14 • Proverbs 3:26 • Proverbs 3:5-6 CEV
Romans 5:5 TPT • Proverbs 16:3 AMPC • Psalm 84:11 TPT • Matthew 22:39

108

Perseverance in Prayer

FATHER, the course that You have set before me is clear. You have called me into this prayer group to respond to the many prayer requests we receive from those who need agreement or who don't know how to pray for themselves.

Lord, You are the Vinedresser, Jesus is the Vine, and I am the branch. I remain in You, and You remain in me, and my prayers bear much fruit. Apart from You, I can do nothing.

Father, at times I am tempted to grow weary and overburdened with the pain and heartache of others. Help me to remember that Jesus said, "Come to me, all you who are weary and burdened, and I will give you rest" (Matt. 11:28 NIV). I take His yoke upon me and learn from Him, for He is gentle and humble in heart, and I will find rest for my soul. His yoke is easy, and His burden is light.

Lord, Jesus said that I ought always to pray and not to turn coward, faint, lose heart, or give up. I am earnest and unwearied and steadfast in my prayer life, being alert and intent in my praying with thanksgiving.

Therefore, because I am surrounded by such a great cloud of witnesses, I throw off everything that hinders and the sin that so easily entangles, and I run with perseverance the race marked out for me. I fix my eyes on Jesus, the Author and Perfecter of my faith. For the joy set before, Jesus endured the cross, scorning its shame, and sat down at the right hand of Your throne. I consider Him who endured such opposition from sinful men, so that I will not grow weary and lose heart during times of intercession. In His name I pray, amen.

SCRIPTURE REFERENCES

John 15:1-7 AMPC • Colossians 4:2 AMPC • Matthew 11:29-30 NIV
Hebrews 12:1-3 NIV • Luke 18:1 AMPC

109

Pleasing God Rather Than People

FATHER, I desire to please You rather than people. Forgive me for loving human praise more than the praise of God. It's your stamp of approval I seek.

Fear and intimidation is but a trap that holds me back. I will not fall into the trap, but I will trust the Lord who keeps me safe. I am bold and confident to say, "The Lord is my Helper. Why should I be afraid of what people can do to me?"

Father, just as You sent Jesus into the world, You have sent me. You are ever with me, and I always seek to do what pleases You. In Jesus' name, amen.

SCRIPTURE REFERENCES

John 12:43 NLT • John 17:18 AMPC • Proverbs 29:25 TPT
John 8:29 AMPC • Hebrew 13:6 ESV • Psalm 37:5-6 MSG

~ 110 ~

Communication with Group Members

FATHER, to as many as received Jesus, You gave the power to become Your sons and daughters. I am learning to be straightforward in my communication with my brothers and sisters in Christ, my co-laborers in the Lord. I have the power to be direct, honestly expressing my feelings and desires, because Jesus has been made unto me wisdom. Wisdom from above is straightforward, objective, and free from doubts, wavering, and insincerity.

I am Your creation, Father, and You created me to actively share my faith. In Jesus' name my conversation will always be full of grace, seasoned with salt, so that I may know how to answer everyone. I am content with my own reality—not complaining about having too little but satisfied in any circumstance—so that others are comfortable in my presence. I will speak truly, deal truly, and live truly, expressing the truth in love.

As Your children and co-laborers, we walk in the ever-developing maturity that enables us to be in perfect harmony in what we say, perfectly united in our common understanding and in our opinions. And if on some point we think differently, You will make it clear to us. We live up to what we have already attained in our individual lives and in our group. We will let our yes be simply yes, and our no be simply no. In Jesus' name, amen.

SCRIPTURE REFERENCES

John 1:12 • Philippians 4:11 AMPC • 1 Corinthians 1:30
Ephesians 4:15 AMPC • James 3:17 AMPC • 1 Corinthians 1:10 AMPC
Philemon 6 NIV • Philippians 3:15-17 NIV • Colossians 4:6 NIV
Matthew 5:37 AMPC

GOD'S
People, Ministers, and Ministries

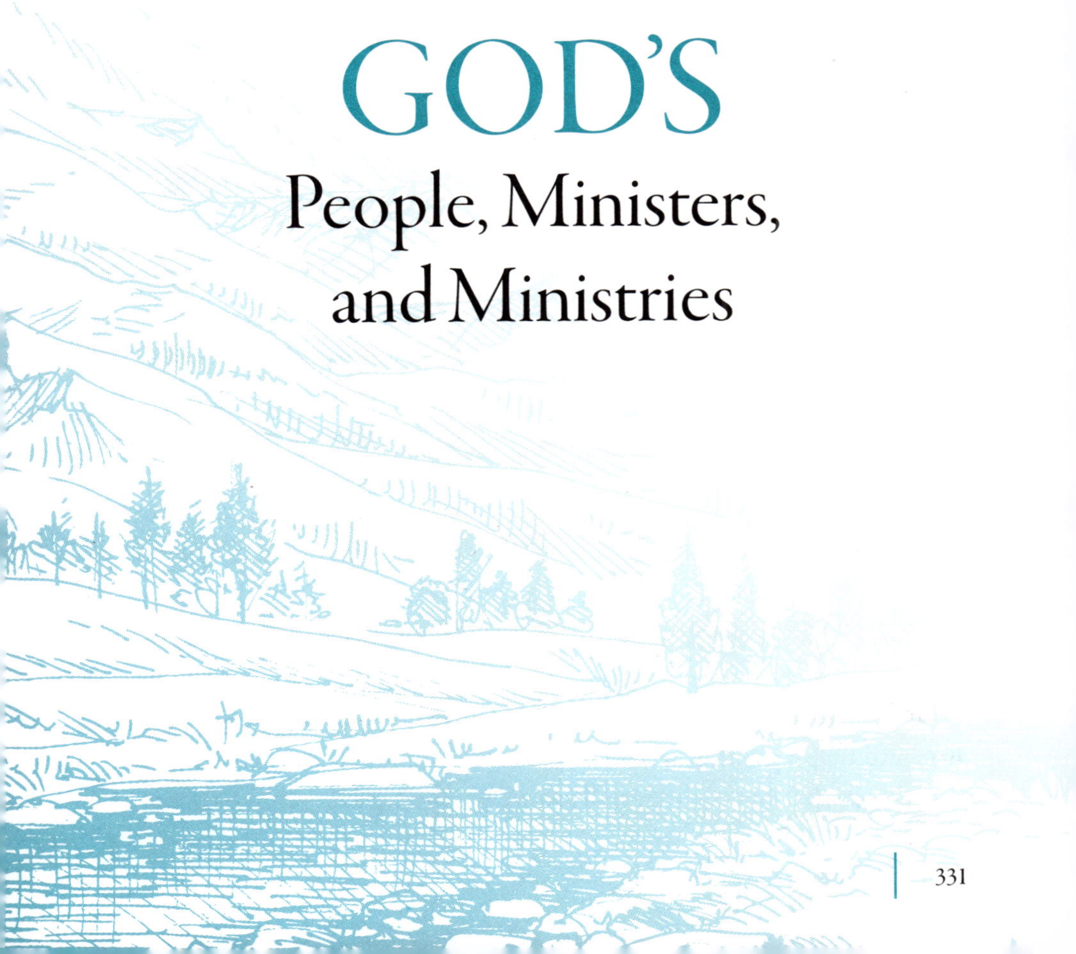

111

The Body of Christ

FATHER, You put all things under the feet of Jesus and gave Him to be head over all things to the Church, which is His Body, the fullness of Him who fills all in all. We were dead in trespasses and sins, but You made us alive! Christ is our Peace, and we are no longer strangers and foreigners, but fellow citizens with the saints and members of the household of God. Jesus is our Cornerstone.

Father, You want us to grow up, to know the whole truth and tell it in love—like Christ in everything. We take our lead from Christ, who is the Source of everything we do. He keeps us in step with each other. His very breath and blood flow through us, nourishing us so that we will grow up healthy in God, robust in love.

May we be filled with the knowledge of Your will in all wisdom and spiritual understanding. As the elect of God, holy and beloved, we put on tender mercies, kindness, humility, meekness, and longsuffering. We bear with one another and forgive one another. If we have a complaint against another, even as Christ forgave us, so we also must forgive. Above all things, we put on love, which is the bond of perfection, and let the peace of God rule in our hearts, to which also we were called in one Body, and we are thankful.

Full of belief, confident that we're presentable inside and out, we keep a firm grip on the promises that keep us going. Father, You always keep Your Word. Now we will see how inventive we can be in encouraging love and helping out, not avoiding worshiping together as some do, but spurring each other on, especially as we see the big Day approaching.

Because we are all called to travel on the same road and in the same direction, we will stay together, both outwardly and inwardly. We have one Master, one faith, one baptism, one God and Father of all, who rules over all, works through all, and is present in all. Everything we are and think and do is permeated with oneness.

Father, we commit to pray for one another, keeping our eyes open and keeping each other's spirits up, so that no one falls behind or drops out. Also, we pray for our spiritual leaders that they will know what to say and have the courage to say it at the right time. We are one in the bond of love, in the name of Jesus.

SCRIPTURE REFERENCES

Ephesians 1:22-23 NKJV • Hebrews 10:23-25 MSG
Ephesians 4:15-16 MSG • Ephesians 4:4-6 MSG
Colossians 3:12-15 NKJV • Ephesians 6:18-19 MSG

112

Unity and Harmony

FATHER, in the name of Jesus, this is the confidence that we have in You—that if we ask anything according to Your will You hear us; and because we know that You hear us, whatsoever we ask, we know that we have the petitions that we desire of You.

Holy Spirit, teach us how to agree (harmonize together and make a symphony) about anything and everything so that whatever we ask will come to pass and be done for us by our Father in heaven.

As a part of the body of Christ, we will live with tender humility and quiet patience, always demonstrating gentleness and generous love toward one another, especially toward those who may try our patience.

This is the goal—to live in harmony with one another and demonstrate affectionate love, sympathy, and kindness toward other believers. Let humility describe who we are as we dearly love one another. We will never repay evil for evil or retaliate with insults when people insult us. Instead, we will pay them back with a blessing. That is what God has called us to do, and He will bless us for doing it.

Father, thank You that Jesus has given to us the glory and honor that You gave Him. I pray that we may all be one, just as You and Jesus are one so that we experience such perfect unity that the world will know that You sent Jesus and that You love them as much as You love Him. Father, I pray Your will is done in earth as it is in heaven. Amen, and so be it.

SCRIPTURE REFERENCES

1 John 5:14-15 • 1 Peter 3:8-9 NLT • 1 Corinthians 1:10 AMPC
John 17:22-23 NLT • Matthew 18:19 AMPC • Matthew 6:10
Ephesians 4:2-3 TPT

113

Vision for a Church

FATHER, in the name of Jesus, we come into Your presence thanking You for __________ (name of church). You have called us to be saints in __________ (name of city) and around the world. As we lift our voices in one accord, we recognize that You are God and everything was made by and for You. We call into being those things that be not as though they were.

We thank You that we all speak the same thing. There is no division among us; we are perfectly joined together in the same mind. Grant unto us, Your representatives here, a boldness to speak Your Word, which You will confirm with signs following. We thank You that we have workmen in abundance. Each department operates in the excellence of ministry and intercessions. We have in our church the ministry gifts for the edifying of this Body till we all come into the unity of faith and knowledge of the Son of God unto a mature person. None of our people will be children, tossed to and fro and carried about with every wind of doctrine. We speak the truth in love.

Father, we thank You for the ministry facilities that will more than meet the needs of the ministry. Thank You for the faithful giving of Your people. We have more than enough to give food and clothing to those in need. We welcome the stranger into our church. We are here to visit the sick and those in jail. No matter how unimportant they may seem, we purpose to do it for You and in Your name.

We acknowledge that all the authority of the universe has been given to Jesus, the Head of the Church. We will go in His authority and make disciples of all nations, baptizing them in the name of the Father, the Son, and the Holy Spirit. We purpose to faithfully follow all that You have commanded us to do, and we thank You for being with us every day, even to the completion of this age.

We have everything we need to carry out Your Great Commission and reach the ___________ (name of city or county) area for Jesus. Thank You for our missionary teams that go into other nations to make disciples. We are a people of love as love is poured out in our hearts by the Holy Spirit. We thank You that the Word of God is living big in all of us, and Jesus is Lord!

We are a supernatural church, composed of supernatural people doing supernatural things, for we are laborers together with God. We thank You for Your presence among us, and we lift our hands and praise Your holy name! Amen.[18]

SCRIPTURE REFERENCES

Acts 4:24 • Ephesians 4:11-15 • Romans 4:17 • Philippians 4:19
1 Corinthians 1:10 • Romans 5:5 • Acts 4:29 • 1 Corinthians 3:9
Mark 16:20 • Psalm 63:4 • Exodus 35:33 • Matthew 25:37-50 CEV
Matthew 28:18-20 TPT

18 Parts of this prayer were written by and used with the permission of T.R. King, Valley Christian Center, Roanoke, Virginia.

— 114 —

A Pastor's Prayer for the Congregation

FATHER, as the pastor of __________, I approach the throne of grace on behalf of the membership. I thank my God in all my remembrance of them. In every prayer of mine, I always make my entreaty and petition for them all with joy and delight. I thank You for their fellowship, cooperation, and partnership in advancing the Good News of the gospel. I am sure of this very thing—You have begun a good work in them and will continue until the day of Jesus Christ's return.

In the name of Jesus, I pray with confidence because my congregation holds a permanent place in my heart as they have partnered with me in Your wonderful grace. Father, You are my witness. You know how I long for and pursue them all with love, in the tender mercies of Christ Jesus Himself!

So, this is my prayer: that their love will flourish and that they will not only love much but love well. They learn to love appropriately, using their heads and testing their feelings so that their love is sincere and intelligent, not sentimental gush. Father, I pray that each one will live a lover's life, circumspect and exemplary. They live a life Jesus will be proud of—bountiful in fruits from the soul, making Jesus Christ attractive to all, and getting everyone involved in the glory and praise of God.

Father, may the membership be filled with the fruits of righteousness—right standing with God and right doing—which come through Jesus

Christ, the Anointed One, to the honor and praise of God—that Your glory may be both manifested and recognized.

I commit myself to You, Father, and to them anew. I shall stay by them to promote their progress and joy in believing, so that in me they may have abundant cause for exultation and glorifying in Christ Jesus. In the name of Jesus, they will be sure as citizens to conduct themselves so that their manner of life will be worthy of the gospel of Christ.

Father, thank You that they are standing united, singular in vision and purpose, striving side by side for the Good News of the gospel. They will never be shaken or intimidated by the opposition that rises up against us. This will be a clear sign to their enemies of their impending destruction but a sure sign to the congregation of salvation, even by God Himself.

The membership of ____________________ makes me truly happy by agreeing wholeheartedly with each other, loving one another, and working together with one mind and purpose. In Jesus' name, amen.

SCRIPTURE REFERENCES

Philippians 1:4-7 AMPC • Philippians 1:25-28 NLT, TPT
Philippians 1:8-11 MSG • Philippians 2:2 NLT

114

Ministers

FATHER, in the name of Jesus, we pray that the Spirit of the Lord will rest upon these ministers of the gospel with wisdom, understanding, counsel, might, and knowledge. We ask You to make them of quick understanding because You, Lord, have anointed and qualified these men and women to preach the Gospel to the meek, the poor, the wealthy, and the afflicted. You have sent them to bind up and heal the brokenhearted, to proclaim liberty to the physical and spiritual captives, and to open the prison and the eyes of those who are bound.

The ministers for whom we are now praying shall be called priests of the Lord. We pray and believe that no weapon formed against those who are called according to Your will shall prosper and any tongue that rises against them in judgment shall be shown to be in the wrong. We pray that they hold fast and follow the pattern of wholesome and sound teaching in all faith and love, which is for us in Christ Jesus. May they at all times guard and keep with the greatest love the precious and excellently adapted truth entrusted to them by the Holy Spirit, who makes His home in their hearts.

Lord, we pray and believe that everyday freedom of utterance is given to these ministers to open their mouths boldly and courageously to get the Gospel to the people. Thank You, Lord, for the added strength, which comes superhumanly, that You have given to them.

According to the grace that we have been given, we shall stand behind and undergird them in prayer. We will say only that good thing that will edify those who minister to us, and if we have questions, we will ask them. We will not judge them, but we will continue to intercede and pray blessings upon them in the name of Jesus. Thank You, Jesus, for the answers. Hallelujah! Amen.

SCRIPTURE REFERENCES

Isaiah 11:2-3 • 2 Timothy 1:13-14 AMPC • Isaiah 61:1,6 AMPC
Ephesians 6:19-20 AMPC • Isaiah 54:17 AMPC • 1 Peter 3:12

— 115 —

Missionaries

FATHER, we lift before You those missionaries in the Body of Christ who are out in the field carrying the good news of the Gospel not only in this country, but also around the world. We lift those in the Body of Christ who are suffering persecution and those who are in prison for their beliefs.

Father, Your grace is always more than enough for all, and Your power finds its full expression through human weakness. When surrounded with troubles on every side and facing persecution because of love for Christ, Your missionaries are made yet stronger.

As these missionaries who have been called according to Your will adapt to a new culture, we pray that with the help of the Holy Spirit, they will constantly chase after the realm of God's kingdom and the righteousness that proceeds from Him. Then all less important things will be given to them abundantly.

You have placed eternity in the hearts of all people everywhere. We pray You will reveal to Your representatives the basic essentials of the Good News of the Gospel that will be understood by the people. Reveal and deliver missionaries from any false religious ideas that would promote pious nitpicking, which chips away at the faith wearing everyone out. We pray they will always concentrate on doing their best for God, always lay out the truth plain and simple. Let every word the missionaries speak be drenched with grace and compassion. May their words be seasoned with salt, friendly, clear, and make people thirsty for truth.

Father, keep these precious missionaries in tune with You. May our brothers and sisters schedule personal retreats where they can rest, have fellowship with others, and pray. Thank You, Lord God, for giving them instruction and the right words to encourage those who are weary. When You awaken them each morning, they will be eager to learn Your teaching and instructions.

Father, we know that You watch over Your Word to perform it. It always produces fruit. Your Word accomplishes all You want it to, and it prospers everywhere You send it. As we pray here, others receive answers there by the Holy Spirit.

Thank You, Father, for revealing unto Your people the integrity of Your Word. You are their Light, Salvation, Refuge, and Stronghold. We ask You to hide these missionaries in Your shelter and set them high upon a rock. Lord, increase their prayerful and financial supporters and meet all their needs according to Your riches in Christ Jesus. May they be strong in You and the power of Your might. Keep them in good health. Keep them safe and set a table before them in the presence of their enemies. You have anointed them to set the prisoners free, feed the hungry, execute justice, rescue, and deliver. Together with these missionaries, we reinforce their faith by taking a decisive stand against the devil, resisting his every attack with strong, vigorous faith.

Lord, we ask You to send ministering spirits to help and assist these heirs of salvation. Your mighty angel heroes hearken to the voice of Your Word, so we give voice to Your Word and declare these far-off ministers of the Gospel are strong in the power of Your might, quenching every dart of the devil in Jesus' name.

Father, we use our faith to cover these in the Body of Christ with Your Word. No weapon formed against them shall prosper, and any tongue that rises against them in judgment will be shown in the wrong. This peace, security, and triumph over opposition is their inheritance as Your children. This is the righteousness they obtain from You, Father. They are far from even the thought of destruction; for they shall not fear, and terror shall not come near them.

Father, You will keep these missionaries steady and strong to the end, maturing their character so they will be found innocent on the day of our Lord Jesus Christ. They will not be anxious or wonder how to defend themselves in any situation, for the Holy Spirit will supply the words—the right words at the right time. They are not anxious beforehand how they shall reply in defense or what they are to say, for the Holy Spirit teaches them in that very hour and moment what they ought to say to those in the outside world, their speech being seasoned with salt.

We commit unto You, Father, our brothers and sisters in the Lord. We deposit them into Your charge, entrusting them to Your protection and care, for You are faithful. You strengthen them, set them on a firm foundation, guard them, and bless them. Greater are You who is in us that he who is in the world. For this, we join our voices in praise to You, Most High! In Jesus' name we pray, amen.

SCRIPTURE REFERENCES

Jeremiah 1:12 • Ephesians 6:10,16 • Isaiah 55:11 • Isaiah 54:14,17
1 Peter 5:9 • 1 Corinthians 1:8 • Psalm 27:1,5 • Luke 12:11-12
3 John 2 • Colossians 4:6 • 1 John 5:4-5 • Acts 20:32 • Psalm 146:7
2 Thessalonians 3:3 • Psalm 144:7 • Psalm 8:2 • Matthew 18:18
1 John 4:4 • Hebrews 1:14 • Matthew 6:33 TPT • 2 Timothy 2:14-18 MSG
Colossians 4:7 • Isaiah 50:4 CEV • 2 Corinthians 12:9-10 TPT

116

Church Teachers

FATHER, we come in the name of Jesus, asking You for anointed teachers and facilitators who are called according to Your will to our small groups, classes, and choirs. We thank You for teachers who are filled with the Spirit of God in wisdom and ability, in understanding and intelligence, and in knowledge and craftsmanship. We thank You that these teachers appointed by You devise skillful methods for teaching us and our children the Word of God. They are teachers who give themselves to teaching.

Father, may these teachers recognize that they must assume the greater accountability. According to Your Word, teachers will be judged by a higher standard and with greater severity than others. So we thank You that our teachers will not offend in speech or say the wrong things—that they may have fully developed characters, each one able to control his/her own body and to curb his/her entire nature.

Thank You that our teachers are part of the fivefold ministry to equip the saints for the work of ministry. They build up the body of Christ, until we all attain the unity of the faith and the knowledge of the Son of God, to mature manhood, to the measure of the stature of the fullness of Christ.

Thank You, Father, that we are no longer children, tossed like ships back and forth. We are enfolded in love, growing up in every way and in all things into Him, who is the Head—even Christ, the Messiah, the Anointed One.

Father, You are effectually at work in our teachers—energizing and creating in them the power and desire—both to will and to work for Your good pleasure and satisfaction and delight. In the name of Jesus, their power and ability are from You. You have qualified them and made them fit to be ministers and dispensers of a new covenant. They are not ministers of the law that kills but of the Holy Spirit who makes alive.

Father, we rejoice over our teachers and surround them with our faith and love. We will not judge or criticize them, but we will speak excellent and noble things concerning them. We only speak true and right words—not one syllable twisted or skewed.

Thank You, Father, that our teachers and the other members of our church are joined together in perfect unity—one heart, one passion, and united in love. We walk together in harmonious purpose. Our teachers are compassionate shepherds who tenderly care for God's flock and feed them well. They are responsible to guide, protect, and oversee the flock (the congregation). They consider it their pleasure not a religious duty because they lead from the heart under God's leadership.

Thank You, Father, for the performance of Your Word in our midst. In the name of Jesus, amen.

SCRIPTURE REFERENCES

Exodus 31:3-4 • 2 Corinthians 3:5-6 AMPC • Romans 12:7
Proverbs 8:6 MSG • James 3:1-2 • Philippians 2:2,4-5 TPT
Ephesians 4:12-15 ESV • 1 Peter 5:2-3 • Philippians 2:13 • Jeremiah 1:12

117

A Christian Counselor

FATHER, in the name of Jesus, I pray for __________ to exhort and counsel the emotionally wounded. I ask in faith that Your Spirit—the Spirit of wisdom and understanding, the Spirit of counsel and might—will rest upon ______________. Give this counselor insight and knowledge for understanding the counselees' responses to circumstances.

Thank You, Father, that _______________ is a good listener to those who are seeking help. Give each counselor discernment and wisdom to comprehend the unfolding of past hurts that influence reactions to current situations.

Lord, we pray that ____________ will not judge by natural sight or decide only by natural hearing. We pray for counselors who will judge the needy and give decisions with justice. Righteousness will be his/her belt, and faithfulness the sash around his/her waist. He/she will be clothed with fairness and with truth.

Thank You that _______________ is a promoter of peace and is filled with joy. Grant Your counselor, out of the rich treasury of Your glory, to be strengthened and reinforced with mighty power in the inner man by the Holy Spirit Himself indwelling his/her innermost being and personality.

You will not leave _____________ without support as he/she gives his/her time and concern, helping to complete the forgiveness process. He/she will be confident about his/her convictions, knowing excellent things, and will have the knowledge to assist Your children in knowing the certainty of the words of truth. In Jesus' name, amen.

SCRIPTURE REFERENCES

Isaiah 11:2-3 AMPC • Ephesians 3:16 AMPC • Isaiah 11:4-5 NIV
Proverbs 22:20-21 AMPC • Isaiah 11:5 TLB

118

Prosperity for Ministering Servants

FATHER, in the name of Jesus, we pray and believe that those who have sown spiritual gifts among the people will reap material gifts in return. For You, Lord, have ordered that those who preach the Good News should be supported by those who benefit from it.

The people's gifts are the fragrant odor of an offering and sacrifice that You welcome and in which You delight. You will liberally supply—fill to the full—the people's every need according to Your riches in glory in Christ Jesus.

Father, we pray that Your people will not get tired of doing what is good, for at just the right time they will reap a harvest of blessing if they don't give up. Therefore, whenever they have the opportunity, they do good to everyone—especially to those in the family of faith. Help us to remember that a stingy planter gets a stingy crop; a lavish planter gets a lavish crop.

But it is You, dear Father, who is able to make all grace, every favor and earthly blessing, come to Your people in abundance, so we are always and under all circumstances possessing enough to require no aid or support and furnished in abundance for every good work and charitable donation.

As Your people give, their deeds of justice and goodness and kindness and benevolence go on and endure forever. You provide the seed for the sower and bread for the eating, so You also will provide and multiply the people's resources for sowing and increase the fruits of their righteousness. Your people are enriched in all things and in every way so that they can be generous, and their generosity, administered by Your teachers, will bring thanksgiving to God.

As they give, it will be given to them packed down, shaken together to make room for more, running over, and spilling over into their laps. For You have said the measurement of generosity becomes the measurement of return because a stingy planter gets a stingy crop; a lavish planter gets a lavish crop. Praise the Lord! In Jesus' name, amen.

SCRIPTURE REFERENCES

Galatians 6:6-10 NLT • 2 Corinthians 9:6-11 MSG
1 Corinthians 9:11-14 NIV, NLT • Luke 6:38 CEV • Philippians 4:17-19 AMPC

— 119 —

A Ministry in Need of Finances

FATHER, we believe all the needs of ____________________ are supplied from Your glorious riches, which have been given to us in Christ Jesus. We believe that You will return their gifts pressed down, shaken together to make room for more, running over, and poured into their lap. You have said that the measurement of generosity becomes the measurement of their return.

In the name of Jesus, we ask on the authority of Your Word that those in Your Body who have sown spiritual gifts among the people should expect to reap material gifts as a harvest. For You, Lord, have ordered that those who preach the Good News should be supported by those who benefit from it.

We confess that Your ministers with __________ ministry seek and are eager for the fruit that increases to the people's credit—the harvest of blessing that is accumulating to their account. The people's gifts are the fragrant odor of an offering and sacrifice that You welcome and in which You delight. You will liberally supply (fill to the full) the people's every need according to Your riches in glory in Christ Jesus.

Father, we call forth partners who will respond to Your call to support this ministry prayerfully and financially.

Lord, we thank You for directing the leader ___________, who seeks Your ways, teaching him/her the fortitude of Your Word and the steadfastness of its truth. Your anointing, which destroys the yoke of bondage, abides in him/her permanently. Teach him/her to pray for the people and the government of our land. Thank You for Your Word, which brings freedom to the hearers, and thank You for preparing the hearts of the people to receive the good news of the Gospel.

Lord, strengthen (complete, perfect) and make __________ what he/she ought to be, equipping him/her with everything good that he/she may carry out Your will; while You Yourself work in him/her and accomplish that which is pleasing in Your sight, through Jesus Christ the Messiah, to whom be the glory forever and ever (to the ages of the ages). In His name we pray, amen.

SCRIPTURE REFERENCES

Luke 6:38 NLT • Isaiah 10:27 • 1 Corinthians 9:11,13 NIV, NLT
1 Timothy 2:1-3 AMPC • Philippians 4:17-19 NLT • John 8:32
Matthew 9:38 AMPC • Hebrews 13:21 AMPC

— 120 —

Prayers for Ministry Partners

I.

FATHER, we thank You for our partners and for their service and dedication to serve You. Thank You that they bring forth the fruit of the Spirit—love, joy, peace, longsuffering, gentleness, goodness, faith, meekness, and temperance.

Thank You that our partners are good ground, that they hear Your Word and understand it, and that the Word bears fruit in their lives. They are like trees planted by rivers of water that bring forth fruit in their season. Their leaves shall not wither, and whatever they do shall prosper.

From the first day we heard of our partners, we haven't stopped praying for them, asking God to give them wise minds and spirits attuned to His will, and so acquire a thorough understanding of the ways in which God works. Our partners are merciful as our Father is merciful. They will judge only as they want to be judged. They do not condemn, and they are not condemned. Our partners forgive others, and people forgive them.

They give, and men will give to them—yes, good measure, pressed down, shaken together, and running over will blessings pour into their laps. For whatever measure they use with other people, they will use in their dealings with them. In Jesus' name we pray, amen.

SCRIPTURE REFERENCES

Colossians 1:9 MSG • Matthew 7:1 AMPC • Galatians 5:22-23
Luke 6:37-38 • Psalm 1:3

II.

Father, we ask You to bless our partners with all spiritual blessings in heavenly places that goodwill might come to them. They are generous and lend freely. They conduct their affairs with justice.

Lord, Your Word says that surely they will never be shaken. They are righteous men and women who will be remembered forever. They will not fear bad news; their hearts are steadfast, trusting in You, Lord.

We ask that Your plans be fulfilled in their lives, and we thank You for Your mercies on their behalf. In the name of Jesus, amen.

SCRIPTURE REFERENCES

Psalm 112:5-8 NIV • Jeremiah 29:11 NIV • Colossians 1:9 MSG

121

Overcoming Prejudice

FATHER, in the name of Jesus, we come before You, asking Your forgiveness for being intolerant of one another because of the colors of our skin. Forgive us for tolerating prejudice in the household of faith, for we are no longer outsiders or aliens, but fellow citizens with every other Christian—we belong now to the household of God (Eph. 2:19 PHI). Set us free from the influence of public opinion that we may live out our glorious, Christ-originated faith where the unity of the Spirit prevails. Red, yellow, black, and white—we stand together—precious in Your sight.

Forgive us for segregating ourselves by color, gender, measure of wealth or intellect. We are all Your children, the sheep of Your pasture. You made us, not we ourselves.

We are one blood, redeemed by the blood of the Lamb, who was slain before the foundation of the world. We are baptized *into* Christ and have put on the family likeness of Christ.

We call for an end to division and segregation in Christ's family—may there be no division into Jew and non-Jew, slave and free, male and female. Among us we are all equal. That is, we are all in a common relationship with Jesus Christ.

Thank You, Father, for bringing us together in Christ through His death on the cross. The cross got us to embrace, and that was the end of the hostility.

Lord, Jesus came and preached peace to us outsiders and peace to us insiders. He treated us as equals and so made us equals. Through Him we share the same Spirit and have equal access to You, Father.

The Kingdom of faith is now our home country, and we are no longer strangers or outsiders. We *belong* here.

Lord, You are building a home. You are using us all—irrespective of how we got here—in what You are building. You are fitting us in with Christ Jesus as the Cornerstone who holds all the parts together. Father, we see it taking shape day after day—a holy temple built by You—and all of us built into it, a temple in which You are quite at home.

Father, You have called us all to travel on the same road and in the same direction, so we will stay together, both outwardly and inwardly. We have one Master, one faith, one baptism, one God and Father of all—who rules over all, works through all, and is present in all. Everything we are and think and do is permeated with oneness.

Father, we imitate You. We walk in love, esteeming and delighting in one another. We walk as children of the light, leading the lives of those native-born to the light. We look carefully how we walk! We live purposefully and worthily and accurately, making the very most of the time buying up each opportunity, because the days are evil.

We speak out to one another in psalms and hymns and spiritual songs, offering praise with voice and instruments and making melody with all our hearts to You, Lord, at all times and for everything, giving thanks in the name of our Lord Jesus Christ to You, Father. By love we serve one another.

Thank You, Father, that prejudice is being rooted out of the Body of Christ. In the name of Jesus, amen.

SCRIPTURE REFERENCES

James 2:1 MSG • Ephesians 2:13-22 MSG • Psalm 100:3
Ephesians 4:3-6 MSG • 1 Peter 1:18-19 NIV • Ephesians 5:1-2,8 AMPC
Galatians 3:27-28 PHI • Ephesians 5:15-16,19-20 AMPC
Galatians 3:28 MSG • Galatians 5:13 AMPC

122

Office Staff

FATHER, we begin this day rejoicing in You and thanking You for Your goodness, mercy, and grace toward us as individuals and as a ministry. We confess and proclaim that this is the day that You have made, and we purpose to rejoice and be glad in it.

Father, we lift up the day with its activities, its relationships, its decisions, and its creativity. We offer it all up to You, acknowledging Jesus as Lord of all and asking You by Your Holy Spirit to use it for Your glory and honor. We pray for Your will to be done in us individually and as a ministry.

We plead the blood of Jesus over this property, all staff members, every phone call, email, text, or electronic contact, every person who enters these doors, and the entire ministry network, including all those for whom we pray. We thank You for delivering us from the authority of darkness and translating us into the kingdom of Your dear Son. We are living and growing up in the kingdom of light.

Father, You have given us choices, and we choose life and blessings. You are our Strength, our Confidence, and our Courage. We are courageous, boldly proclaiming that Your anointing—Your burden-removing, yoke-destroying power—is abiding in us individually and collectively. This anointing is working in, on, and through us this day to accomplish Your will. May You be glorified in all that we do.

Thank You for Your love. We are imitators of You—walking in love, in truth, in light, and in wisdom inside and outside these offices. We are well-balanced and enduring in all things.

We are asking for and expecting the former and latter rains to be poured out on this ministry to fulfill Your assignments. You have called us by Your grace for such a time as this. We rejoice in the outpouring of Your Spirit on this ministry. In the name of Jesus, amen.

SCRIPTURE REFERENCES

Psalm 33:1 • 1 John 2:27 • Psalm 118:24 • 1 Corinthians 6:20
1 Corinthians 12:3 • Ephesians 5:1-2 AMPC • Matthew 6:10
James 5:7 • Colossians 1:13 • 1 Peter 5:10 • Deuteronomy 30:19
Esther 4:14 • Isaiah 10:27 • Acts 2:17

123

Ministry in Nursing Homes

FATHER, thank You for calling me to minister to Your children in nursing homes. I purpose to keep on going by Your power, for You first saved me and then called me to this holy work. It was a gift prepared for me in Jesus long before I knew anything about it.

But I know it now. Since the appearance of our Savior, nothing could be plainer—death defeated, life vindicated in a steady blaze of light, all through the work of Jesus. I couldn't be more sure of my ground—the One I've trusted in can take care of what He's trusted me to do right to the end.

Thank You for Your Word—the entrance of Your Word brings light, and Your light is the life of men. The words that I speak are spirit and life, and I pray that the light of the Gospel will illumine the minds of those to whom I minister. Father, Your anointing abides within me permanently—thank You for an unction from the Holy One.

Thank You, Lord, for those who welcome me, reaching out for prayer, encouragement, and hugs. I pray that the light in my eyes will bring joy to their hearts. Help me to exhort and teach them to continue in their desire to be useful, fulfilling Your call on their lives. Father, You have a purpose for them—it is not Your will that they be set aside. You have said gray hair is a crown of splendor attained in the way of righteousness. You want them to continue bringing forth fruit in their old age, so help me to bring understanding to them.

Father, thank You that You have touched my hands with Your anointing, and when I lay hands on the sick, they will be healed. They shall experience the healing that flows from Your throne and recover a spiritual tone of mind and spirit. I yield to You as an instrument of righteousness, bringing salvation, wholeness, healing, deliverance, and comfort to the sick and the elderly.

Father, You execute justice for the fatherless and the widow, and You are a Judge and Protector (champion) of the widow. You protect, preserve, and uphold the fatherless and widow, and You set them upright. I am claiming these promises for all those I minister to, believing You always uphold Your Word and keep Your promises.

Lord, Your arm is not shortened that You cannot save, and nothing is too hard for You. I ask You for the wisdom and common sense I need to be a vessel of honor, sanctified and fitting for Your use and prepared for every good work.

I do not go in my own strength but in Yours, Father. True spirituality that is pure in the eyes of our Father God is to make a difference in the lives of the orphans and widows in their troubles. Real Christianity, the kind that passes muster before God the Father, is this: Reach out to the homeless and loveless in their plight.

Thank You, Lord, that I eat the good of the land because You created in me a willing and obedient spirit. I serve You with a glad heart and a joyous spirit. I choose to do whatever You call me to do. Thank You for equipping me with all that I need to accomplish it. In the name of Jesus, amen.

SCRIPTURE REFERENCES

2 Timothy 1:8-10 MSG • Romans 6:13 • Deuteronomy 10:18 AMPC
Psalm 68:5 AMPC • Psalm 119:130 • Psalm 146:9 AMPC
John 1:4 • Jeremiah 1:12 AMPC • John 6:63 • Isaiah 39:1
2 Corinthians 4:4 AMPC • Genesis 18:14 • 1 John 2:20,27 AMPC
James 1:27 MSG • Mark 16:18 NLT • 2 Timothy 2:21 • Psalm 92:14
Isaiah 1:19 • Mark 4:2

124

Ministry to the Incarcerated

FATHER, You said that everyone who calls on the name of the Lord will be saved. Yet, how can people have faith in the Lord and ask Him to save them if they have never heard about Him? And how can they hear, unless someone tells them? And how can anyone tell them without being sent by the Lord? The Scriptures say it is a beautiful sight to see even the feet of someone coming to preach the good news.

So we thank You, Father, for sending Your ministers who are willing to go and preach deliverance to the incarcerated. Grant to them out of the rich treasury of Your glory to be strengthened and reinforced with mighty power in the inner man by the Holy Spirit. Anoint their lips to preach the good news of the Gospel.

Father, send Your Holy Spirit to go before the ministers, anointing the ears of the hearers and preparing their hearts to hear, receive, love, and obey Your Word. Thank You that the light of the Gospel shines in their hearts so as to beam forth the light for the illumination of the knowledge of Your majesty and glory so everyone who calls on Your name shall be saved.

Father, thank You for creating a desire within Your ministers to diligently study Your Word that they might receive your approval and correctly explain the word of truth. They are living witnesses to those who are not yet obedient to the Gospel.

Father, we thank You for an outpouring of Your Spirit upon the staff and inmates of this facility. We know that faith comes by hearing and hearing by Your Word. And we are thankful for the Holy Spirit who reveals truth to sinners, convicting and convincing them of sin, righteousness, and judgment. We thank You for the salvation and deliverance of all those who call upon Your name.

Now we release Your mercy, Your love, and Your grace to those within these walls that they might be saved through faith in God. Salvation is Your gift to man—not anything we have done on our own. Thank You, Lord, for hearing our prayer in behalf of the people at this correctional facility/prison. In Jesus' name, amen.

SCRIPTURE REFERENCES

Romans 10:13-14 CEV • Romans 15:18 • Matthew 9:38
Acts 2:18 • Ephesians 3:16 AMPC • Romans 10:17 • 2 Corinthians 4:6 AMPC
John 16:8,13 • Romans 10:13 • Ephesians 2:8 • 2 Timothy 2:15

125

Revival

FATHER, revive us again and give us fresh life that we may rejoice in You. Give us a fresh start! Thank You for showing us Your love and saving us! Give me again the joy that comes from Your salvation. Let my passion for life be restored, tasting joy in every breakthrough You bring to me. Hold me close to You with a willing spirit that obeys whatever You say.

Thank You for all the promises You have made to us! Your great promises are ours, so let us purify ourselves from everything that makes body or soul unclean. Let us be completely holy by living in awe of You. We carefully read the map of Your Word, and we single-mindedly pursue You. Don't let us miss the road signs you've posted or wander or step aside. We've banked your promises in the vault of our hearts so sin will not bankrupt us.

Jesus, thank You for cleansing us through the Word—the teachings that You have given us. We delight ourselves in Your statutes; we will not forget Your Word. We thank You that we walk in abundance of life that we may always live to obey Your truth.

Father, in the name of Jesus, we are doers of the Word and not merely listeners to it. You revive us with Your Word just like You promised You would. Barricade the road that goes Nowhere; grace me with Your clear revelation. I choose the true road to Somewhere, and I post Your road signs at every curve and corner.

Everything with the old way of life has to go! It's rotten through and through, and we choose to get rid of it! Father, we take on an entirely new way of life—a God-fashioned life, a life renewed from the inside and working itself outside as Your character reproduces in us. Hallelujah! Amen.

SCRIPTURE REFERENCES

Psalm 85:6-7 CEV • James 1:22 • Psalm 51:10,12-13 TPT • Psalm 119:25 MSG
Psalm 119:9-11 MSG • Psalm 119:37,40,50 • 2 Corinthians 7:1
Ephesians 4:22-24 MSG • John 15:3 • 2 Corinthians 4:16
Psalm 119:16-17 TPT

126

Success of a Meeting

FATHER, in the name of Jesus, we approach the throne of grace boldly and confidently. May the Word of God come forth accurately and in love during the _____________ meeting. We ask You to anoint each speaker to teach and preach the Word of God in simplicity, with boldness and with accuracy during the entire meeting. We ask that those who hear will not be able to resist the wisdom and the inspiration of the Holy Spirit spoken through Your ministers of the Gospel.

As Your Word is taught, we ask You to cause people to open their spiritual eyes and ears that they might turn from darkness to light—from the power of Satan to You, Father—and that they will personally confess Jesus as their Savior and Lord.

We commit this meeting to You, Father. We deposit it into Your charge—entrusting this meeting, the people who will hear, and the people who will speak into Your protection and care. Your gracious Word, Father, can make us into what You want us to be and give us everything we could possibly need. Your Word will build up the people and cause them to realize that they are joint-heirs with Jesus.

We believe, Father, that as Your Word comes forth, an anointing will be upon the speaker(s), and _________ (name) will be submitted completely to the Holy Spirit, for the Word of God that is spoken is alive and full of power, making it active, operative, energizing and effective, being sharper than any two-edged sword. We ask You to meet the need of every person spiritually, physically, mentally, and financially.

Thank You and praise You, Father, because we have asked, agreed and now believe that these petitions come to pass. Thank You that You always watch over Your Word to perform it and that not a word of Your good promise ever fails to come to pass. We believe that all the earth's people will know that You are God, and there is none other! Hallelujah! Amen.

SCRIPTURE REFERENCES

James 5:16 • Acts 26:18 • Matthew 18:19 • Acts 20:32 • Ephesians 6:19
Hebrews 4:12 AMPC • Acts 6:10 • Philippians 4:19 • Ephesians 1:18
1 Kings 8:56 NKJV • Jeremiah 1:12

127

Success of a Conference

FATHER, we pray that those who hear the messages at the ____________ conference will believe—adhere to, trust in, and rely on Jesus as the Christ—and that all those You have called to attend the conference will be there and receive what You have for them.

Let it be known and understood by all that it is in the name and through the power and authority of Jesus Christ of Nazareth that this conference is successful.

Jesus said what we bind on earth is bound in heaven, and what we loose on earth is loosed in heaven. Therefore, we declare in Jesus' name that freedom of utterance is given to every individual who holds a microphone that they boldly proclaim the good news of the Gospel. Every speaker, psalmist, usher, and worker has an unction from the Holy One. Each person involved with the organization and operation of the conference has his/her eyes flooded with light and has a spirit of wisdom and revelation in the knowledge of You. When the people see the boldness and unfettered eloquence of the speakers, they shall marvel and recognize that they have been with Jesus.

Father, in the name of Jesus, the people will praise and glorify God for what occurs at this conference. By the hands of the ministers, numerous and startling signs and wonders will be performed among the people. Your bondservants have full freedom to declare Your message fearlessly—while You stretch out Your hand to cure and perform signs and wonders in the name of Jesus.

Thank You, Father, that when we pray, the place where we are assembled will be shaken; we shall all be filled with the Holy Spirit, and Your people shall continue to speak the Word of God with freedom and boldness and courage. More and more individuals will join themselves with us—people coming from the north, south, east, and west, bringing the sick, the depressed, the oppressed, and the brokenhearted. Jesus will cure them all.

I pray for each one participating in this conference. May every attitude be an expression of the fruit of the Spirit—love, joy, peace, patience, kindness, goodness, faithfulness, gentleness, and self-control. Lord, I pray that each one will release rivers of living water, an outflowing of the anointing of Your Holy Spirit.

Thank You, Father, for the performance of Your Word. Your plans and purposes in the lives of everyone in attendance will be accomplished. In the name of Jesus, amen.

SCRIPTURE REFERENCES

Acts 4:10,13,21 • Acts 5:12-13,16 AMPC • Matthew 18:18
Acts 6:3,10 • Galatians 5:22 • Acts 4:29-31 AMPC
Ephesians 1:17-19 AMPC • John 1:20

PEOPLES
and Nations

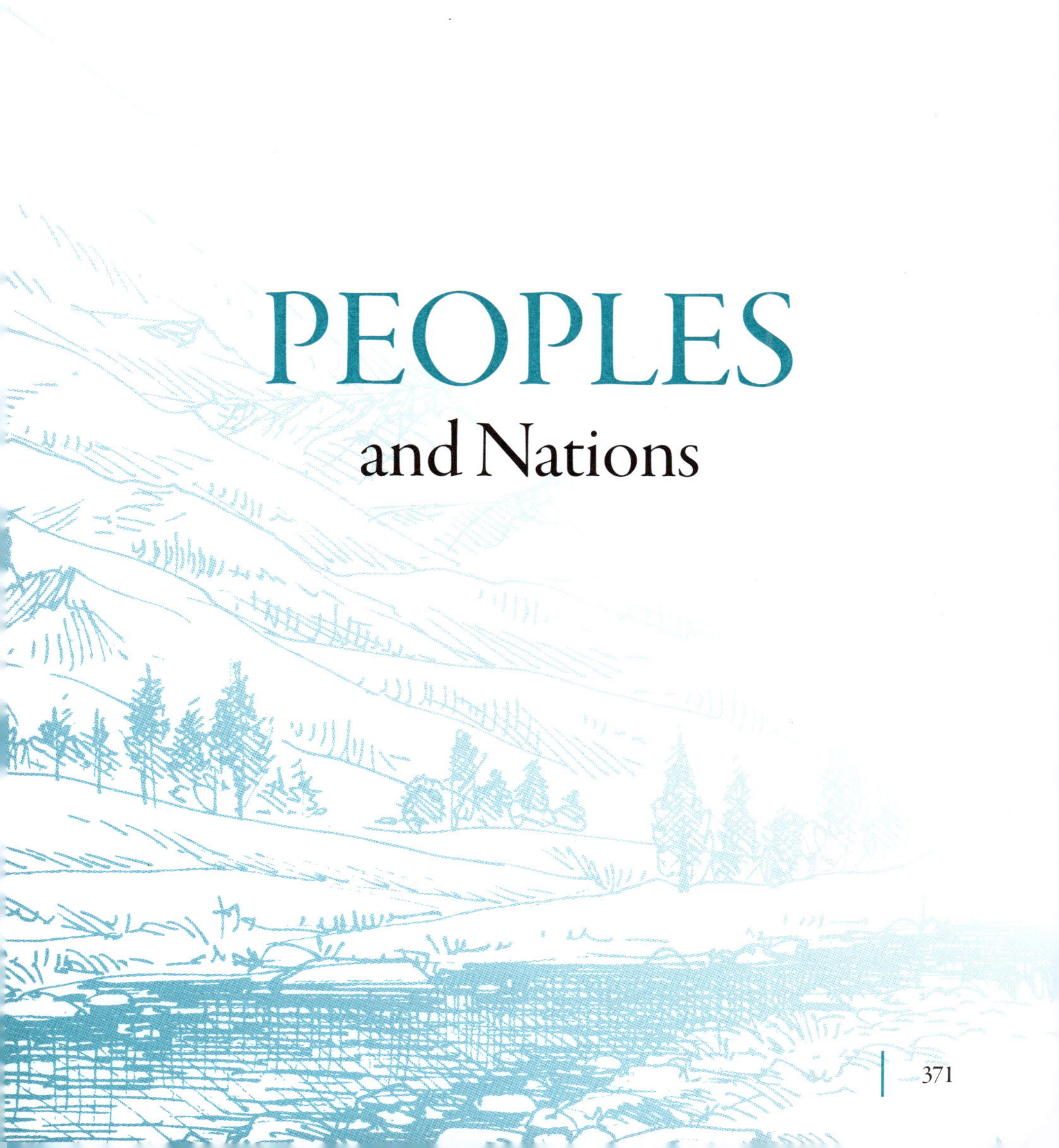

128

Protection and Deliverance of a City

FATHER, in the name of Jesus, we have received Your power—ability, efficiency, and might—because the Holy Spirit has come upon us; and we are Your witnesses in __________ and to the ends, the very bounds, of the earth.

Father, we confidently and boldly draw near to Your throne of grace, that we may receive mercy and find grace to help in time of need on behalf of the city of __________________. Thank You for sending forth Your commandments to the earth. Your Word runs very swiftly throughout ______________ and continues to grow and spread.

Father, we seek the peace and welfare of ________________, where You have planted us to live. We pray to You for the welfare of this city and do our part by getting involved in it. We pray for every political leader and representative, so that we would be able to live tranquil, undisturbed lives, as we worship You, the awe-inspiring God, with pure hearts. It pleases You that we pray for them, for You long for everyone to embrace Your life and return to the full knowledge of the truth.

Holy Spirit, we ask You to make us good citizens, for all governments are under God. Insofar as there is peace and order, it's God's order. Help us to live responsibility as citizens, for decent citizens should have nothing to fear.

Father, we pray for deliverance and salvation for those who are following the course and fashion of this world—who are under the sway of the tendency of this present age—following the prince of the power of the air. Father, forgive them, for they know not what they do.

In Jesus' mighty name we break the power of the devil, the god of this world, who has blinded the minds of those who don't believe and have not received the glorious light of the good news. We pray that the Lord of the harvest send laborers across their paths with the Gospel of Jesus Christ. We pray that the Father of glory, the God of our Lord Jesus Christ, would impart to them the riches of the Spirit of wisdom and the Spirit of revelation to know Him through deepening intimacy. May their hearts be flooded with light until they experience the wealth of God's glorious inheritances.

Thank You, Father, for the guardian angels assigned to this place who war for us in the heavenlies. In the name of Jesus, we stand victorious over the principalities, powers, rulers of the darkness of this world, and spiritual wickedness in high places over ______________.

We ask the Holy Spirit to sweep through the gates of our city and convince the people and bring demonstration to them about sin and about righteousness—uprightness of heart and right standing with God.

Father, You said, "For I know the thoughts and plans that I have for you...thoughts and plans for welfare and peace and not for evil, to give you hope in your final outcome" (Jer. 29:11 AMPC). By the blessing of the influence of the upright and God's favor because of them, the city of ____________ is exalted. Amen.

SCRIPTURE REFERENCES

Acts 1:8 AMPC • Ephesians 1:17-23 TPT • Hebrews 4:16 AMPC
2 Corinthians 4:4 AMPC • Psalm 147:15 AMPC • Ephesians 6:12
Acts 12:24 AMPC • Jeremiah 29:7-8 AMPC • John 16:8 AMPC
Romans 13:1-7 MSG • Jeremiah 29:11 AMPC • Matthew 9:37-38
Proverbs 11:11 AMPC • Ephesians 2:2 AMPC • 1 Timothy 2:2-4 TPT

129

Prayer Against Terrorism

FATHER, we praise You and offer up thanksgiving because Jesus is coming soon. We are here to take our stand against the evil spirits of terrorism, which have come to steal, kill, and destroy. Thank You for the Holy Spirit who rises up within us to super-intercede on our behalf. We are here pleading to You with emotional sighs too deep for words. Father God, You are the searcher of the heart, and You know fully our longings, yet You also understand the desires of the Spirit because the Holy Spirit is passionately pleading before You for us, Your holy ones, in perfect harmony with Your plan and our destiny.

Therefore, we will not fret or have any anxiety about terrorism threatening the lives of unsuspecting and innocent people. We submit to You and resist the temptation to be pulled in different directions or worried about a thing. We are saturated in prayer throughout each day, offering our faith-filled requests before You with overflowing gratitude.

Father, our petition is that terrorism in the heavenlies and on earth be stopped! You have not given us a spirit of fear, but a spirit of love, power, and a sound mind. Therefore, we will not be in fear of those who can kill only the body but not our souls.

> Lord, You know where every terrorist cell is located across this nation. Father, I ask You to cut asunder the cords of this wicked net (Ps. 129:4). And bring disarray, confusion, defection, and a holy fear of God into the enemy camp. Sever their communication network, their financial

funding, and their tracking systems. Diffuse their power and expose their evil schemes and terrorist activities and bring them to justice, in Jesus' name.

Father, I pray that You would target every terrorist leader, and that like Saul of Tarsus, You would knock them off their "high horses" of pride, delusion, and deception. May the brilliance of Your Glory surround them and bring them to their knees in surrender to You! (Acts 9:1-6). I push back the occult cover of darkness that conceals them. For it is written: "Their webs of evil will not become garments; or will they cover themselves with their works." I declare in Jesus' name that their works will be exposed, and the perpetrators apprehended, for theirs are "works of iniquity, and the act of violence is in their hands" (Isa. 49:6).[19]

Father, we offer this prayer to You in the name of Jesus, amen.

SCRIPTURE REFERENCES

Philippians 4:5-6 TPT • Romans 8:31 • Luke 10:19 AMPC
2 Timothy 1:7 AMPC • Ephesians 6:10 AMPC • Psalm 91:5-6 AMPC
Ephesians 2:2 AMPC • Isaiah 54:14 AMPC • Ephesians 6:12 AMPC
Proverbs 3:3 AMPC • Matthew 16:19 • Psalm 50:23
Psalm 56:9 AMPC • Romans 8:26-27 TPT

19 Quoted with permission from Intercessors for America, IFApray.org.

130

Salvation of the Lost

We come to stand in the gap before You and pray for those who are lost and without God. We pray in agreement with Jesus who is able to save to the uttermost those who come to You through Him because He always lives to make intercession for them.

We pray for those who are perishing, for their minds are blinded by the god of this age, leaving them in unbelief. Open their blind eyes that keep them from seeing the dayspring light of the wonderful news of the glory of Jesus Christ. Father, let Your brilliant light shine out of darkness and cascade Your light into them that they might see the knowledge of grace and truth.

We are here to take our stand against the unseen spirits of darkness that have held them in bondage. We pray for their deliverance from the power of darkness and ask You to convey them into the kingdom of the Son of Your love, in whom we have redemption through His blood, the forgiveness of sins.

Father, we know that Satan would prevent these people from hearing truth, if possible. We are human, but we don't wage war with human plans and methods. We use God's mighty weapons to knock down the devil's strongholds. With these weapons we break down every proud argument that keeps people from confessing Jesus as Lord and believing in their hearts that You raised Him from the dead. We pray the people will be saved and come to the knowledge of the truth.

When the Light shines out of darkness, and they hear the Good News of the Gospel, they will call upon the name of the Lord and be saved. Thank You for loving us even when we were Your enemies. You gave Your Son, Your one and only Son, so that no one need be destroyed; by believing in Him, anyone can have a whole and lasting life.

Jesus, You are not late with Your promise to return. The delay reveals Your loving patience toward those who do not yet know You because You do not want any to perish but all to come to repentance.

Lord Jesus, when we look at the nations, we realize that the harvest of souls is huge and ripe! We ask the Owner of the harvest to thrust out many more reapers to harvest His grain!

We confess that they shall see who have never been told of Jesus. They shall understand who have never heard of Jesus. And they shall come out of the snare of the devil who has held them captive. They shall open their eyes and turn from darkness to light—from the power of Satan to You, God! In Jesus' name, amen.

SCRIPTURE REFERENCES

Hebrews 7:25 NKJV • 2 Corinthians 4:1-6 TPT • 1 Corinthians 10:3-5 NLT
Romans 15:21 AMPC • Matthew 9:38 • 2 Timothy 2:26 AMPC
Colossians 1:13 NKJV • 2 Peter 3:8-10 TPT

131

Nations and Continents

FATHER, Jesus is our Salvation. He is the God-revealing light to the non-Jewish nations and the light of glory for Your people Israel. As members of the Body of Christ, we are asking You to give us the nations for an inheritance and the ends of the earth for our possession. All kings shall fall down before You; all nations shall serve You. In the name of Jesus, we bring before You the nation (or continent) of __________________ and her leaders. We ask You to rebuke leaders for our sakes, so that we may live a quiet and peaceable life in all godliness and honesty.

We pray that skillful and godly wisdom will enter the heart of _____________________'s leaders and that knowledge shall be pleasant to them, that discretion will watch over them, and that understanding will keep them and deliver them from the way of evil and from the evil men.

We pray that the upright shall dwell in the government(s), that men and women of integrity, blameless and complete in Your sight, Father, shall remain; but the wicked shall be cut off and the treacherous shall be rooted out. We pray that those in authority winnow the wicked from among the good and bring the threshing wheel over them to separate the chaff from the grain, for loving-kindness and mercy, truth, and faithfulness preserve those in authority, and their offices are upheld by the people's loyalty.

Father, we ask that You direct the decisions made by these leaders, and that present leaders who are men and women of discernment, understanding, and knowledge will remain in office so the stability of _______________ will long continue. We pray that the uncompromisingly righteous will be in authority in _______________ so the people can rejoice.

Father, it is an abomination for leaders to commit wickedness. We pray that their offices be established and made secure by righteousness and that right and just lips are a delight to those in authority and that they love those who speak what is right.

We pray and believe that the good news of the Gospel is published in this land. We thank You for laborers of the harvest to publish Your Word that Jesus is Lord in _______________. We thank You for raising up intercessors to pray for _______________ in Jesus' name. Amen.[20]

SCRIPTURE REFERENCES

1 Timothy 2:1-2 • Proverbs 28:2 AMPC • Psalm 105:14
Proverbs 29:2 AMPC • Proverbs 2:10-15 AMPC • Acts 12:24
Proverbs 2:21-22 AMPC • Psalm 68:11 • Proverbs 20:26,28 AMPC
Luke 2:30-32 MSG • Proverbs 21:1 • Psalm 2:8
Proverbs 16:10,12-13 AMPC • Psalm 72:11

20 For a complete list of nations to incorporate in your prayer time and additional prayers for the nations, we direct you to *Prayers That Avail Much® for the Nations.*

132

The People of Our Land

FATHER, in the name of Jesus, we come before You to claim Your promise in 2 Chronicles 7:14 AMPC: "If My people, who are called by My name, shall humble themselves, pray, seek, crave, and require of necessity My face and turn from their wicked ways, then will I hear from heaven, forgive their sin, and heal their land."

We humble ourselves before you in prayer. We seek You, and we crave Your presence. We are Your people, called by Your name, and we return to You—our first love. We turn from our wicked ways. And we thank You for hearing our prayers and moving by Your Spirit in our land.

Father, we pray that a spirit of humility and a passion to pray will be fueled to an even greater measure in Christians far and wide throughout the land. As the Body of Christ, we rise to bless our cities and our nation under You. Proverbs 11:11 says, "When right-living people bless the city, it flourishes; evil talk turns it into a ghost town in no time" (MSG). We thank You, dear Father, for healing our land and causing our nation to flourish once again.

Forgive us our sins of judging inappropriately, complaining about, and criticizing our leaders. We pray for rulers and governments to rule well so we the people can live peaceful and quiet lives marked by godliness and dignity. Touch our lips with coals from Your altar that we may pray prayers that avail much for all men and women everywhere. We pray the people of our land prosper in every way and continually enjoy good health just as their souls prosper in You.

Lord, we desire to release rivers of living water for the healing of the nations. In the name of Jesus, amen.

SCRIPTURE REFERENCES

Luke 21:11,25-26 • Psalm 51:7 NIV • Matthew 16:3 • Isaiah 6:6-7 NIV
Matthew 26:41 • James 5:16 • James 4:10 • 1 Timothy 2:1
1 Peter 3:4 • John 7:38 • Matthew 5:5 • Psalm 139:23 • Revelation 22:1-2

133

American Government

FATHER, in Jesus' name, we give thanks for the United States and its government. We hold up in prayer before You the men and women who are in positions of authority. We pray and intercede for the president, the representatives, the senators, the judges of our land, the policemen and the policewomen, as well as the governors and mayors, and for all those who are in authority over us in any way. We pray that the Spirit of the Lord rests upon them.

We believe that skillful and godly wisdom has entered into the heart of our president and knowledge is pleasant to him. Discretion watches over him; understanding keeps him and delivers him from the way of evil and from evil men.

Father, we ask that You compass the president about with men and women who make their hearts and ears attentive to godly counsel and do that which is right in Your sight. We believe You cause them to be men and women of integrity who are obedient concerning us that we may lead a quiet and peaceable life in all godliness and honesty. We pray that the upright shall dwell in our government—that men and women blameless and complete in Your sight, Father, shall remain in these positions of authority, but the wicked shall be cut off from our government and the treacherous shall be rooted out of it.

Your Word declares that "blessed is the nation whose God is the Lord" (Ps. 33:12). We receive Your blessing. Father; You are our Refuge and Stronghold in times of trouble, high cost, destitution, and desperation. So we declare with our mouths that Your people dwell safely in this land,

and we *prosper* abundantly. We are more than conquerors through Christ Jesus!

It is written in Your Word that the heart of the king is in the hand of the Lord and that You turn it whichever way You desire. We believe the heart of our leader is in Your hand and that his decisions are divinely directed of the Lord.

We give thanks unto You that the good news of the Gospel is published in our land. The Word of the Lord prevails and grows mightily in the hearts and lives of the people. We give thanks for this land and the leaders You have given to us, in Jesus' name.

Jesus is Lord over the United States! Amen.

SCRIPTURE REFERENCES

1 Timothy 2:1-3 • Deuteronomy 28:10-11 • Proverbs 2:10-12,21-22
Romans 8:37 AMPC • Psalm 33:12 • Proverbs 21:1 • Psalm 9:9 • Acts 12:24

134

School Systems and Children

FATHER, we thank You that the entrance of Your Word brings light and that You watch over Your Word to perform it. Father, we bring before You the _________________ school system(s) and the men and women who are in positions of authority within the school system(s).

We offer petitions, prayers, requests, and thanksgivings in behalf of these leaders. We ask You to give them skillful and godly wisdom to conduct affairs of the school system(s), the schools, and in the best interest of our children. Thank You that men and women of integrity—blameless and complete in Your sight—remain in these positions. Those who do wrong and cannot be trusted will be rooted out in the name of Jesus. Father, we also thank You for born-again, Spirit-filled people in these positions whenever possible.

We bring our children, our young people, before You, Father. We speak forth Your Word boldly and confidently that we and our households are saved in the name of Jesus. We are redeemed from the curse of the law, for Jesus was made a curse for us. As parents, we train our children in the way they should go, and when they are old they shall not depart from it.

Father, we pray that our children will choose to shrink from whatever might offend You and discredit the name of Christ. We pray that they show themselves to be blameless and innocent children of God without blemish in the midst of a crooked and twisted generation, among whom they shine as bright lights in a dark world. Thank You, Father, that You give them knowledge and skill in all learning and wisdom and bring them into favor with those around them.

Father, we pray and intercede that these young people, their parents, and the leaders in the school system(s) separate themselves from contact with contaminating and corrupting influences and cleanse themselves from everything that would contaminate and defile their spirits, souls, and bodies. We confess that they shun immorality and all sexual looseness—flee from impurity in thought, word, or deed—and they live and conduct themselves honorably and becomingly as in the open light of day in Jesus' name.

Father, we ask You to commission the ministering spirits to go forth and police the area, dispelling the forces of darkness.

Father, thank You that in Christ our spiritual wealth is stored up like hidden treasure waiting to be discovered—heaven's wisdom and endless riches of revelation. We praise You for working in the hearts of our children, giving them the desire to honor You by living holy lives. Those in error will believe the truth, and complainers will be willing to be taught. It is our prayer that You, Father, will always occupy first place in their hearts. We surround our children with our faith. They are reborn from above and spiritually transformed, taking paths You prepared ahead of time that they should walk in them living the good life that you made ready for us to live.

Thank You, Father, that You are the delivering God. Thank You that the good news of the Gospel is published throughout our school system(s). Thank You for intercessors to stand on Your Word and for laborers of the harvest to preach Your Word in Jesus' name. Praise the Lord! Amen.

SCRIPTURE REFERENCES

1 Timothy 2:1 AMPC • Psalm 119:130 • 2 Timothy 2:21 AMPC
Jeremiah 1:12 • 2 Corinthians 7:1 AMPC • Proverbs 2:10-12 AMPC
1 Corinthians 6:18 AMPC • Proverbs 2:21-22 AMPC • Romans 13:13 AMPC
Acts 16:31 • Ephesians 5:4 • Galatians 3:13 • 2 Timothy 2:22
Matthew 18:18 • Proverbs 22:6 AMPC • 2 Timothy 2:26
Philippians 2:15-16 AMPC • Hebrews 1:14 • Daniel 1:17 AMPC
Colossians 2:3 TPT • Daniel 1:9 • 1 John 2:16-17 AMPC
Ephesians 2:10 AMPC • Isaiah 29:23-24 TLB

135

Members of the Armed Forces

FATHER, our troops have been sent into _____________ as peacekeepers, and we petition You for their safety according to Psalm 91.

This is no afternoon athletic contest that our armed forces will walk away from and forget about in a couple of hours. This is for keeps, a life-or-death fight to the finish against the devil and all his angels. We look beyond human instruments of conflict and address the forces and authorities and rulers of darkness and powers in the spiritual world. As children of the Most High God, we enforce the triumphant victory of our Lord Jesus Christ.

Our Lord stripped principalities and powers, making a show of them openly. Thank You, Jesus, for defeating the evil one and his forces of darkness for us and giving us authority to proclaim your name that is above every name. All power and authority both in heaven and earth belong to you. Righteousness and truth shall prevail, and nations shall come to the light of the Gospel.

We petition heaven to turn our troops into a real peacekeeping force by pouring out the glory of God through our men and women in that part of the world. Use them as instruments of righteousness to defeat the plans of the devil.

Lord, we plead the power of the blood of Jesus, asking You to manifest Your power and glory. We entreat You on behalf of the citizens in these countries on both sides of this conflict. They have experienced pain and heartache; they are victims of the devil's strategies to steal, kill, and destroy. We pray that they will come to know Jesus, who came to give us life and life more abundantly.

We stand in the gap for the people of the war-torn, devil-overrun land. We expect an overflowing of Your goodness and glory in the lives of those for whom we are praying. May they call upon Your name and be saved.

You, Lord, make known Your salvation; Your righteousness You openly show in the sight of the nations.

Father, provide for and protect the families of our armed forces. Preserve marriages, cause the hearts of the parents to turn toward their children, and the hearts of the children to turn toward the fathers and mothers. We plead the blood of Jesus over our troops and their families. Provide a support system to undergird, uplift, and edify those who have been left to raise children by themselves. Jesus has been made unto these parents wisdom, righteousness, and sanctification. Through Your Holy Spirit, comfort the lonely and strengthen the weary.

Father, we are looking forward to that day when the whole earth shall be filled with the knowledge of the Lord as the waters cover the sea. In Jesus' name, amen.[21]

SCRIPTURE REFERENCES

Ephesians 6:12 MSG • Psalm 98:2 AMPC • Colossians 2:15
Malachi 4:6 • John 10:10 • 1 Corinthians 1:30 • Ezekiel 22:30
Isaiah 11:9 • Acts 2:21

21 A portion of this prayer was based on a letter dated January 22, 1996, written by Kenneth Copeland of Kenneth Copeland Ministries in Fort Worth, Texas, and sent to his partners. Used by permission.

136

The Nation and People of Israel

LORD, You will not cast off nor spurn Your people, neither will You abandon Your heritage. You have regard for the covenant You made with Abraham. Father, remember Your covenant with Abraham, Isaac, and Jacob.

Father, we pray for the peace of Jerusalem: "May they prosper who love you [the Holy City]! May peace be within your walls and prosperity within your palaces! For my brethren and companions' sake, I will now say, Peace be within you! For the sake of the house of the Lord our God, I will seek, inquire for, and require your good" (Ps. 122:6-9 AMPC).

Father, we thank You for bringing the people of Israel into unity with each other and for bringing Your Church (both Jew and Gentile) into oneness—one new man. Thank You for the peace treaties with Israel's former enemies. May these treaties be used for good to make way for the good news of the Gospel as we prepare for the coming of our Messiah.

We intercede for those who have become callously indifferent, blinded, hardened, and made insensible to the Gospel. We pray that they will not fall to their utter spiritual ruin. It was through their false step and transgression that salvation has come to the Gentiles. Now, we ask that the eyes of their understanding be enlightened that they may know the Messiah who will make Himself known to all of Israel.

We ask You to strengthen the house of Judah and save the house of Joseph. Thank You, Father, for restoring them because You have compassion on them. They will be as though You had not rejected them, for You are the Lord their God, and You will answer them. We thank You for Your great mercy and love to them and to us, in the name of Yeshua, our Messiah.

Father, thank You for saving Israel and gathering them from the nations, that they may give thanks to Your holy name and glory in Your praise. Praise be to You, Lord, the God of Israel, from everlasting to everlasting. Let all the people say, "Amen!" Praise the Lord. In Jesus' name.

SCRIPTURE REFERENCES

Psalm 94:14 AMP • Psalm 74:20 AMP • Romans 11:7 AMP
Romans 11:11 AMP • Leviticus 26:42 • Ephesians 1:18 • Psalm 122:6-9 AMP
Ephesians 2:14 AMP • Zechariah 10:6,12 NIV • Psalm 106:47-48 NIV

137

Peace of Jerusalem

FATHER, in the name of Jesus and according to Your Word, I long and pray for the peace of Jerusalem. I pray that blind eyes will be opened and deaf ears will hear. Lord, may they recognize You as their refuge and place of safety. Father, Your Word says "multitudes, multitudes in the valley of decision" (Joel 3:14) and whoever calls upon Your name shall be delivered and saved (see Rom. 10:13).

Have mercy upon Israel and be gracious to them. Consider that they fight for their land to be restored. You, Lord, are their Strength and Stronghold in their day of trouble. We pray that they are righteous before You and that You will make even their enemies to be at peace with them. Your Word says through the cleanness of our hands, You will deliver those for whom we intercede who are not innocent. May they realize that their defense and shield depend on You.

Lord, we thank You for Your Word and that You have a covenant with Israel and will take away their sin. They are Your beloved. Your Word also says that Your gifts are irrevocable—You never take back the gifts You have given and when You choose someone and graciously impart gifts to the person, they are never rescinded. Though Israel has been disobedient and rebellious toward You, Lord, we pray that now they will repent and obtain Your mercy and forgiveness through Your Son, Jesus. We praise You, Lord, for Your compassion and forgiveness to Your people. We praise You that they are under Your protection and divine guidance, for they are Your special possession and Your peculiar treasure. You will spare them, for we have read in Your Word that all Israel shall be saved!

I commit to pray for the peace of Jerusalem! Thank You, Father, for delivering us all from every evil work and for the authority You have given us in the name of Jesus. We love You and praise You.

Pray for the peace of Jerusalem! May they prosper that love You—the Holy City! Peace be within your walls and prosperity within your palaces! Amen.

SCRIPTURE REFERENCES

Joel 3:14 • Romans 10:13 • Romans 11:28-29 TPT

138

Prayer of Protection in Destructive Weather and Natural Disaster

FATHER, we are ever grateful that not one word of Your good promise has ever failed to come to pass. You are a loving Father who is good and faithful to Your children. You protect us from every sort of evil in Jesus' name.

Earthquakes, famines, hurricanes, tornadoes, droughts, fires, tsunamis, floods, and more are the results of sin and its effects on a planet that is groaning and travailing in pain under the bondage of corruption.

You gave the earth to man and woman, who were to fill it and govern it. Through Adam's disobedience, suffering and death were unleashed upon the human race. In some cases, man's own neglect of our planet has brought harm to planet Earth. Father, the devil is called the god of this world, but we know that Jesus defeated Him when He was raised from the dead! Dear Father, You have imparted to us the same mighty power that raised Christ from the dead and seated Him in the place of honor at Your right hand in the heavenly realms.

During the flood in the days of Noah, the planet was shaken to its core—dramatically altered from Your original design. Now these natural disasters and weather patterns bring death and destruction to millions. But we know, Father, that You do not send them. Every gift from You is good, perfect, and wholesome, streaming down from above. You are the Father of lights who shines from the heavens with no hidden shadow or darkness and is never subject to change.

We cannot control the events that transpire in this fallen world. We cannot declare there will be no more natural disasters or destructive weather. Your Word even predicts these events as we draw closer to the return of Jesus. You said "there will be terrible earthquakes—seismic events of epic proportion, horrible epidemics and famines in place after place. This is how the first contractions and birth pains of the new age will begin" (Matt. 24:7-8 TPT).

But, Father, we thank You that we can prevent them from coming to our homes and our property. We can minimize their damage with our prayers and our words. We can rebuke the wind and the waves and speak "peace be still" to storms just as Jesus did (Mark 4:37-31). We can speak to the elements just as Elijah did (see James 5:17-18). And we can receive Your safety and protection!

Father, thank You for the first responders who lay down their lives for others. Be a shield round about them as they go to rescue those who need help. When floods roar like thunder and lift their pounding waves, we shout to You, our God. You are mightier than the violent raging of the seas, mightier than the breakers on the shore—You, Lord, are mightier than these! You are a present help in time of trouble.

Thank you for the provisions of Psalm 91 (TPT). We pray Your promises of protection over our lives, proclaiming: My family and I sit enthroned under the shadow of Shaddai. We are hidden in Your strength, God Most High. You are the hope that holds us and the Stronghold that shelters us. You are the only God for us and our great confidence. You rescue us from every hidden trap of the enemy and protect us from false accusation and any deadly curse. Your massive arms are wrapped around us, protecting us. We can run under Your covering of majesty and hide. Your arms of faithfulness are a shield keeping us from harm.

We will never worry about an attack of demonic forces at night, nor will we fear a spirit of darkness coming against us. We don't fear a thing!

Whether by night or by day, demonic danger will not trouble us, nor will the powers of evil launch against us.

Even in a time of disaster, with thousands and thousands being killed, we will remain unscathed and unharmed. We will be a spectator as the wicked perish in judgment, for they will be paid back for what they have done! When we live our lives within Your shadow, Most High, our secret hiding place, we will always be shielded from harm. How then could evil prevail against us or disease infect us? It cannot!

Thank You for sending angels with special orders to protect us wherever we go, defending us from all harm. If we walk into a trap, they'll be there for us and keep us from stumbling. We even walk unharmed among the fiercest powers of darkness, trampling every one of them beneath our feet!

For here is what You have spoken: "Because you have delighted in me as my great lover, I will greatly protect you. I will set you in a high place, safe and secure before my face. I will answer your cry for help every time you pray, and you will find and feel my presence even in your time of pressure and trouble. I will be your glorious hero and give you a feast. You will be satisfied with a full life and with all that I do for you. For you will enjoy the fullness of my salvation!" (Ps. 91:14-16 TPT). In Jesus' name we pray, amen.

SCRIPTURE REFERENCES

2 Kings 5:8 • 1 Kings 8:56 • James 1:17 TPT • Romans 8:21-22 WEB
Psalm 93:3-4 NLT • Psalm 115:16 • Psalm 107:20 NKJV • Psalm 8:4-6
Matthew 24:7 TPT • Genesis 1:26-28 • Mark 4:37-41 • 2 Corinthians 4:4
James 5:17-18 • Hebrews 2:14 • Psalm 91 TPT • Ephesians 2:6

PRAYING
for One Another

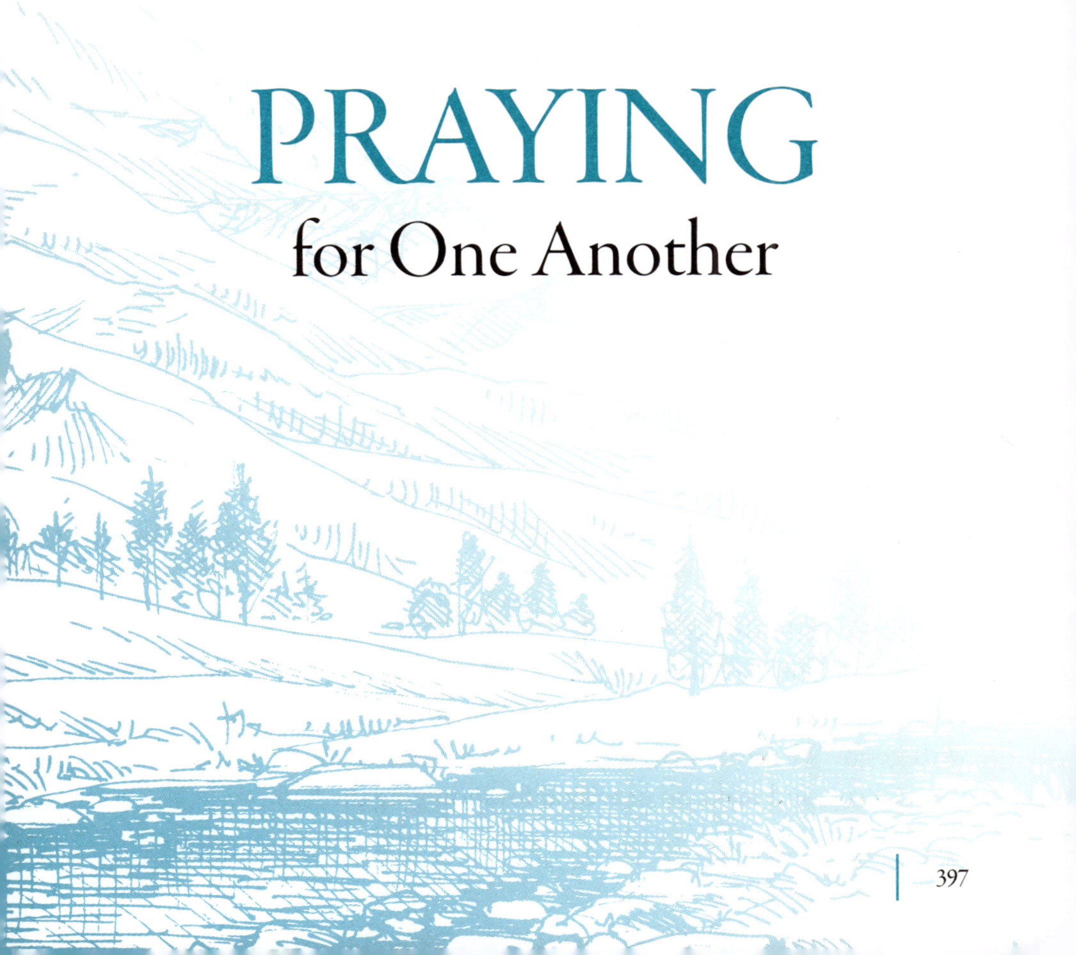

139

Spirit-Controlled Life

FATHER, I pray for all saints everywhere. Help us remain teachable that we may receive instruction from the apostles, prophets, evangelists, pastors, and teachers. We will be Your children equipped for the work of ministry, for the edifying of the Body of Christ. Bring us to the unity of faith and knowledge of the Son of God, to a perfect man, to the measure of the stature of the fullness of Christ.

Father, there is now no condemnation to those who walk according to the Spirit, because through Christ Jesus the law of the Spirit of life sets us free from the law of sin and death. Grant us the grace to live the life of the Spirit. Father, You condemned sin in the flesh—subdued, overcame, and deprived it of its power over us. Now the righteous and just requirement of the Law is fully met in us who live and move in the ways of the Spirit—our lives governed and controlled by the Holy Spirit.

We purpose to live according to the Spirit, and we are controlled by the desires of the Spirit. We set our minds on and seek those things which gratify the Holy Spirit. We no longer live the life of the flesh; we live the life of the Spirit. The Holy Spirit of God really dwells within us, directing and controlling us.

On the authority of Your Word, we declare that we are more than conquerors gaining a surpassing victory through Jesus who loves us. We refuse to be overcome with evil, but we will overcome and master evil with good. We have on the full armor of light, clothed with the Lord Jesus Christ, and make no provision for indulging the flesh.

Father, we choose to be doers of Your Word. We draw forth Your wisdom in prayer and walk in it. We are peace-loving, full of compassion and good fruit. We walk in faith because it's impossible to please You without it. We choose to be imitators of You in everything You do—representing You as a son or daughter. And we live a life filled with love, following the example of Jesus.

Lord, we are strong in the power of Your might. Therefore, we take our stand against the devil and resist him; he flees. We draw close to You, and You draw close to us. We have Your word on it. We do not fear, for You never leave us.

In Christ, we are filled with the Godhead—Father, Son, and Holy Spirit. Jesus is our Lord!

SCRIPTURE REFERENCES

Romans 8:2,4,9,14,31,37 AMPC • Romans 12:21 • Hebrews 13:5
Hebrews 11:6 • Ephesians 5:1 TPT • Romans 13:12,14 • Ephesians 6:10
James 1:22 • James 4:7-8 • James 3:17 AMPC • Colossians 2:10

140

Prayer for Renewed Fellowship

FATHER, Thank You that You watch over Your Word to perform it. I pray and believe that ____________ is a disciple of Christ, taught of You and obedient to Your will. Great is his/her peace and undisturbed composure. ______________ has You for his/her Teacher. We pray that You will give _______________ a teachable spirit and a listening ear so he/she will learn from You and return to his/her first love, Jesus.

I pray that ________________ will choose to advance in strength with the truth wrapped around his/her heart, faithful to the things he/she has been taught and has believed. From childhood he/she has been wise enough to have known the Holy Scriptures that are able to make him/her wise enough to have faith in Christ Jesus and be saved. Jesus gives _______________ real and eternal life, and no one has the power to snatch him/her out of His hands.

Father, create a desire in _________'s heart to submit to You and resist the devil who would keep him/her blinded to the truth. I pray that the light of God will illuminate the eyes of his/her imagination, flooding his/her eyes with the light that comes from the Good News of the Gospel of Jesus Christ. I pray and believe that ______________ comes to his/her senses and escapes out of the snare of the devil.

I am here to stand in the gap and build up the hedge for ________ until he/she is confident that there is nothing in the universe with the power to separate him/her from God's love. There is no power above ______ or beneath him/her—no power that could ever be found in the universe that can distance ___________ from God's passionate love, which is lavished upon him/her through our Lord Jesus, the Anointed One! In Jesus' name, amen.

SCRIPTURE REFERENCES

Jeremiah 1:12 ESV • 2 Timothy 2:26 • John 6:45
1 Corinthians 11:31 • Isaiah 54:13 AMPC • Matthew 18:18
2 Timothy 3:14-15 TPT • Hebrews 3:14 AMPC • Isaiah 57:18
Hebrews 10:35 AMPC • John 10:28-29 • Ephesians 1:18 TPT
1 John 5:16 • 1 John 1:3 • 2 Corinthians 4:4 • Ezekiel 22:30
Romans 8:38 TPT

— 141 —

Deliverance from Satan and His Demonic Forces

If the person for whom you are interceding has not confessed Jesus as Savior and Lord, pray specifically for his/her salvation if you have not already done so. Stand and thank the Father that it is done in the name of Jesus. Then pray:

Father, in the name of Jesus, I come boldly to Your throne of grace and present ___________ before You. I stand in the gap and intercede in behalf of ___________, knowing that the Holy Spirit within me takes hold together with me against the evils that would attempt to hold ___________ in bondage. I unwrap ___________ from the bonds of wickedness with my prayers and take my shield of faith and quench every fiery dart of the adversary that would ensnare ___________. Father, You say that whatever I bind on earth is bound in heaven, and whatever I loose on earth is loosed in heaven.

In the name of Jesus, I bind ________'s body, soul, and spirit to the will and purposes of God for his/her life. I bind ___________'s mind, will, and emotions to the will of God. I bind him/her to the truth and to the blood of Jesus. I bind his/her mind to the mind of Christ, that the very thoughts, feelings, and purposes of His heart would be within his/her thoughts.

> I loose every old, wrong, ungodly pattern of thinking, attitude, idea, desire, belief, motivation, habit, and behavior from him/her. I tear down, crush, smash, and

> destroy every stronghold associated with these things. I loose any stronghold in his/her life that has been justifying and protecting hard feelings against anyone. I loose the stronghold of unforgiveness, fear, and distrust from him/her. I bind and loose these things in Jesus' name.[22]

Father, I ask You to commission Your ministering spirits to go forth and provide the necessary help and assistance for __________.

Father, by faith I take hold of __________'s salvation and his/her confession of the Lordship of Jesus Christ. I speak of things that are not as though they were, for I choose to look at the unseen—the eternal things of God. In Jesus' name, Satan shall not get an advantage over __________, for I am not ignorant of Satan's devices. I am submitted to God and resist Satan's attempt to hold ______________ in bondage; the devil runs in terror in the name of Jesus. I plead the blood of the Lamb over __________, for Satan and his cohorts are overcome by that blood and Your Word. I thank You, Father, that I tread on serpents and scorpions and over all the power of the enemy on __________'s behalf. __________ is delivered from this present evil world. He/she is delivered from the powers of darkness and translated into the Kingdom of Your dear Son!

Father, I ask You now to fill those vacant places within __________ with Your redemption, Your Word, Your Holy Spirit, Your love, Your wisdom, Your righteousness, and Your revelation knowledge in the name of Jesus.

I thank You, Father, that __________ is redeemed out of the hand of Satan by the blood of Jesus. He/she is justified and made righteous by the blood of Jesus and belongs to You—spirit, soul, and body. I thank You that every enslaving yoke is broken, for he/she will not become the slave of anything or be brought under its power in the name of Jesus. ____________ has escaped the snare of the devil who has held him/her

22 Liberty Savard, *Shattering Your Strongholds*, (North Brunswick, NJ: Bridge-Logos Publishers, 1992), 171-172.

captive and henceforth does Your will, Father, which is to glorify You in his/her spirit, soul, and body.

Father, thank You that Jesus was manifested that He might destroy the works of the devil. Satan's works are destroyed in __________'s life in the name of Jesus. Hallelujah! __________ walks in the Kingdom of God, which is righteousness, peace, and joy in the Holy Spirit! Praise the Lord! Amen.[23]

SCRIPTURE REFERENCES

Hebrews 4:16 • 2 Corinthians 2:11 • Ezekiel 22:30 • James 4:7 • Romans 8:26
Ephesians 4:27 • Isaiah 58:6 • Revelation 12:11 • Ephesians 6:16
Luke 10:19 • Matthew 18:18 • Galatians 1:4 • Mark 16:17
Colossians 1:13 • Ephesians 6:12 • Matthew 12:43-45 • Colossians 2:15
1 Corinthians 6:12 • Matthew 12:29 • 2 Timothy 2:26 • Hebrews 1:14
1 John 3:8 • Romans 4:17 • Romans 14:17 • 2 Corinthians 4:18

23 This prayer may be prayed as many times as necessary. It takes time to realize the faith that leads you into a position of praise and thanksgiving. Stand firm, fixed, unmovable, and steadfast, remembering that greater is He that is in you than he that is in the world.

142

Deliverance from Cults

FATHER, in the name of Jesus, we come before You in prayer and in faith, believing that Your Word runs swiftly throughout the earth, for the Word of God is not chained or imprisoned. We bring before You ______________ (those involved in cults and their families).

Father, stretch forth Your hand; rescue and deliver ________________ from these dark powers—barbarians who lie through their teeth, who shake your hand and then knife you in the back. They must be silenced because they subvert and turn whole families away from the truth by their false and corrupt teachings, all for their dishonest greed. Nothing will come of these latest imposters; everyone will see through their hoax.

Execute justice for the oppressed, precious Father. Set the prisoners free, open the eyes of the blind, lift up the bowed down, heal the brokenhearted, and bind up their wounds. Lift up the humble and downtrodden, and cast the wicked down to the ground in the mighty name of Jesus.

Turn back the hearts of the disobedient, incredulous, and unpersuadable to the wisdom of the upright and the knowledge of the will of God, in order to make ready for You, Lord, a people perfectly prepared in spirit. Kindle devout understanding among hardened skeptics to get the people ready for Jesus' appearing.

Father, we refrain our voices from weeping and our eyes from tears, for our prayers shall be rewarded and ___________ shall return home from the enemy's land. You will save our offspring from the land of their exile;

our sons and daughters will return. We shall see __________ walking in the truth of God's Word, revering Your name, Father. Those who got off track will get back on track, and complainers and whiners will learn gratitude. They will accept instruction in the Way—Jesus. Father, You contend with those who contend with us, and You give safety to ______________. I pray that ________________ will choose life and live the abundant life Jesus provided.

In the name of Jesus, I bind ___________'s feet to the paths of righteousness, that his/her steps would be steady and sure. I bind ______________ to the work of the Cross, with all of its mercy, grace, love, forgiveness, and dying to self.

> I loose the power and effects of deceptions and lies from him/her. I loose the confusion and blindness of the god of this world from ____________'s mind that have kept him/her from seeing the light of the gospel of Jesus Christ. I call forth every precious word of Scripture that has ever entered into his/her mind and heart, that it would rise up in power within him/her. I loose the power and effects of any harsh or hard words (word curses) spoken to, about, or by __________.
>
> Jesus gave me the keys and the authority to bind and loose these things in His name. Thank You, Lord, for the truth.[24]

Father, we ask You to commission the ministering spirits to go forth and dispel these forces of darkness and bring _______________ home in the name of Jesus.

Father, we believe and confess that __________ has had knowledge of and been acquainted with the Word, which was able to instruct him/her and give him/her the understanding for salvation that comes through faith in Christ Jesus. Lord, we pray and believe that You certainly will

24 Liberty Savard, *Shattering Your Strongholds,* (North Brunswick, NJ: Bridge-Logos Publishers, 1992), 171-172.

deliver __________ from every assault of evil and draw __________ to Yourself and preserve and bring __________ safe into Your heavenly Kingdom. Glory to You, Father, who deliver those for whom we intercede in Jesus' name! Amen.[25]

SCRIPTURE REFERENCES

Psalm 147:15 • Isaiah 43:5-6 • 2 Timothy 2:9 • Isaiah 29:23-24 MSG
Psalm 144:7-8 MSG • Isaiah 49:25 AMPC • Deuteronomy 30:19
John 10:10 • Titus 1:11 NLT, NIV • Matthew 18:18 • 2 Timothy 3:9 MSG
2 Timothy 3:2-9 • Psalm 146:7-8 • Hebrews 1:14 • Psalm 147:3-6
2 Timothy 3:15 • Luke 1:17 MSG • 2 Timothy 4:18 • Jeremiah 31:16-17
Job 22:30 • Jeremiah 46:27

25 Pray this prayer until faith arises in you. Then you will know that God shall perform His Word in the life of the one for whom you are interceding. The Holy Spirit is your Helper. When you perceive the intercession is completed, surround the individual with songs and shouts of deliverance in your prayer closet.

143

Deliverance from Habits

FATHER, in the name of Jesus and according to Your Word, I believe in my heart and say with my mouth that Jesus is Lord of my life. Because all truth is in Jesus, I strip myself of my former nature; I put off and discard my old, unrenewed self. I desire to be free from the habit(s) of __________ in the name of Jesus. Father, the habit(s) is/are not helpful (good for me, expedient, and profitable). I no longer desire to be the slave of wrong habits and behaviors or be brought under their power.

Father, these self-destructive habits are symptoms of a flaw in my soul, my character, and I confess them as sin. I don't want to habitually make the same mistakes over and over. Father, Your Word exposes the wrong thought patterns that are driving me to continue acting out in ways that are contrary to Your Word. I desire to be continually filled with and controlled by the Holy Spirit.

Thank You, Father, for translating me into the Kingdom of Your dear Son. Now I am Your garden under cultivation. In the name of Jesus, I throw all spoiled virtue and cancerous evil into the garbage. In simple humility, I purpose to let You, my Gardener, landscape me with the Word, making a salvation-garden of my life.

I arm myself with the full armor of God, the armor of a heavily armed soldier, which God has supplied for me—the helmet of salvation, loins girded with truth, feet shod with the preparation of the gospel of peace, the shield of faith, and the Sword of the Spirit, which is the Word of God.

With God's armor on, I am able to stand up against all the strategies and deceits and fiery darts of Satan, in the name of Jesus.

Clothed in Your armor, I discipline my body and subdue it. With every temptation I choose the way of escape that You provide. Greater is He that is in me than he that is in the world.

Thank You, Lord. I praise You that I am growing spiritually and that Your engrafted Word is saving my soul. I strip away the old nature with its habits, and I put on the new man created in Christ Jesus. Hallelujah! Amen.

SCRIPTURE REFERENCES

Romans 10:9-10 • 1 Corinthians 10:13 • Ephesians 4:21-22 AMPC
Ephesians 6:13-17 • 1 Corinthians 6:12 AMPC • 1 John 4:4
1 Corinthians 3:9 AMP • 2 Corinthians 5:17 • James 1:21 MSG

144

Deliverance from Corrupt Companions

FATHER, in the name of Jesus, I ask You to open the eyes of ___________'s understanding, that he/she might not be deceived by the influence of corrupt and depraved people. Thank You for causing him/her to come alive and awakening ______________________ that he/she might return to sober sense and his/her right mind.

Father, I come before You asking for mercy—mercy that triumphs over judgment. Thank You for drawing ______________ to Yourself with cords and bands of love and for leading him/her to repentance with Your goodness. Then ______________________ will separate himself/herself from contact with contaminating influences and cleanse himself/herself from everything that would defile spirit, soul, and body.

In the name of Jesus, I bind ______________________'s mind to the mind of Christ, that he/she might live and conduct himself/herself honorably and becomingly as in the open light of the day. I loose him/her from the wrong thought patterns of his/her former lifestyle that were controlled by a set of values inspired by the adversary, who misleads those who have not come alive to Christ.

I ask You to give ______________ a willing heart, that he/she might be loyally subject submissive to the governing civil authority—not resisting nor setting himself/herself up against them. He/she shall be obedient, prepared, and willing to do any upright and honorable work. He/she shall walk as a companion with wise men, and he/she shall be wise.

__________ is pardoned through the name of Jesus and because he/she confesses His name. He/She is victorious over the wicked one because he/she has come to know and recognize and be aware of the Father.

As ___________'s mind is renewed by the Word, the Word dwells and remains in him/her, and he/she dwells in the Son and in the Father always. God's nature abides in __________; His principle of life remains permanently within him/her, and he/she cannot practice sinning because he/she is born of God. The law of the Spirit of life in Christ Jesus has made ___________ free from the law of sin and death. Thank You, Father, for watching over Your Word to perform it, in Jesus' name! Amen.

SCRIPTURE REFERENCES

1 Corinthians 15:33-34 • Proverbs 28:7 • 2 Timothy 2:21 AMPC
1 Thessalonians 5:22 • 2 Corinthians 7:1 • 1 John 2:12-16 AMPC
Romans 13:13 AMPC • 1 John 2:21,24 • 1 Peter 2:1 • 1 John 3:9 AMPC
Romans 13:1-2 AMPC • Romans 8:2 • Titus 3:1 AMPC
Jeremiah 1:12 • Proverbs 13:20

145

Deliverance from Mental Disorder

FATHER, in the name of Jesus, I fearlessly and confidently and boldly draw near to the throne of grace, that I may receive mercy and find grace to help in good time for ___________.

Father, I commit to pray on ___________'s behalf, making up the hedge and standing in the gap before You for him/her, that Your mercy might triumph over judgment. Jesus, You defeated the devil for __________, and we take back everything Satan has stolen from him/her.

It is You, Father, who delivers ____________ from the pit and corruption of ____________________ (name of disorder: schizophrenia, paranoia, manic depression, etc.). Father, You have not given ___________________ a spirit of timidity—of cowardice, of craven and cringing and fawning fear—but You have given him/her a spirit of power and of love and of a calm and well-balanced mind and discipline and self-control.

In the name of Jesus, I forgive his/her sins and stand in the gap for ________________ until he/she comes to his/her senses and escapes out of the snare of the devil, who has held _______________ captive.

Because Jesus defeated principalities and powers and made a show of them openly, I stand against the forces of darkness, which have been assigned to ________________. Thank You, Father, for delivering ________________ from the authority of darkness and translating him/her into the Kingdom of your dear Son.

I decree and declare that the law of the Spirit of life in Christ Jesus has made _____________ free from the law of sin and death. ______________ shall no longer be of two minds—hesitating, dubious, irresolute—unstable and unreliable and uncertain about everything (he/she thinks, feels, and decides). ______________ shall get rid of all uncleanness and the rampant outgrowth of wickedness, and in a humble (gentle, modest) spirit receive and welcome the Word, which, implanted and rooted in his/her heart, contains the power to save his/her soul (mind, will, and emotions).

In the name of Jesus, grace be to __________ and peace from God our Father and from the Lord Jesus Christ, who gave Himself for his/her sin so that He might deliver him/her from this present evil world, according to the will of God and our Father, to whom be glory for ever and ever. Amen.

SCRIPTURE REFERENCES

Hebrews 4:16 AMP • Ephesians 6:12 • Psalm 50:15 • Colossians 1:13
Psalm 56:13 • Romans 8:2 • Psalm 103:4 AMP • James 1:8,21 AMP
2 Timothy 1:7 AMP • Galatians 1:3-5 • John 20:23 AMP • Ezekiel 22:30
2 Timothy 2:26 AMP

146

Hedge of Protection

FATHER, in the name of Jesus, we lift up __________ to You and pray a hedge of protection around him/her. We thank You, Father, that You are a wall of fire round about __________ and that You set Your angels round about him/her.

We thank You, Father, that __________ dwells in the secret place of the Most High and abides under the shadow of the Almighty. We say of You, Lord, You are his/her refuge and fortress, in You will he/she trust. You cover __________ with Your feathers, and under Your wings shall he/she trust. __________ shall not be afraid of the terror by night or the arrow that flies by day. Only with his/her eyes will __________ behold and see the reward of the wicked.

Because __________ has made You, Lord, his/her refuge and fortress, no evil shall befall him/her—no accident will overtake him/her—neither shall any plague or calamity come near him/her. For You give Your angels charge over __________, to keep him/her in all Your ways.

Father, because You have set Your love upon ______________, therefore will You deliver him/her. ______________ shall call upon You, and You will answer him/her. You will be with him/her in trouble and will satisfy __________ with a long life and show him/her Your salvation. Not a hair of his/her head shall perish. Amen.

SCRIPTURE REFERENCES

Ezekiel 22:30 • Psalm 91:4-5 AMPC • Zechariah 2:5 • Psalm 91:8-11 AMPC
Psalm 34:7 • Psalm 91:14-16 AMPC • Psalm 91:1-2 AMPC • Luke 21:18

147

Finding Favor with Others

FATHER, in the name of Jesus, You make Your face to shine upon and enlighten __________ and are gracious (kind, merciful, and giving favor) to him/her. __________ is the head and not the tail. __________ is above only and not beneath.

Thank You for favor for __________ who seeks Your Kingdom and Your righteousness and diligently seeks good. __________ is a blessing to You, Lord, and is a blessing to __________ (name them: family, neighbors, business associates, etc.). Grace (favor) is with __________, who loves the Lord Jesus in sincerity. __________ extends favor, honor, and love to __________ (names). __________ is flowing in Your love, Father. You are pouring out upon __________ the spirit of favor. You crown him/her with glory and honor, for he/she is Your child—Your workmanship.

__________ is a success today. __________ is someone very special with You, Lord. __________ is growing in the Lord—waxing strong in spirit. Father, You give __________ knowledge and skill in all learning and wisdom.

You bring __________ to find favor, compassion, and loving-kindness with __________ (names). __________ obtains favor in the sight of all who look upon him/her this day in the name of Jesus. __________ is filled with Your fullness—rooted and grounded in love. You are doing exceedingly abundantly above all that __________ asks or thinks, for Your mighty power is taking over in __________.

Thank You, Father, that _______________ is well-favored by You and by man, in Jesus' name! Amen.

SCRIPTURE REFERENCES

Numbers 6:25 AMPC • Psalm 8:5 • Deuteronomy 28:13
Ephesians 2:10 • Matthew 6:33 • Luke 2:40 • Proverbs 11:27
Daniel 1:17 • Ephesians 6:24 • Daniel 1:9 AMPC • Luke 6:38
Esther 2:15,17 • Zechariah 12:10 AMPC • Ephesians 3:19-20

148

Improving Communication Skills

FATHER, for too long I have not understood the power of words. Forgive me for using words as weapons. Too often I have not expressed myself with love, and all my words were reduced to the hollow sound of nothing more than a clanging cymbal. For too long being right was more important than my relationships.

Grant me the wisdom to be quick to listen, slow to speak, and slow to become angry. It is from the abundance of my heart that I speak, and I am ready to abandon everything morally impure. Teach me to speak beautiful, life-giving words that will release sweetness to our souls and inner healing to our spirits. I am ready to absorb Your Word with a sensitive spirit because Your Word of Life has the power to continually save my soul (my personality, emotions, and thoughts). I pray that Your Word will always be like poetry written and fulfilled by my life! May my body language and my words agree revealing the motive and intent of my heart.

I am here before You and eager to discard every form of dishonesty and lying so that I will be known as one who always speaks the truth, for we all belong to one another. I choose to bind my emotions to the control of the Holy Spirt and thank You that those passions can no longer lead me to sin. Now and forever may my words be beautiful gifts that encourage others. May I speak words of grace to help them, in Jesus' name.

SCRIPTURE REFERENCES

1 Corinthians 13:1 TPT • James 1:13-22 TPT • James 3:2-17 TPT
Proverbs 16:24 • Ephesians 4:25-29 TPT

149

Prayer for Employment

FATHER, in Jesus' name, we believe and confess Your Word over __________ today, knowing that You watch over Your Word to perform it. Your Word prospers in __________'s life where it's sent. You are his/her Source of every consolation, comfort, and encouragement. __________ is courageous and grows in strength.

His/her desire is to owe no man anything but to love him. Therefore, __________ is strong and his/her hands are not weak or slack, for his/her work shall be rewarded. His/her wages are not counted as a favor or a gift, but as something owed to him/her. __________ makes it his/her ambition and definitely endeavors to live quietly and peacefully and minds his/her own affairs. ______________ is correct and honorable and commands the respect of the outside world, being self-supporting, dependent on nobody, and having need of nothing. You, Father, supply to the full his/her every need.

He/she works in quietness, earns his/her own food and other necessities. He/she is not weary of doing right and continues in well-doing without weakening. __________ learns to apply himself/herself to good deeds—to honest labor and honorable employment—so that he/she is able to meet necessary demands whenever the occasion may require.

Father, You know the record of his/her works and what he/she is doing. You have set before __________ a door wide open, which no one is able to shut. __________ does not fear and is not dismayed, for You, Father, help and strengthen him/her. In Jesus, __________ has perfect peace and confidence and is of good cheer, for Jesus overcame the world and deprived it of its power to harm __________. He/she does not fret or have anxiety about anything, for Your peace, Father, mounts guard over his/her heart and mind. _______________ knows the secret of facing every situation, for he/she is self-sufficient in Christ's sufficiency. ______________ guards his/her mouth and his/her tongue, keeping himself/herself from trouble.

_______________ prizes Your wisdom, Father, and acknowledges You. You direct, make straight and plain his/her path, and You promote him/her. Therefore, Father, __________ increases in Your wisdom in broad and full understanding and in stature and years and in favor with You, Father, and with man! Amen.

SCRIPTURE REFERENCES

Jeremiah 1:12 • Titus 3:14 AMPC • Isaiah 55:11 • Revelation 3:8 AMPC
2 Corinthians 1:3 AMPC • Isaiah 41:10 AMPC • 1 Corinthians 16:13 AMPC
John 16:33 AMPC • Romans 13:8 AMPC • Philippians 4:6-7 AMPC
2 Chronicles 15:7 AMPC • Philippians 4:12-13 AMPC • Romans 4:4 AMPC
Proverbs 21:23 AMPC • 1 Thessalonians 4:11-12 AMPC • Proverbs 3:6 AMPC
2 Thessalonians 3:12-13 AMPC • Proverbs 4:8 AMPC • Luke 2:52 AMPC

150

Overcoming Negative Work Attitudes

THANK You, Father, in Jesus' name, for watching over Your Word until its accomplished. __________ is obedient to his/her employers—bosses or supervisors—having respect for them. He/she is eager to please them, in singleness of motive and with all his/her heart, as service to Christ, not in the way of eye service—as if they were watching him/her—but as a servant (employee) of Christ, doing the will of God heartily and with his/her whole soul.

__________ readily renders service with goodwill to the Lord and not to men. He/she knows that for whatever good he/she does, he/she will receive his/her reward from the Lord.

__________ will live a cheerful life and do everything without grumbling or arguing or division. He/she is blameless so no one can criticize him/her. He/she lives a clean, innocent life as children of God, shining like a bright light in a world full of crooked and perverse people and offering them the words of eternal life.

______________ honors the Lord, and his/her work is a sincere expression of devotion to Him. Whatever the task or job may be, ______________ works with a smile on his/her face, always keeping in mind that no matter who happens to be giving the orders, he/she is really serving God. Good work will get __________________ good pay from the Master. Amen.

SCRIPTURE REFERENCES

Jeremiah 1:12 VOICE • Colossians 3:22-24 PHI • Ephesians 6:5-8 MSG
Philippians 2:14-15 TPT, NLT

151

Comfort for a Person Who Has Lost a Christian Loved One

FATHER, I thank You that we have a High Priest who is able to understand and sympathize and have a fellow feeling with __________'s grief over the loss of his/her __________.

Father, I thank You that __________ does not grieve like people who have no hope because he/she believes that Jesus died, rose again, and will return. Father, You have said when Jesus returns, He will bring with Him all who had faith in Jesus before they died.

Jesus, You have come to heal the brokenhearted. It is in the name of Jesus that You, Father, comfort __________ because You have loved him/her and have given him/her everlasting consolation and good hope through grace.

All praises belong to the God and Father of our Lord Jesus Christ. For He is the Father of tender mercy and the God of endless comfort, who comforts ______________. Father, You always come alongside us to comfort us in every suffering so we can come alongside those who are in any painful trial. We can bring them this same comfort that God has poured out upon us.

Father, thank You for granting ______________ beauty for ashes, the oil of joy for mourning, the garment of praise for the spirit of heaviness, that he/she might be called a tree of righteousness, the planting of the Lord, that You might be glorified. In Jesus' name, amen.

SCRIPTURE REFERENCES

Hebrews 4:15-16 AMPC • 2 Thessalonians 2:16
1 Thessalonians 4:13-14 NLT • 2 Corinthians 1:3-4 TPT • Matthew 5:4
Isaiah 61:3 • Luke 4:18

152

Healing of the Handicapped

FATHER, we come before you boldly and confidently, knowing that You are not a man that You should lie and that You watch over Your Word to perform it. Therefore, Father, we bring before You those who are called handicapped and ill—mentally and physically. By the authority of Your Word, we know without a doubt that it is Your will for these people—babies, children, and adults—to be made completely whole and restored in the name of Jesus.

Although Satan, the god of this world, comes against Your handiwork, we know You are the God of miracles, the God of love, power, and might. Through Your redemptive plan, we are redeemed from the curse of the law. The law of the Spirit of life in Christ Jesus has made us free from the law of sin and death. We are seated with Christ in heavenly places far above all satanic forces. We bring those who have been attacked mercilessly—mentally and/or physically—before Your throne of grace. We intercede on their behalf, and for their families and loved ones.

We proclaim the victory Jesus won at Calvary when He disarmed the principalities and powers that were waged against us. We believe that everyone who has the opportunity this day to make Jesus their Lord and Savior will call upon His name and be saved. We bind their spirits, souls, and bodies to the will of God, to the blood of Jesus, to mercy, grace, and truth. We destroy strongholds of unforgiveness, fear, and distrust. In the name of Jesus, we loose unbelief, fear, discouragement, tradition, depression, and oppression from the minds of the parents, children, and individuals involved.

Father, we pray for born-again, Spirit-filled individuals in positions of authority—administrators, teachers, doctors, nurses, orderlies, attendants, and volunteers. We pray that men and women of integrity, blameless and complete in Your sight, remain in these positions, but that the wicked be cut off and the treacherous be rooted out. Father, we pray for laborers of the harvest to go forth preaching the good news to the lost and to the Body of Christ.

We pray that You quicken these individuals to Your Word—that they may be filled with wisdom and revelation knowledge concerning the integrity of Your Word, speaking faith-filled words and doing faith-filled actions. We pray for the infilling of the Holy Spirit, divine health, the fruit of the recreated human spirit, the gifts of the Holy Spirit, and deliverance. May they know that Jesus is their Source of every consolation, comfort, and encouragement, and that they are to be sanctified—spirit, soul, and body. We confess that they are redeemed from the curse of the law—redeemed from every sickness, disease, malady, affliction, defect, deficiency, deformity, injury, and every demon.

We speak healing to unborn infants in the wombs of mothers, for children are a heritage of the Lord and the fruit of the womb is their reward.

We speak restoration to damaged brain cells and activation of dormant brain cells. We speak normal intellect for one's age. We speak creative miracles to parts of the body and healing to all wounds. We speak words of life and say that they shall live in victory in this life and not die. We speak perfect soundness of mind and wholeness in body and spirit. We say that tongues are loosed and speech is distinct. We say ears hear and eyes see in the name of Jesus. We say demons are cast out, bowing to the name of Jesus. We speak deliverance to bodies and minds, for You, Lord God, are the Help of their countenance and the Lifter of those bowed down—the joy of the Lord is their strength and stronghold!

We commission God's ministering spirits to go forth as they hearken to God's Word to provide the necessary help and assistance to those for whom we are praying! Father, no word of Yours is void of the power that it takes to cause itself to come to pass! We establish Your Word on this earth, for it is already forever settled in heaven. Nothing is too hard or impossible for You. All things are possible to us who believe. We pray for more intercessors to stand with us. Let our prayers be set forth as incense before You—a sweet fragrance to You! Praise the Lord! In Jesus' name we pray, amen.

SCRIPTURE REFERENCES

Romans 3:4 • Mark 16:17 • Mark 11:23-24 • Jeremiah 1:12 • Psalm 42:11
1 Peter 2:24 • Acts 3:16 • Psalm 146:8 • Matthew 8:17 • 2 Corinthians 4:4
Nehemiah 8:10 • Mark 7:35 • John 10:10 • Psalm 103:20
Proverbs 20:12 • Galatians 3:13 • Matthew 9:37-38 • Luke 1:37
Romans 8:2 • Ephesians 1:17-18 • Psalm 119:89 • Ephesians 2:6
2 Corinthians 1:3 • Jeremiah 32:27 • Matthew 18:18
1 Thessalonians 5:23 • Mark 9:23 • Proverbs 2:21-22 • Psalm 127:3
Psalm 141:2

153

Those Involved in Abortion

Introduction

Through our ministry, a dear child of God shared with us the following Scriptures, which continue to bring her through periods of grief and sorrow. God's grace and love have proven to be the balm necessary for healing the emotional pain incurred by an act that cannot be reversed. The memory of the decision will never be erased. Reminders are all around—at church, in the media, and in everyday life.

The prayer as written has a twofold application: (1) for a people—a nation—who have permitted the legalization of abortion on demand; (2) for both the man and woman involved in the decision-making process. During moments of intercession for women and men who are dealing with past mistakes, we have identified with them in their pain. God's Word is the medicine that heals and the salvation of souls.

Prayer

This prayer can also be prayed in the singular "I" form by the individual person involved in abortion.

Father, in the name of Jesus, forgive us as a nation for disregarding the sanctity of life. We recognize that each person is uniquely created by You, Lord—marvelously made! You know each one inside and out; You know every bone in the body. You know exactly how we are made, bit by bit, and how we are sculpted from nothing into something. All the stages of a life are spread out before You, and the days are prepared before a child even lives one day. Because we now see clearly, we value the life You give.

Father, each of us is an open book to You; even from a distance, You know what we are thinking. We are never out of Your sight. When we look back, we realize that You were there. You were present when we put to death the being/beings to whom You gave life.

Lord, we repent of our sin and the sin of our nation. Be merciful unto us, O Lord. We ask Your forgiveness, and You are faithful and just to forgive us and cleanse us from all unrighteousness.

Unless Your law had been our delight, we would have perished in our affliction. We will never forget Your precepts (how can we?), for it is by them You have quickened us (granted us life).

We are ready to halt and fall; our pain and sorrow are continually before us. For we do confess our guilt and iniquity; we are filled with sorrow for our sin.

So instead of further rebuke, now we desire rather to turn and be graciously forgiven and comforted and encouraged to keep us from being overwhelmed by excessive sorrow and despair.

We look to Jesus as our Savior and Consolation and welcome His peace and completeness to our souls. We cannot bring our child/children back again; we shall go to them; they will not return to us.

We are awaiting and looking for the fulfillment and the realization of our blessed hope, even the glorious appearing of our great God and Savior, Christ Jesus (the Messiah, the Anointed One). In His name we pray, amen.

SCRIPTURE REFERENCES

Psalm 139:14-16 MSG • Psalm 119:92-93 AMPC • Psalm 38:17-18 AMPC
2 Corinthians 2:7 AMP • Psalm 139:2-5 MSG • 2 Samuel 12:23 AMPC
1 John 1:9 • Titus 2:13

154

An AIDS Patient

I. Prayer for the Child of God

FATHER, You sent Jesus to bind up _____________'s heartaches and to heal his/her emotional and physical pain. The Bible says that You sent Your Word to heal him/her and to deliver _________________ from all his/her destructions.

Lord, we believe; help our unbelief. We ask You to give _____________ a spirit of wisdom and revelation of insight into mysteries and secrets in the deep and intimate knowledge of Jesus, the Messiah.

Father, as ________ grows in grace and the knowledge of the Lord Jesus Christ, help him/her to receive all the spiritual blessings given by You. Thank You for giving him/her peace that the world cannot take away.

Lord, Your Son, Jesus, gave His life for _________. He/she has received Him as his/her Lord and is born again, desiring to give the glory to You and to continue to fellowship with Your family. Jesus lives in his/her heart, and he/she loves You and loves others as he/she loves himself/herself. Thank You that __________ finds plenty of support from the Body of Christ so that he/she will find encouragement, edification, and comfort.

Heavenly Father, in Your mercy strengthen ______________ and help him/her with his/her physical problems. Let him/her be aware that he/she is not alone, for there is nothing that can separate him/her from the love of Christ—not pain or stress or persecution. He/she will come to the top of every circumstance or trial through Jesus' love.

Father, ____________ is trusting in You and doing good; so shall he/she dwell in the land and feed surely on Your faithfulness, and truly he/she shall be fed. ________________ delights himself/herself also in You, and You will give him/her the desires and secret petitions of his/her heart. We ask You to give ___________ the grace to commit his/her way to You, trusting in You, and You will bring it to pass.

Help _________ to enter into Your rest, Lord, and to wait for You without fretting himself/herself. May he/she cease from unrighteous anger and wrath.

Father, You have not given _____________ a spirit of fear, but of power and of love and of a sound mind. Neither shall he/she be confounded and depressed. You have given him/her beauty for ashes, the oil of joy for mourning, and the garment of praise for the spirit of heaviness, that You might be glorified.

The chastisement needful to obtain __________'s peace and wellbeing was upon Jesus, and with the stripes that wounded Him, he/she was healed and made whole.

As Your child, Father, __________________ has a joyful and confident hope of eternal salvation. This hope will never disappoint or delude him/her, for Your love has been poured out in his/her heart through the Holy Spirit who has been given to him/her. In the name of Jesus, amen.

SCRIPTURE REFERENCES

Luke 4:18 AMPC • Romans 8:35-37 • Psalm 107:20 • 2 Corinthians 2:14
Mark 9:24 • Psalm 37:3-5,7-8 AMPC • Ephesians 1:17 AMPC
2 Timothy 1:7 • 2 Peter 3:18 • Isaiah 54:4 AMPC • Ephesians 1:3
Isaiah 61:3 • John 14:27 • Isaiah 53:5 AMPC • John 3:3
Romans 5:4-5 AMPC • John 13:34

II. Prayer for One Who Does Not Know Jesus as Lord

Thank You for calling us to be Your agents of intercession for ________________. By the grace of God we will build up the wall and stand in the gap before You for ______________ that he/she might be spared from eternal destruction.

Lord, we acknowledge Your Son, Jesus, as the Lamb of God who takes away _______________'s sins. Thank You for sending the Holy Spirit who goes forth to convince and convict ________________ of sin, righteousness, and judgment. Your kindness leads him/her to repent—to change his/her mind and inner man to accept Your will. You are the One who delivers ____________ and draws him/her to Yourself out of the control and dominion of darkness and transfers him/her into the Kingdom of the Son of Your love.

Lord of the harvest, we ask You to thrust the perfect laborer into ______________'s path, a laborer to share Your Gospel in a special way so that he/she will listen and understand it. We believe that he/she will come to his/her senses—come out of the snare of the devil who has held him/her captive—and make Jesus the Lord of his/her life.

Father, as ________ grows in grace and the knowledge of the Lord Jesus Christ, help him/her to receive all the spiritual blessings given by You. Thank You for giving him/her peace that the world cannot take away.

Heavenly Father, in Your mercy strengthen _____________ and help him/her with his/her physical problems. Let him/her be aware that he/she is not alone, for there is nothing that can separate him/her from the love of Christ—not pain or stress or persecution. He/she will come to the top of every circumstance or trial through Jesus' love.

Help _______________ to enter into Your rest and to wait for You without fretting himself/herself. May he/she cease from unrighteous anger and wrath.

Father, You sent Jesus to bind up _____________'s heartaches and to heal his/her emotional and physical pain. The Bible says that You sent Your Word to heal him/her and to deliver ____________ from all his/her destructions. We ask You to give him/her a spirit of wisdom and revelation of insight into mysteries and secrets in the deep and intimate knowledge of Jesus, the Messiah.

The chastisement needful to obtain __________'s peace and wellbeing was upon Jesus, and with the stripes that wounded Him, he/she was healed and made whole. As Your child, Father, ________________ has a joyful and confident hope of eternal salvation. This hope will never disappoint or delude him/her, for Your love has been poured out in his/her heart through the Holy Spirit who has been given to him/her. In the name of Jesus, amen.

SCRIPTURE REFERENCES

Ezekiel 22:30 AMPC • John 14:27 • John 1:29 • Romans 8:35-37
John 16:8-12 AMPC • 2 Corinthians 2:14 • Romans 2:4 AMPC
Psalm 37:7-8 AMPC • Colossians 1:13 AMPC • Luke 4:18 AMPC
Matthew 9:38 AMPC • Psalm 107:20 • 2 Timothy 2:26 NIV
Ephesians 1:17 AMPC • 2 Peter 3:18 • Isaiah 53:5 AMPC
Ephesians 1:3 • Romans 5:5 AMPC

155

Prison Inmates

Introduction

The following prayers were written in response to letters from prisoners requesting prayers to be used by them in special circumstances. They may be prayed in agreement with a prayer partner or intercessor.

I. Prayer for an Inmate's Protection and Future

Father, I pray that I may become useful and helpful and kind to those around me, tenderhearted (compassionate, understanding, loving-hearted), forgiving others readily and freely, as You, Father, in Christ forgave me my sins.

It is my desire to be an imitator of You, Lord. With the Holy Spirit as my Helper, I will copy You and follow Your example as a well-beloved child imitates his/her father. I purpose to walk in love, esteeming and delighting in others as Christ loves me. As I attend to Your Word, I depend on Your Holy Spirit to teach me to live a life of victory in Christ Jesus my Lord.

In the name of Jesus, I am Your child. I am dwelling in the secret place of the Most High and abiding under the shadow of the Almighty. I say of You, Lord, that You are my Refuge and Fortress—my God; in You will

I trust. You cover me with Your feathers, and under Your wings shall I trust; Your truth is my shield and buckler.

Because You are my Lord, my Refuge and Habitation, no evil shall befall me—no accident will overtake me—neither shall any plague or calamity come near me. You give Your angels special charge over me, to keep me in all of my ways of obedience and service.

Thank You for hearing my prayer. You are with me in trouble; You deliver me and satisfy me with long life and show me Your salvation. In Jesus' name, amen.

SCRIPTURE REFERENCES

Ephesians 4:32 AMPC • Psalm 91:9-11 AMPC
Ephesians 5:1-2 AMPC • Psalm 91:15-16 • Psalm 91:1-2,4

II. Prayer for an Incarcerated Parent and His/Her Children

Listen, God, I'm calling at the top of my lungs: "Be good to me! Answer me!"

When my heart whispered, "Seek God," my whole being replied, "I'm seeking Him!" Don't hide from me now.

I didn't know it before, but I know now that You've always been right here for me; don't turn Your back on me now. Don't throw me out and don't abandon me; You've always kept the door open.

Thank You for sending ministers to tell me about You and Your love for me.

My children say they hate me; they feel abandoned and alone. Even though their father/mother walked away from them, I ask You, Father, to take them in.

Lord of the harvest, I ask You to send laborers of the harvest and wise counselors to my children, who have been hurt by my actions.

Father, I have sinned against You, against my children, and against myself. I repent of the sins that have so easily beset me and ask You to forgive me.

Father, Your Word assures me that You forgive me and cleanse me from all unrighteousness. Thank You for forgiving me. I pray that my children will be willing to forgive me so that we may be a family again.

In the name of Jesus, I cast the care of my children on You and rest in the assurance that You will perfect that which concerns me. I put on the garment of praise and delight myself in You. Teach me Your ways, Lord, that I may walk and live in Your truth. In Jesus' name, amen.

SCRIPTURE REFERENCES

Psalm 27:7-10 MSG • Isaiah 61:3 • Matthew 9:38 • 1 John 1:9
Psalm 86:11 AMPC • 1 Peter 5:7 • Psalm 138:8 • Hebrews 12:1

III. Prayer for an Inmate to Pray for His/Her Family and Caregiver

Father, I have sinned against You, against my children, and against myself. I repent of the sins that have so easily beset me and ask for Your forgiveness.

Father, Your Word assures me that You forgive me and cleanse me from all unrighteousness. Thank You for forgiving me. I pray that my children will be willing to forgive me so that we may be a family again.

Thank You for the one who has assumed responsibility for my children while I am away. I pray that You will strengthen ________________ and fill him/her with Your Spirit who gives him/her great wisdom, ability, and skill in rearing the children You gave to me. I repent for failing to assume my responsibility to my children, and I ask You to reward the one who is taking care of them.

____________________'s mouth shall speak of wisdom; and the meditation of his/her heart shall be understanding. I thank You that he/she is in Christ Jesus, who has been made unto him/her wisdom from You—his/her righteousness, holiness, and redemption. He/she is filled with the knowledge of Your will in all spiritual wisdom and understanding so that he/she may live a life worthy of You and may please You in every way, bearing fruit in every good work.

Father, I am responsible for my own actions, and I recognize that what I have done has hurt my entire family. Forgive me for dishonoring You, my family, my friends, and my children. Give me the grace to pay my debt and do my assigned work as unto You. Help me to develop diligence and patience, giving myself to prayer, study, and meditation in Your Word.

Lord, there is violence within these walls, but I look to You. Hide me in the secret place of Your presence, safe from the plots and schemes of those who conspire against me. Shelter me in your presence, far from accusing tongues. In the name of Jesus, I pray.

SCRIPTURE REFERENCES

1 John 1:9 • Colossians 1:9-10 AMPC • Psalm 49:3
Colossians 3:23-24 • Psalm 31:20 NLT

Testimonies

Oh, how your *Prayers That Avail Much* changed my life. I met Germaine at a Bible study hosted by Carolyn Munsey in Marietta in the early 1980s. I never knew anyone could pray the way you taught us that Thursday morning. Then I bought your book. I prayed it over so many situations, mainly my own, and saw my life change because of the power of God. When I taught on prayer, I used it as a reference that everyone should keep in their "spiritual arsenal." Thank you, thank you, thank you for your obedience to the Lord.

—Susan Walker Allen
Haleyville, AL

For me, this book became a reference for me. I'm often asked to pray for random and unusual situations, married folks, those with children, etc. I haven't experienced every lifestyle; therefore, this book gives a glimpse of God's heart and Holy Spirit completes the download. I appreciate you, Germaine Copeland!

—Charise Adams, Elder
The Embassy,
Atlanta, GA

I started following Germaine in 1977, before *Prayers That Avail Much* books were available. I went to several of her Bible studies, prayer groups, and seminars. I was born again at age 10 and was always a prayer warrior. In 1979, I received the baptism in the Holy Spirit in her seminar in Atlanta.

Then I started using the "little yellow book" regularly and learned how to pray God's Word effectively. I have learned so much from *Prayers That Avail Much* books and Germaine's teachings. I have had many answered prayers for healing and other situations in my life because I use the scriptural prayers in the *Prayers That Avail Much* books. Germaine has been a huge blessing to me and my family!

—Karen Gray Beasley,
Prayer Partner with Word Ministries, Inc.
Bowdon, GA

My first adventure in real effective intercession was under the tutelage of Germaine Copeland. Her book, *Prayers that Avail Much*, was my primer for intercession. It taught me how to use the written Word of God as a foundation for powerful intercessory prayers that truly availed much for those I was lifting up before the Lord. I began to see how to apply scripture to the lives of those I knew and loved as a prayer to open a way for them to walk in their divine destiny. *Prayers that Avail Much* gave me a firm foundation in effective prayer. I am so thankful to have been a small part of that ministry for many years. It changed my life and opened the door to my own destiny. Thank you, Germaine, for being a catalyst in my growth as a young Christian.

—Angela Brown
Marietta, GA
Author of *His Footstool, Secrets from the Sanctuary, I AM, Who Am I?*

Prayers That Avail Much is a MUST HAVE. I spent one whole year reading prayers five to six days a week out of this book. At first it was hard, and I would fall asleep. I kept trying though. Within two months, I began to see God answering some of these prayers. I would write in my book when I noticed God answering. This book of prayers renewed my mind first thing every morning and really began to put the truth on the inside of me. Chains were beginning to break!

There were times during these prayers that I would cry my way through them because the presence of the Lord was so strong. I have learned that when I pray God's Word, it does not return void to Him but will accomplish what He desires. So my prayers began to be answered, and it changed my life.

Also, I noticed when I would pray out loud in a group setting, I would catch myself saying the same things that were in my *Prayers That Avail Much* book. This book really helped me began the healing process in my life, and I'm very grateful. I now am praying out of the *Prayers that Avail Much for Leaders*, and I already see God working on my leadership skills. I'm super excited to see how He answers these prayers through the next season of my life.

—Britany C., Restoration House
Goliad, TX

I would defiantly say *Prayers That Avail Much* has helped me! Every morning when I wake up, I grab my prayer book and find a quiet place to read my prayers! For so many years, I was stuck in bondage—hurt and broken. But when I started reading these prayers out loud, something amazing began happening to me in my life. It felt like a heavy weight was being lifted off of me!

Not only did I read these prayers for me, but I also used them to intercede for my friends and family members as well as those God would put on my heart. There would be days when I was feeling sad and gloomy, and I would grab my book and begin to read those prayers out loud, and right then, I knew God was there with me answering every prayer. I have recommended *Prayers That Avail Much* books to so many people. I have a family member that is doing time in prison, and he is now praying these prayers also.

—Sara C., Restoration House
Goliad, TX

I was one of the group of ladies who had a desire to learn to pray God's Word in 1976. I received Jesus as my Lord and Savior as a child but never had instructions on how to pray and did not know for sure that my prayers would be answered. Learning to pray God's Word changed my life.

My daughter-in-law carried a baby for eight months and lost it. There were many complications with this baby, and they were told not to have any more children without going through certain tests. She was determined to have another baby and didn't pay any attention to the doctor. I knew the dangers and started praying what I was learning at Word Ministries, standing firm on His Word. I asked God to show me that He was in control of this baby. Christopher was born on Palm Sunday in 1977—a perfect baby boy with a strawberry cross on his neck.

My daughter-in-law wanted another baby three years later. Again, I knew the dangers and started praying. Danielle was born on Thanksgiving Day in 1980. *Prayers That Avail Much* was birthed for anyone who wanted answered prayers in their lives. People wanted to know they were praying God's Word for whatever situation they might have. Praise God for moving on Word Ministries and Germaine Copeland to step out and answer the call to write *Prayers That Avail Much.*

—Jan Duncan,
Former business manager and board member, Word Ministries, Inc.
Mulberry, FL

I was a brand-new believer when I started attending Bible study with Germaine as the teacher. That was in 1977 if I remember correctly. My life was totally changed as she opened the Word of God to me. I was there as the Word of God was put into prayer form. Exciting times! My foundation for a life of prayer was set in place during these years. The value of the original prayer book (*Prayers That Avail Much*) cannot be measured except in eternity. I was blessed to be a part of Word Ministries for years. I saw the favor of God poured out in Bible studies, conferences, and more prayer books. Who can even imagine the ripple effect of the years of Germaine's faithfulness? She not only stirred hearts to pray but also wrote books on prayer that made sure people would pray! I thank God for Germaine and *Prayers That Avail Much.* I write as one whose life was changed by these prayer books and the author.

—Molly Hintz, Bible teacher
Marietta, GA

This book is full of God's truth and promises, and it helped me in my prayer life a lot. It has also helped me have more confidence in praying with strangers and others. I remember first coming to the program and reading what seemed like an empty page with no full meaning behind it. But after a couple of weeks went by, I started realizing this book was so powerful, and no matter what, my prayers were not void. They were surely God's words, and I was being heard by God!

This book is very useful when you're broken and hurting because it allowed me to see specifically what to pray about and how to fight off the enemy. I was also able to look up the verses at the bottom of the pages which helped me pick a few verses to memorize when needed. I still use this book daily, and I have bought two as gifts for people. I think this book is where my healing began.

—Ashley K., Restoration House
Goliad, TX

I've been in ministry almost 40 years, and I still have one of the original books. It's used most every day! I love praying the Word of God.

—Carol Lain
Nashville, TN

Over 30 years ago, I was introduced to Germaine Copeland's *Prayers That Avail Much*, and it changed my prayer life. In fact, very few books have influenced my life as much as the *Prayers That Avail Much* series. I still have my first version to prove it—although it's a bit dog-eared with tabs throughout. To this day, every time I pray for others, I hear the influence of this book come out my mouth.

Whether you've been a Christian for years or you're a new believer, the simple truth of drawing from scriptures to pray is so important. As a young Christian, *Prayers That Avail Much* made prayer less daunting for me, and as I matured, *Prayers That Avail Much* inspires me with a passion to pray. Germaine's wisdom from years of praying for others has given her the ability to pen prayers that will help guide the reader to an effective and life-long passionate prayer life.

Prayers That Avail Much is a constant on my desk, and each of my family members has his or her own copy of her bestselling commemorative edition. I am truly grateful to God for the gift of Germaine's life and her influence on my life. Germaine is a precious and humble servant of God who has taught millions of people how to pray scripturally through her standard-setting—yet simple—prayer books.

—Kyle Loffelmacher, Sales Manager
Harrison House and Destiny Image
Tulsa, OK

It was 1985. My son and I knelt by my bed. My husband of almost thirty years had left. Such shock and numbness. I picked up my well-worn copy of *Prayers That Avail Much,* realizing that years before God had led Germaine to write this book, and of course, years before He had seen my son and me so heartbroken. Could we even pray? I picked up my well-worn book with His words arranged for us by an author He had chosen. That morning we were comforted by the precious Holy Spirit. My son has the old copy, and the new one I bought years ago is worn. Guess it's time to get another one. Thank You, Germaine.

—Cathy Chastain Lowman
Canton, GA

I have the 25th anniversary edition and several of the individual books. I use them all. My favorite of them has to be the prayer for leaders. They have been passed around, and I have purchased several for friends. I was also blessed to be part of her weekly prayer groups while Germaine met in Roswell and Tucker. One becomes an intimate, eternal friend with those they pray with and for.

—Linda Cross Posi
Marietta, GA

I started with the green book—your very first book! It taught the ladies and me in my prayer group how to pray! Over the years, I've started writing my own prayers—all because of the *Prayers That Avail Much* books! The Word comes alive in my heart when I pray them. Thank you, Germaine Griffin Copeland, for your obedience and sacrifice!

—Trisha Tippin, Word Ministries, Inc. Board Member
Phoenix, AZ

As an altar worker at church, I was gifted with the 25th anniversary commemorative gift edition of *Prayers That Avail Much* back in the 1990s. A huge answer to prayer came as I prayed the prayer for selling real estate. Not long after that, I met Germaine in person as we had both moved the same year to the same location!

—Georgia Toomey Wieler
Eatonton, GA

Journal

About Germaine Copeland

GERMAINE Copeland is the author of the bestselling *Prayers That Avail Much®* book series. Founder and president of Word Ministries, Inc., Germaine has traveled nationally and internationally conducting prayer schools and speaking at churches and conferences. Today, her ministry reaches around the world through her books and teaching videos. Germaine and her husband, Everette, have four children, eleven grandchildren, and a growing number of great-grandchildren and great-great grandchildren.

Mission Statement

Word Ministries, Inc.

To motivate individuals to spiritual growth and emotional wholeness, encouraging them to become more deeply and intimately acquainted with Father God as they pray prayers that avail much.

Contact Word Ministries by writing:

Word Ministries, Inc.

P. O. Box 289

Good Hope, GA 30641

(770) 267-7603

www.prayers.org

Please include your testimonies
and praise reports when you write!

Other Bestselling Books in the *Prayers That Avail Much*® series

Prayers That Avail Much® Gold-Letter Gift Edition

Prayers That Avail Much® Volume 1

A Global Call to Prayer

Prayers That Avail Much® for New Believers

Prayers That Avail Much® for Your Family

Prayers That Avail Much® for Women – pocket edition

Prayers That Avail Much® for Men – pocket edition

Prayers That Avail Much® for Parents

Prayers That Avail Much® for Moms – pocket edition

Prayers That Avail Much® for Mothers

Prayers That Avail Much® for Grandparents

Prayers That Avail Much® for Young Adults

Prayers That Avail Much® for the College Years

Prayers That Avail Much® for Teens

Prayers That Avail Much® for the Workplace

Prayers That Avail Much® for Leaders

Prayers That Avail Much® 365-Day Devotional

365 Days to a Prayer-Filled Life

Prayers That Avail Much® for America

Prayers That Avail Much® for the Nations

Prayers That Avail Much® for Graduates

The Harrison House Vision

Proclaiming the truth and the power
of the Gospel of Jesus Christ with excellence.
Challenging Christians
to live victoriously,
grow spiritually,
know God intimately.